Issues in Supply
and Contracting

T

Christian Alexander Ullrich

Issues in Supply Chain Scheduling and Contracting

Springer Gabler

Dr. Christian A. Ullrich
Bielefeld, Germany

Dissertation Bielefeld University, 2013

ISBN 978-3-658-03768-0   ISBN 978-3-658-03769-7 (eBook)
DOI 10.1007/978-3-658-03769-7

The Deutsche Nationalbibliothek lists this publication in the Deutsche Nationalbibliografie;
detailed bibliographic data are available in the Internet at http://dnb.d-nb.de.

Library of Congress Control Number: 2013950220

Springer Gabler
© Springer Fachmedien Wiesbaden 2014

Printed on acid-free paper

Springer Gabler is a brand of Springer DE.
Springer DE is part of Springer Science+Business Media.
www.springer-gabler.de

Foreword

This dissertation adds its insights to two growing areas of research in Operations Management, Supply Chain Scheduling and contract design in R&D supply chains.

While it is a, if not the, core paradigm of supply chain management literature that supply chain members should co-operate to enhance the efficiency of their collective effort, it does provide but little indication of how to do so on an operational level. The first, and larger part of Christian Ullrich's dissertation strives to fill this gap with respect to different supply chain scheduling scenarios. The question driving his analysis is: What is the size, in economic terms, of the advantage of commonly scheduling manufacturing and transportation operations by subsequent supply chain members? This question is answered by extensive numerical studies, employing newly devised algorithms for the different scenarios under scrutiny, like linear supply chains or supply networks. The high quality and efficiency of these heuristics are shown. They hence turn out to be useful not only for gaging the cost saving potential of supply chain scheduling but also as a tool for solving some of the aforementioned tasks of operational supply chain management. Moreover, some of the algorithms are formulated as spread sheet models. Due to the ubiquity of spread sheet tools in company offices this opens a route to the practitioner's day to day application of the supply chain scheduling tools developed here.

There is ample indication available that especially SMEs are often characterized by a considerable in-house production depth and high innovation intensity at the same time. At first glance, this phenomenon does not fit well into the modern perspective of concentration on the firm's core competencies. The final part of the dissertation tries to find an explanation for this observation by exploring the benefits of sharing the R&D investment among the supplier and the manufacturer in a two-stage innovative supply chain. Christian Ullrich illuminates, analytically and numerically, the parameter set-

FOREWORD

tings under which sharing the R&D investment is advantageous for both supply chain partners.

I hope this book will find the broad audience it deserves.

Oerlinghausen, July 2013   Hermann Jahnke

Preface

This dissertation[1] is based on four papers written during my term of employment at Bielefeld University. The following abstracts summarize the problems investigated, the solution methodologies, and the most important findings.

- **Integrated machine scheduling and vehicle routing with time windows**[2]

  This paper integrates production and outbound distribution scheduling in order to minimize total tardiness. The overall problem consists of two subproblems. The first addresses scheduling a set of jobs on parallel machines with machine-dependent ready times. The second focusses on the delivery of completed jobs with a fleet of vehicles which may differ in their loading capacities and ready times. Job-dependent processing times, delivery time windows, service times, and destinations are taken into account. A genetic algorithm approach is introduced to solve the integrated problem as a whole. Two main questions are examined. Are the results of integrating machine scheduling and vehicle routing significantly better than those of classic decomposition approaches which break down the overall problem, solve the two subproblems successively, and merge the subsolutions to form a solution to the overall problem? And if so, is it possible to capitalize on these potentials despite the complexity of the integrated problem? Both questions are tackled by means of a numerical study. The genetic algorithm outperforms the classic decomposition approaches in the case of small-size instances and is able to generate relatively good solutions for instances with up to 50 jobs, 5 machines, and 10 vehicles.

---

[1]Examiners: Prof. Dr. Hermann Jahnke, Prof. Dr. Reinhold Decker, and Prof. Dr. Christian Stummer (Bielefeld University, Faculty of Business Administration and Economics)

[2]Published in *European Journal of Operational Research*, Volume 227, Issue 1, May 2013, pages 152-165. Chapter 3 contains this paper in a revised and supplemented version.

PREFACE

- **The cost-cutting potential of Supply Chain Scheduling**
  Co-authored by Dr. Jan Herrmann

  Supply Chain Scheduling deals with the coordination of the machine and delivery schedules of two or more supply chain stages. The objective is to improve the supply chain's competitiveness measured in total logistics costs or the supply chain makespan, for example. However, the potential for improvement has never been properly quantified. If performance improvements did not suffice to compensate for the cost of coordination, Supply Chain Scheduling would be unprofitable and thus expendable. This paper aims to assess the cost-cutting potential of Supply Chain Scheduling. The investigation focusses on a supplier and a manufacturer, both of whom face a machine and delivery scheduling problem. The sum of tardiness, inventory holding, and transportation costs that result if the companies schedule on their own is compared to the total costs incurred if they schedule jointly. On average, Supply Chain Scheduling cut costs by up to 35%.

  Since the complexity of the examined scheduling problems can lead to extremely long computation times, only small-size instances are solvable using a commercial optimization software. Hence, a Microsoft Excel-based heuristic approach is developed that enables us to handle real-world-size instances as well. To the best of our knowledge there is currently no appropriate spreadsheet approach to scheduling problems that does not rely on expensive add-on software packages. This paper's heuristic can be easily transferred to a large number of batching, sequencing, routing, and scheduling problems. Since Excel is an omnipresent software and such problems occur almost everywhere, the proposed approach provides enormous opportunities for practitioners. (co-authored by Dr. Jan Herrmann)

- **Supply Chain Scheduling: Makespan reduction potential**[3]

  This paper also addresses the optimization potential of Supply Chain Scheduling. Focusing on the overall makespan of a four-stage supply chain, eight scheduling scenarios are compared by means of a numerical study. The simplest scenario is characterized by separate scheduling of all stages. The most promising scenario is a joint scheduling approach that treats the supply chain as a flow shop. In the other six scenarios, different subsets of stages coordinate their schedules. Joint Supply Chain Scheduling of all stages significantly outperforms the other

---

[3]Published in *International Journal of Logistics Research and Applications*, Volume 15, Issue 5, October 2012, pages 323-336. Chapter 5 contains this paper in a revised and supplemented version.

PREFACE

seven scenarios. This result holds for the case with a single machine as well as for two identical parallel machines at each stage. Owing to the complexity of some scheduling problems, the numerical investigation of the four-stage supply chain scenario is limited to small-size instances which are still solvable using a commercial optimization software. However, a second study deals with a simpler two-stage supply chain structure that allows for the investigation of real-world-size instances. Since the shortest processing time priority applied at the first stage leads to permutation schedules which on average result in near-optimum makespans, a joint Supply Chain Scheduling approach based on Johnson's algorithm turns out to be unreasonable.

- **How to benefit from an R&D investment sharing contract with a supplier**
  Co-authored by Dipl.-Kffr. Rabab Mitri

  Despite a tendency to concentrate on one's core business, especially companies that are known for their innovative products are often found to have an exceptionally high in-house production depth. Focusing on such a company, we model various factors that influence the make-or-buy decision for a component required for a new product. As many innovating companies aim to produce high-quality goods on principle, the component's quality plays an important role in the model. Investment in R&D is another important factor since these sunk costs can weaken the innovating company's position when negotiating with a potential supplier on the component price. Consistent with the observation that innovative companies tend to produce specific components on their own, we identify cases in which in-house production is advantageous. However, in-house production as well as a classic wholesale price contract with a specialized supplier often turn out to be inefficient. This paper demonstrates that, under certain conditions, both the innovative company and the supplier can benefit from sharing the associated R&D investment.

Bielefeld, August 2013   Christian Ullrich

Contents

List of Figures

List of Tables

LIST OF TABLES

6.5   Bargaining scenario for the supplier's investment share g (scenario 6.4.2) . . 134

6.6   Bargaining scenario with anticipated profits (scenario 6.4.2) 134

6.7   Bargaining scenario with anticipated profits (scenario 6.4.3.1) 136

6.8   Bargaining scenario with anticipated profits (scenario 6.4.3.2) 137

6.9   Summary of the example 138

6.10 Frequency of occurrence and average parameter values 139

6.11 Effects of R&D investment sharing 142

List of Abbreviations

BHG	Biskup, Herrmann, Gupta
CPU	Central processing unit
EDI	Electronic data interchange
ERP	Enterprise resource planning
FCFS	First come first served
GHz	GigaHertz
LPT	Longest processing time
MB	Megabyte
MV	1. Machine scheduling, 2. Vehicle routing
M1, M2	Machine 1 and 2, respectively
NP-hard	Non-deterministic polynomial-time hard
O1, O2	Offspring 1 and 2, respectively
P1, P2	Parent 1 and 2, respectively
RAM	Random access memory
RD	Rectangular distribution
R&D	Research and development
RFID	Radio-frequency identification
SPT	Shortest processing time
V1, V2	Vehicle 1 and 2, respectively
VMV	1. Vehicle routing, 2. Machine scheduling, 3. Vehicle routing

Abbreviations of the Three-Field Notation

asym	Asymmetric
ETP	Sum of earliness and tardiness penalties
F2	Two-stage flow-shop
HFS	Hybrid flow-shop scheduling

HF2	Two-stage hybrid flow-shop
HF3	Three-stage hybrid flow-shop
HF4	Four-stage hybrid flow-shop
IC	Inventory holding costs
IP	Identical parallel machines
IP2	Two identical parallel machines
mT	Multiple tours
TC	Transportation costs
twhs	Time windows with hard lower and soft upper bounds

List of Symbols

Symbols used in the Outline

$f(\cdot)$ Function depending on the numbers $x_1, x_2, ..., x_n$

x_i The ith number $(i = 1, ..., n)$

Symbols used in Chapter 3

Latin symbols

c_v Loading capacity of vehicle v

C_j Completion time of job j

d_j Processing due date of job j

D_j Delivery time of job j

fit_{ind} Fitness of individual ind

Fit Total fitness of all individuals

g_{jvt} Binary variable which takes the value 1 if job j is delivered on the tth tour of vehicle v

NP Class of non-deterministic polynomial-time hard problems

n Input size of a given instance

obj_{ind} Objective value of individual ind

$O(\cdot)$ Big O notation. $O(n^2)$ means that the genetic algorithm's worst case computation time can be approximated by a quadratic function depending on the input size n (the number of jobs)

p_j Processing time of job j

P	Class of polynomial-time hard problems
q	Sufficiently large number
r_m	Ready time of machine m
$\hat{r}_v$	Ready time of vehicle v
s_j	Service time at the destination of job j
S_{vt}	Start time of the tth tour of vehicle v
t_{ij}	Travel time from the destination of job i to the destination of job j
T_j	Tardiness of job j
u_j	Size of job j
$\underline{w}_j, \overline{w}_j$	Lower and upper bound of job j's delivery time window
x_{ij}	Binary variable which takes the value 1 if job i is processed before job j and no other job is processed in between on that machine
$x_{j,J+1}$	Binary variable which takes the value 1 if job j is the last job processed on a machine
y_{mj}	Binary variable which takes the value 1 if job j is the first job processed on machine m
z_{ijvt}	Binary variable which takes the value 1 if job i is delivered before job j on the tth tour of vehicle v

Greek symbols

δ_1, δ_2	Time window adjustment parameters
γ	Release date parameter of vehicle 1
κ_j	Upper time window parameter of job j
λ	Service time adjustment parameter
μ	Capacity adjustment parameter
π_j	Lower time window parameter of job j
ρ	Maximum processing time
τ_v	Capacity parameter of vehicle v

Symbols used in Chapter 4

Latin symbols

A_c	Company c's additional Supply Chain Scheduling costs
b_{fix}	Fixed batch delivery costs
b_{fix_c}	Company c's fixed batch delivery costs
b_{var}	Variable batch delivery costs per time unit
b_{var_c}	Company c's variable batch delivery costs
$\bar{b}$	Batch capacity
$\bar{b}_c$	Company c's batch capacity
B_k	Maximum number of delivery batches for customer k
B_{ck}	Company c's maximum number of delivery batches for customer k
C_j	Completion time of job j
C_{cj}	Completion time of job j at company c
d_j	Due date of job j
d_{cj}	Company c's due date of job j
$\underline{h}_j$	Job j's inventory holding costs per time unit before processing
$\underline{h}_{cj}$	Company c's inventory holding costs of job j before processing
$\bar{h}_j$	Job j's inventory holding costs per time unit after processing
$\bar{h}_{cj}$	Company c's inventory holding costs of job j after processing
E_j	Earliness of job j
E_{cj}	Company c's earliness of job j
g_{jkb}	Binary variable which takes the value 1 if job j is delivered within the bth batch to customer k
g_{cjkb}	Binary variable which takes the value 1 if company c delivers job j within the bth batch to customer k
$K_c(\cdot)$	Company c's logistics costs
$L(\cdot)$	Lump sum
M	Number of identical parallel machines
M_c	Number of identical parallel machines owned by company c
NP	Class of non-deterministic polynomial-time hard problems
p_j	Processing time of job j
p_{cj}	Company c's processing time of job j

P	Class of polynomial-time hard problems
q	Sufficiently large number
r_j	Release date of job j
r_{cj}	Release date of job j at company c
R^2	Statistical coefficient of determination
S_j	Start time of the delivery of job j
S_{cj}	Job j's delivery start time at company c
t_k	Travel time to customer k
t_{ck}	Travel time from company c to customer k
T_j	Tardiness of job j
T_{cj}	Company c's tardiness of job j
u_j	Size of job j
u_{cj}	Size of company c's job j
w_{jk}	Binary parameter which has the value 1 if job j is ordered by customer k
w_{cjk}	Binary parameter which has the value 1 if customer k has ordered job j from company c
x_{ij}	Binary variable which takes the value 1 if job i is processed before job j and no other job is processed in between on that machine
x_{cij}	Binary variable which takes the value 1 if company c processes job i before job j and no other job is processed in between on that machine
$x_{j,J+1}$	Binary variable which takes the value 1 if job j is the last job processed on a machine
x_{cj,J_c+1}	Binary variable which takes the value 1 if job j is the last job processed on a machine of company c
x_{0j}	Binary variable which takes the value 1 if job j is the first job processed on a machine
x_{c0j}	Binary variable which takes the value 1 if job j is the first job processed on a machine of company c
y_j	Real number assigned to job j
y_j^*	Once modified number of job j
y_j^{**}	Twice modified number of job j
Z_{kb}	Variable which takes the value 1 if at least one job is assigned to the bth batch shipped to customer k

Z_{ckb} Variable which takes the value 1 if at least one job is delivered within the bth batch from company c to customer k

Greek symbols

α_{BHG}	First due date parameter used by Biskup et al. (2008)
α_j	Job j's earliness penalty per time unit
α_{cj}	Company c's earliness penalty of job j
β_{BHG}	Second due date parameter used by Biskup et al. (2008)
β_j	Job j's tardiness penalty per time unit
β_{cj}	Company c's tardiness penalty of job j
δ	Batch number used to explain the Excel-based heuristic
ϵ_j	Manufacturer's second release date parameter
γ_j	Supplier's due date parameter
κ_j	Manufacturer's due date parameter
π_j	Manufacturer's first release date parameter
σ_c	Transportation cost adjustment parameter of company c
τ	Supplier's customer parameter
v_{cj}	Company c's penalty adjustment parameter of job j
ϕ	Supplier's bargaining power
ω	Overall schedule resulting from separate planning (sep) and Supply Chain Scheduling (SCS), respectively

Symbols used in Chapter 5

Latin symbols

C_{sj}	Completion time of job j at stage s
C_{max}	Maximum completion time at the last stage
M_s	Number of identical parallel machines at stage s
p-value	Probability of obtaining a test statistic that is at least as extreme as the observed one
p_{sj}	Job j's processing time at stage s

q	Sufficiently large number
r_j	Job j's release date at the first stage
t_s	Travel time from stage s to stage $s+1$
x_{sij}	Binary variable which takes the value 1 if job i is processed before job j on the same machine of stage s and no other job is processed in between
$x_{j,J+1}$	Binary variable which takes the value 1 if job j is the last job processed on a machine at stage s
x_{s0j}	Binary variable which takes the value 1 if job j is the first job processed on a machine at stage s

Greek symbols

α	Level of significance

Symbols used in Chapter 6

Indices

c	Central control
e	External procurement
i	In-house production
is	Investment sharing
M	Manufacturer
qd	Quantity discount
rs	Revenue sharing
S	Supplier
tp	Two-part tariff
$*$	Optimum

Latin symbols

A	Investment in in-house production
b	Variable quality assurance costs
B	Investment in external procurement
c	R&D investment effect parameter

LIST OF SYMBOLS XXVII

d	Parameter of the quantity discount contract
f	Difference between the manufacturer's and the supplier's variable unit costs of producing the component
g	Supplier's R&D investment share
$\underline{g}$	Threshold that indicates whether investment sharing or the threat point scenario is more profitable for the manufacturer
$\overline{g}$	Threshold that indicates whether investment sharing or the threat point scenario is more profitable for the supplier
I^2	R&D investment in the product innovation
k_M	Manufacturer's variable unit costs of completing the product (the component's variable costs are not included)
k_S	The supplier's variable unit costs of producing the component
L	Lump sum of the two-part tariff
$p(\cdot)$	Price-demand function
q	Quantity of the product innovation to be sold on the market
s	Percentage of the revenue, the manufacturer pays to the supplier
w	Component price

Greek symbols

$\delta_1, \delta_{1a}, \delta_{1b}$	Thresholds that indicate whether in-house production or external procurement is more profitable
δ_2	Threshold that indicates whether in-house production or central control is more profitable
$\delta_3, \delta_{3a}, \delta_{3b}$	Thresholds that indicate whether the manufacturer's threat point in the negotiation for the component price is in-house production or discontinuation of the project
κ_M	The manufacturer's total variable unit costs in case of in-house production
$\pi(\cdot)$	Profit function

Chapter 1

Outline

Since the 1980s, strategic supply chain management issues, such as the selection of production sites, out- or offshore-sourcing decisions, and long-term business relationships, have always attracted a high level of interest in literature (Thomas and Griffin, 1996). Comparatively little attention has been paid to short-term problems at an operational level. Assuming an enormous cost-cutting potential, Thomas and Griffin (1996) therefore requested the development of approaches to improve the cross-company coordination of logistics operations. In response to this call for research, Hall and Potts (2003), Kreipl and Pinedo (2004), and Agnetis et al. (2006) established *Supply Chain Scheduling* as a new field of study.[1] Supply Chain Scheduling deals with the coordination of the machine and delivery schedules of two or more supply chain stages. The objective is to enhance the supply chain's competitiveness by improving overall performance measured in the total logistics costs, for example.

Chapters 3–5 of this dissertation focus on current issues in Supply Chain Scheduling. Although this research area has existed for approximately ten years, the savings potential has never been properly quantified. If the achievable improvements in supply chain performance did not justify at least the costs of coordination that inevitably accompany a joint scheduling approach, Supply Chain Scheduling would be uneconomical. The three chapters on Supply Chain Scheduling investigate various scenarios with the aim of identifying cases in which joint cross-company scheduling is beneficial and possible in face of the complexity of the arising scheduling problems.

Chapter 3 refers to a broad definition of the term 'supply chain.' This definition already considers production and subsequent delivery operations as a simple form of a

---

[1] In response to the increasing interest, the *Annals of Operations Research* dedicated a special volume to Supply Chain Coordination and Scheduling (161 (1), 2008).

two-stage supply chain, even if the machines and the delivery vehicles belong to the same company. Enterprise resource planning (ERP) systems are usually based on decomposition approaches (Stadtler and Kilger, 2005; Stadtler et al., 2012). Production and delivery operations are successively planned. The partial solutions are then joined to form a solution to the overall problem. However, decomposition approaches are at risk of producing poorly coordinated composite schedules leading to many tardy deliveries. Aiming to reduce total tardiness, Chapter 3 introduces a genetic algorithm that tackles a machine scheduling and vehicle routing problem simultaneously. Two questions motivate this research project. Are the solutions produced by the simultaneous approach significantly better than the composite solutions provided by classic decomposition approaches? And if so, is it possible to capitalize on the optimization potential despite the integrated problem's complexity?

Chapters 4–6 are based on a more common definition of the term 'supply chain.' The supply chains examined here consist of several production sites which may be owned by legally separated companies that maintain supplier-buyer business relationships with one another.

Chapter 4 focusses on one manufacturer and one supplier which are embedded in a larger supply network environment, meaning that they also maintain business relationships with other companies at the various supply chain stages. Both the supplier and the manufacturer face a production/distribution scheduling problem similar to the integrated problem investigated in Chapter 3. An innovative Microsoft Excel-based heuristic is developed that is able to cope with the single companies' problems as well as the joint overall problem. It is hence possible to assess the cost-cutting potential of Supply Chain Scheduling on the basis of a comparison between the total logistics costs resulting from the joint scheduling approach and the costs that are incurred when both companies schedule only on their own.

Note that the spreadsheet heuristic turns out to be very effective. Since Excel is an omnipresent software and the approach can be easily adjusted to many batching, sequencing, scheduling, and routing problems, the heuristic provides enormous opportunities for practitioners.

Whereas Chapter 4 studies a supply network environment organized as a pull system, Chapter 5 deals with a multiple-stage linear supply chain consisting of several consecutive production stages that push the intermediate products downstream. First, a four-stage supply chain is investigated. Using a commercial optimization software package, eight different scheduling scenarios are compared with regard to their effects on the supply chain makespan. All four stages schedule for themselves in the status-quo scenario. In the most promising scenario, all stages schedule jointly. In the remaining six scenarios, different subgroups of the stages collaborate. Since the complexity of the arising scheduling problems limits this investigation to small-size instances,[2] a second investigation concentrates on a simpler two-stage supply chain. Thanks to the existence of some well-known rules, such as *Johnson's rule* (Johnson, 1954), it is possible to handle real-world-size instances, too.

The last part of this dissertation addresses *Supply Chain Contracting*. From an overall supply chain perspective, optimality is often only reachable if one party puts itself into a worse position. For example, improving the supply chain's competitiveness in terms of service levels may require reducing flow times. To this end, materials, parts, and components should be passed down the supply chain as fast as possible. On the other hand, grouping of components to form delivery batches may substantially diminish a company's transportation costs. Since delivery can start only when all components assigned to a batch are ready, the flow times of all but the last component completed are negatively affected by transportation batching. If the company did not or only marginally benefit from a reduction in the supply chain flow times, there is no incentive for it to abstain from delivery batching and incur higher transportation costs. To align one single company with the whole supply chain's interests, compensation needs to be provided by a well-designed cost or profit sharing mechanism.

This example shows that, sometimes, preparatory contractual arrangements are crucial for the success of supply chain management instruments such as Supply Chain Scheduling. As mentioned in the quote below, disparate incentives, different interests, information asymmetries, etc. can cause the objectives and decisions of the companies in a supply chain to be incongruent. The resulting inefficiencies threaten the supply chain's competitiveness. However, in many cases, well-designed contracts that ensure win-win situations can encourage all companies involved to comply with the requirements of the overall supply chain.

> *"Optimal supply chain performance requires the execution of a precise set of actions. Unfortunately, those actions are not always in the best interest of the members in the supply chain, i.e., the supply chain members are primarily concerned with optimizing their own objectives, and that self-serving focus often results in poor per-*

---

[2]The term 'instance' refers to a specific problem of the general problem in focus. Assume the general problem is to multiply the numbers $x_1, x_2, ..., x_n$, $f(x_1, x_2, ..., x_n) = \prod_{i=1}^{n} x_i$, then small-size instances of this general problem are $f(2,5) = 2 \cdot 5$ and $f(4,2,9) = 4 \cdot 2 \cdot 9$, for example. Specific problems dealing with many numbers, say $n = 1\,000$, are large-size instances.

formance. However, optimal performance is achievable if the firms coordinate by contracting on a set of transfer payments such that each firm's objective becomes aligned with the supply chain's objective." Cachon (2003), p. 229

Inspired by Bhaskaran and Krishnan (2009) and the real-life examples mentioned therein, Chapter 6 examines a new type of contract. Many companies that are known for their product innovations, such as Miele or Apple, exhibit exceptionally high production depth. Even parts and components that these innovating companies do not specialize in are produced in-house. Viewed in the context of the last decades' trend towards global corporate networks, this phenomenon is hardly immediately intuitive. For example, the core competency approach by Prahalad and Hamel (1990) implies that companies should rather concentrate on their key skills and leave everything else to specialized suppliers. Chapter 6 develops a model which can partly explain the high production depths of many innovating companies. However, the investigation also shows that the chosen production depth can nevertheless be suboptimal from an overall supply chain perspective. In many cases, cooperation with a specialized supplier bears optimization potential which could be capitalized on given a well-designed contract. Since classic contract types here cannot simultaneously coordinate the supply chain in accordance with the manufacturer's and the supplier's interests, a new type of contract used in the pharmaceutical industry is analyzed. This contract is based on sharing the research and development costs related to a product innovation.

The dissertation is structured as follows. Chapter 2 generally motivates and introduces the research area of supply chain management that covers all topics handled in the subsequent chapters. To provide an uniform understanding of relevant terms and aspects, basic historical and theoretical backgrounds are briefly discussed here. Chapter 2 is followed by the four main chapters 3–6 which have been summarized above. Chapter 7 concludes this dissertation.

Chapter 2

Introduction to Supply Chain Management

"Times have changed since Henry Ford made the River Rouge complex in Dearborn, Michigan, into the ultimate in vertical integration, with iron ore going in at one end and shiny model A's coming out the other. Now vertical dis-integration is the order of the day— in autos, in handheld computers, in pharmaceuticals, in ink-jet printers, in health care, in cameras..." Dolan and Meredith (2001), p. 107

2.1 Historical background and general motivation

The term 'supply chain management' originates from an outlook issued in 1982 by the consultants Oliver and Webber (Oliver and Webber, 1982, reprint: Oliver and Webber, 1992). The first scientific articles to use this term were written by Houlihan (1985) and Jones and Riley (1985). As revealed in Table 2.1, since then there has been an enormous number of publications with this keyword (Burgess et al., 2006; Herrmann, 2010). However, on closer inspection it becomes apparent that many of the problems that are now assigned to the research area of supply chain management were in fact identified much earlier. For example, the first articles on the *bullwhip effect*[1] were already written in the 1950s (Simon, 1952; Forrester, 1958). Nevertheless, it was not before the late 1990s that

---

[1]The bullwhip effect describes an amplification of demand variability further up the supply chain. A company exhibits this effect if it purchases materials and components more variably with regard to quantities and time intervals than it sells its products. Several reasons for this phenomenon are listed by Lee et al. (1997b,a) and Moyaux et al. (2007). Cachon and Kök (2007) and Bray and Mendelson (2012) provide empirical evidence.

this ubiquitous issue in current supply chain management theory and practice (Moyaux et al., 2007; Cachon and Kök, 2007; Bray and Mendelson, 2012) was brought into focus by Lee et al. (1997a,b) who coined the term 'bullwhip effect.' The problem of *double marginalization*[2] was also recognized long before supply chain management was established as a research area (Cournot, 1897; Spengler, 1950; Machlup and Taber, 1960; Tirole, 1988). Cournot (1838) already pointed to this problem in the 19th century.

Table 2.1: Number of scientific publications with the terms 'supply chain' and 'supply chain management' in the title (according to scholar.google)

Years	Supply chain	Supply chain management
1981-1984	8	4
1985-1988	22	5
1989-1992	100	31
1993-1996	718	229
1997-2000	4 670	1 459
2001-2004	10 700	3 190
2005-2008	14 400	3 770
2009-2012	16 100	4 090

What applies to many subjects of the current supply chain management research often applies to the underlying models, too. Many of the models used to describe and solve the problems in focus refer to approaches which were also developed long before the 1980s. For example, the frequently cited article by Corbett and de Groote (2000) on lot sizing conflicts in supply chains uses the *economic order quantity model*[3] by Harris (1913). The *newsvendor model*,[4] on which many studies especially on Supply Chain Contracting are based (Lariviere and Porteus, 2001; Taylor, 2002; Cachon, 2003; Cachon and Kök, 2007; Katok and Yan Wu, 2009; Chiu et al., 2010), can be attributed to Edgeworth (1888) and Arrow et al. (1951).

---

[2]Double marginalization describes a problem of inefficient pricing in monopoly chains. If each supply chain stage sets its product price individually, focusing only on its own profit, under certain circumstances the sum of profits is lower than the total supply chain profit resulting from a joint optimization approach.

[3]Aiming to determine the cost-minimal order (or production) lot size, the economic order quantity model trades off inventory holding costs, which increase in the number of product units per lot, and the one-time order (or set-up) costs incurred by each lot.

[4]Facing stochastic demand, the newsvendor model deals with the problem of determining the optimal order (or production) quantity of a perishable good such as a newspaper, for example. If demand exceeds the order (or processing) quantity, profits are lost. On the other hand, product units unsold after demand is satisfied can still have a salvage value but generally, lead to a loss.

Supply chain management topics have clearly attracted increasing interest since the early 1980s (see Table 2.1). The strong interest finally resulted in the establishment of this new field of study. As discussed above, existing and related subjects and models were pieced together and also viewed in this new research framework. But what caused the sudden interest in cross-company collaboration issues? Empirical studies (Spekman et al., 1998; Ho et al., 2002) confirm that there has been a development from competition between large nationally operating companies towards competition between global supply chains consisting of highly specialized smaller business units (Christopher, 1992; Cooper et al., 1997; Handfield and Nichols, 1999; Barnes, 2006; Mentzer et al., 2007; Stadtler, 2008), a phenomenon that has boosted the interest in supply chain management (Sachan and Datta, 2005; Burgess et al., 2006). But what, in turn, are the reasons for the tendency towards globally networks of interlinked specialists? The core competency theory (Prahalad and Hamel, 1990) argues that it results from the competition-induced necessity to ensure flexibility and to make use of any cost-savings potential. To adapt more quickly to new market situations and more competitive product prices, many companies specialized, concentrated on their core businesses, and outsourced inefficient steps in the production processes. The transaction cost theory (Coase, 1937; Williamson, 1975, 1985, 1991, 2008), which also provides reasons for the development towards smaller business units, deals with the effects of bounded rationality, opportunistic behavior, uncertainty, and product specificity on the decision whether a transaction should take place via the market, within a centrally controlled company, or within a hybrid form between these two extremes. For example, transaction cost theory assumes that the costs of bureaucracy grow disproportionately to a company's size. Many collaborating specialists are hence likely to be more flexible and competitive than a cumbersome large company with an enormous head office that attempts to administrate all activities centrally.

Among other things, the trend towards global supply networks has been supported by the political developments of the last decades. For example, access to the production sites and markets of the Eastern Bloc and China opened up enormous opportunities (Zhao et al., 2007; Sauvant, 2008). Brazil and India are also becoming more and more appealing (Humphrey, 2003). In addition, scientific and technological progress made this global orientation feasible and profitable. The flows of information within and between companies have been facilitated in the extreme by developments such as RFID (Radio-Frequency Identification) technology (Alshawi, 2001; Lancioni et al., 2003; Croom, 2005; Sarac et al., 2010). Schifrin (2001) especially highlights the essential significance of the

Internet in the modern business world:

> *"Good-bye mergers and acquisitions. In a global market tied together by the Internet, corporate partnerships and alliances are proving a more productive way to keep companies growing."* Schifrin (2001), p. 26

The following incidents show how interrelated the global economy actually is these days. Not only did 9/11 impact on financial markets and the US economy, it also severely affected the global flow of materials for a long time. Due to stricter transport regulations, Japanese car manufacturers Honda and Toyota, for example, had difficulties supplying their production sites in North America (Czaja, 2009). The volcanic ash cloud in 2010 and the earthquake in Japan in 2011 caused similar problems to companies all around the world. However, most supply bottlenecks are not just due to socio-political issues or natural catastrophes, they are also the result of human failure or bad planning. Taking appropriate measures, many supply shortages could have been avoided by the supply chains' decision-makers. Defective diesel injection pumps delivered by Bosch, for example, forced BMW and DaimlerChrysler to partly halt production in 2005 (manager magazin, author unknown, 2005b) which entailed enormous costs. Bosch traced the defect to a spare part bought from a Czech supplier and subsequently pledged to improve its quality control (Freitag and Noé, 2005). Later that year, defective power brake units also delivered by Bosch led to a recall by US car manufacturer General Motors (manager magazin, author unknown, 2005a). In September 2012, a workers' riot protesting bad working conditions resulted in the brief closure of one of Foxconn Technologies' largest Chinese plants, which employed almost 50 000 workers. This affected electronic giants such as Apple, Hewlett-Packard, Dell, and Microsoft, all of which source large quantities of components for their products from Foxconn (Barboza and Bradsher, 2012). Note that these incidents also reveal the risks of the *just-in-time*[5] supply concept (Ohno, 1988).

Ever more complex and competitive global markets with enigmatic supplier-buyer-relationships mean that well-coordinated cross-company material, information, and cash flows are essential for success. This argumentation, which is used to motivate almost every publication on supply chain management, is supported by the above and many more real-life examples, explaining why supply chain management has attracted

---

[5]The just-in-time concept, a prevailing supply chain management measure, aims to prevent or at least minimize all waste of resources along the supply chain. However, reducing buffer inventories to minimize tied-up capital, can put some supply chain stages or even the entire supply chain at the risk of supply shortage induced production breakdowns.

so much attention over the last decades. But what can supply chain management actually achieve?

The literature provides numerous hints as to the often enormous potential offered by appropriate supply chain management measures. For example, Cachon and Lariviere (2005) deal with a change in contract design between US home video rental chain Blockbuster and film studios. Shortly after their release, films were often not available due to high demand, causing severe customer frustration. Instead of paying the studios $65 per copy of one video, the parties agreed on a price of only $8 plus a share of the rental fee Blockbuster earned off its home videos. This share was approximately 30–45%. The so-called *revenue sharing contract* made it profitable for both Blockbuster and the film studios to provide a larger number of copies of a new film. Using a specimen calculation, Cachon and Lariviere (2001) show the coordinating effect of this new type of contract on the video rental supply chain. Blockbuster was able to increase its market share from 24 to 40% between 1997 and 2002 (Warren and Peers, 2002). In their introduction, Stadtler and Kilger (2005) mention other impressive examples of successful supply chain management measures at Hewlett-Packard, Campbell Soup, IBM, and BASF (Lee and Chu, 2005; Cachon and Fisher, 1998; Grupp, 1998; Lin et al., 2000). These companies achieved enormous savings by improving material provision along their supply chains.

Brinkhoff and Thonemann (2007) carry out a large-size empirical investigation of the use of supply chain management measures in practice. 57% of the companies questioned stated that they already participated in cross-company collaborations. As many as 97% said they intended to extend their partnerships with other companies to 2012. However, the study also reveals that more than 50% of the supply chain management initiatives failed for various reasons. In one case, an information sharing project with a supplier that served to increase the service level and reduce inventory stocks was stopped at the last minute. Having heard of the project, top management was apprehensive about the high level of data transparency it would entail. This empirical investigation indicates that there is still great potential and demand for research on supply chain management topics such as Supply Chain Scheduling and Contracting.

2.2 Basic definitions

Developing concise definitions can be very painful since there are typically many people with divergent opinions ready to defend their perspectives on the subject in question. The benefit of going to the trouble of producing generally accepted definitions often turns out to be limited relative to the elaborate and extensive discussions this involves. Such definitions have the habit to be very broad and distracting. Nevertheless, the lack of consistency in the literature concerning the definitions of the terms 'supply chain' and 'supply chain management' (Ho et al., 2002; Burgess et al., 2006; Jain et al., 2010) makes it imperative to discuss the way these terms are used here. But note that the aim is not to develop yet another definition. Instead, common definitions are analyzed with regard to their most important elements.

Chopra and Meindl (2012) contribute the following fairly broad definition of the term 'supply chain:'

> "*A supply chain consists of all parties involved, directly or indirectly, in fulfilling a customer request. The supply chain includes not only the manufacturer and suppliers, but also transporters, warehouses, retailers, and even customers themselves. Within each organization, such as a manufacturer, the supply chain includes all functions involved in receiving and filling a customer request. These functions include, but are not limited to, new product development, marketing, operations, distribution, finance, and customer service.*" Chopra and Meindl (2012), p. 13

This definition encompasses two perspectives (Stadtler, 2005):

- The inter-organizational perspective and
- the intra-organizational perspective.

2.2.1   The inter-organizational perspective

The inter-organizational perspective addresses a network of independent, meaning legally separated, companies that is referred to as a supply chain (Ross, 1998), which is the more common definition mentioned in the dissertation's outline. The word 'chain' suggests a linear sequence of companies. However, in practice, the structure of business relationships between companies is generally not linear but arborescent. Since companies often pursue a dual or multiple sourcing strategy,[6] meaning they source required materials and components from several suppliers, 'supply network' would be the more accurate term to describe real-world business structures. Nevertheless, the term 'supply chain,' often meaning a supply network, has became accepted in the literature. Figure 2.1 depicts a classic inter-organizational supply chain structure.

---

[6]A detailed discussion of the reasons for a dual or multiple sourcing strategy follows in Chapter 4 on page 63.

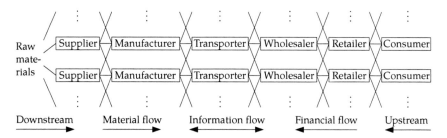

Figure 2.1: A classic inter-organizational supply chain structure

For example, Dr. Oetker, a German manufacturer of food products, purchases ingredients such as pepperoni, cheese, flour, and tomato sauce for frozen pizzas from its suppliers. The suppliers in turn source raw materials such as pork, milk, grain, and tomatoes from farmers. Having passed through Dr. Oetker's production process, the frozen pizzas are stored in central warehouses where third-party transporters pick them up and deliver them to wholesalers. The end-consumers buy the pizzas from retailers who are supplied by the wholesalers. While the material flow generally proceeds down the supply chain, information flows in both directions. For example, orders are given up the supply chain, while the arrival times of the materials are communicated down. The financial flow generally proceeds up the supply chain. Note that Figure 2.1 does not claim to represent all of the supply chain business relationships that exist in practice. In case of product recycling or reverse logistics of load carriers, for example, the material flows down as well as up the supply chain. The same holds for monetary payments. Contractual tardiness penalties can cause downstream financial flows, too. Figure 2.1 only presents a classic structure that is relevant in many branches of industry.

Consistent with the inter-organizational perspective, Simchi-Levi et al. (2008) propose the following definition of supply chain management:

> "Supply Chain Management is a set of approaches utilized to efficiently integrate suppliers, manufacturers, warehouses, and stores, so that merchandise is produced and distributed at the right quantities, to the right locations, and at the right time, in order to minimize systemwide costs while satisfying service level requirements."
> Simchi-Levi et al. (2008), p. 1

This definition contains three key elements (Stadtler, 2008):

- Integration,

- coordination, and

- the goal of supply chain management.

Supply chain **integration** means that several companies enter into a very close collaboration with a cross-company planning focus. Since such commitments are generally made for at least a mid-term time horizon, the careful selection of suitable partners is of fundamental importance to the partnerships' success. Integration aims to facilitate channel **coordination** which implies that the products are processed and distributed in the right quantities, in the right locations, and at the right time. Matching logistics equipment is the first step towards integration and coordination. Real-time data exchange via joint EDI (Electronic Data Interchange) systems (Ho et al., 2002), for example, allows for the exchange of up-to-date information on inventory levels. Improving the coordination of cross-company material flows can contribute towards mitigating the previously mentioned bullwhip effect. Also, the effectiveness of the prevalent just-in-time and *vendor managed inventory*[7] (Çetinkaya and Lee, 2000; Disney and Towill, 2003) approaches strongly depends on well-integrated EDI systems.

Without effective integration and coordination, the competitiveness of a supply chain as a whole is put at risk. Competitors may outperform the supply chain in terms of product quality and service level standards such as lead times, compliance with due dates, and shortfall quantities. Since the overall cost structure directly affects pricing decisions and profits, the system-wide costs, as mentioned in the definition by Simchi-Levi et al. (2008), are also of major importance. Taking into account all of these aspects, the primary **goal** of supply chain management is to improve overall competitiveness. However, when dealing with inter-organizational supply chains, there is the additional constraint of having to ensure Pareto improvements for all companies involved. As described in the dissertation's outline, major conflicts arise if at least one party suffers because it has to comply with the measures required to optimize overall performance. Since it entails cost and profit sharing mechanisms, suitable Supply Chain Contract-

---

[7]The term 'vendor managed inventory' describes a specific logistics concept involving a supplier and a manufacturer. Provided with all relevant information on the manufacturer's material flows, the supplier is in charge of managing the inventory stock of a component that the manufacturer sources from him. The primary aim is to optimize the material flows between the two supply chain partners and thus to reduce logistics costs.

ing is thus especially important in inter-organizational supply chains. Stadtler (2005) emphasizes this:

> *"While hierarchical coordination in globally operating enterprises is already a demanding task, the real challenge arises in an inter-organizational supply chain where hierarchical coordination is no longer possible."* Stadtler (2005), p. 576

To sum up, the task of supply chain management is to provide approaches that efficiently integrate and coordinate the individual supply chain stages. In doing so, it aims to enhance the competitiveness of the supply chain as a whole. In the case of inter-organizational supply chains, it also needs to be ensured that all companies involved benefit from the close collaboration. Note that the inevitable costs of integration and coordination, caused by a need for new software licences and labor input, for example, must be traded off against the resulting improvements in performance.

2.2.2   The intra-organizational perspective

The intra-organizational perspective deals with the supply chain within a company, which can be explained by the *supply chain planning matrix*[8] in Figure 2.2. The focus is on the activities carried out within a company.

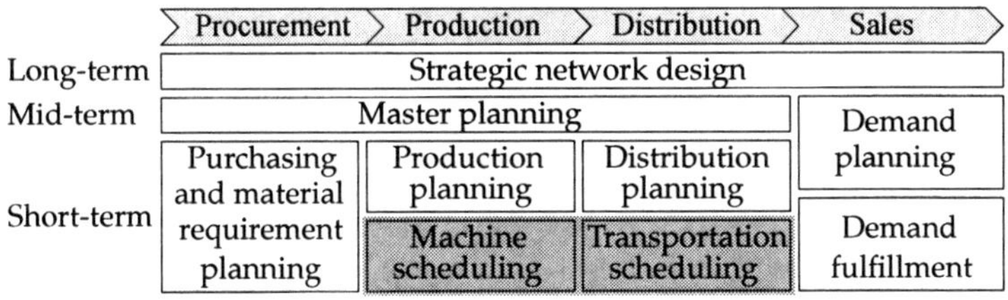

	Procurement	Production	Distribution	Sales
Long-term	Strategic network design			
Mid-term	Master planning			Demand planning
Short-term	Purchasing and material requirement planning	Production planning	Distribution planning	
		Machine scheduling	Transportation scheduling	Demand fulfillment

Figure 2.2: The supply chain planning matrix (Rohde et al., 2000, p. 10)

Assumed to be linked by information flows in all directions, the rectangles represent typical planning issues arising in most industrial companies. The *y*-axis addresses the

---

[8]The supply chain planning matrix focuses on logistics related planning tasks. Business functions such as new product development, marketing, and finance are ignored. Fandel et al. (2009) identify two main groups of definitions of the term 'supply chain management.' While the first group deals with logistics aspects only (Göpfert, 2004), the second also addresses other functions (Cooper et al., 1997). Note that Mentzer et al. (2001) mark out the differences and commonalities between supply chain management and other fields of study such as traditional logistics.

time horizon of these issues (Fleischmann et al., 2008). The x-axis exhibits the material flow through the main activities *procurement, production, distribution,* and *sales*. For example, *strategic network design* requires making structural decisions with a long time horizon. The challenge is to determine capacities, transportation modes, strategic business relationships, and locations of processing sites and warehouses. These decisions should be made simultaneously since they concern procurement, production, distribution, and sales more or less at the same time. A mid-term task is *master planning* which comprises the assignment of production quantities to processing sites, identification of bottlenecks, adjustment of capacities, and contracting with suppliers and third-party transporters. Covering the next sales cycles, master planning is based on demand forecasts provided by the department responsible for *demand planning*. Based on the results of master planning and a bill of materials explosion, the short-term material requirements can be planned and the materials purchased. *Production planning* and *machine scheduling* means determining lot sizes and production schedules for a given week, day, and/or hour. *Distribution planning* and *transportation scheduling* refer to assigning completed products to transportation batches and scheduling deliveries to customers.

Intra-organizational supply chain management focuses on the integration and coordination of the company-internal activities. Its aim is to improve the company's performance and competitiveness. Heizer and Render (2011) propose a definition of 'supply chain management' that is consistent with this definition:

> *"Supply chain management is the integration of the activities that procure materials and services, transform them into intermediate goods and final products, and deliver them to customers."* Heizer and Render (2011), p. 326

Compared with inter-organizational supply chains aligned by coordinating contracts, intra-organizational supply chains seem to have the advantage of a central head office that can issue instructions. However, in practice centrally unmanageable structures often involve the need to split companies into a number of departments with certain degrees of responsibility such as cost centers, profit centers, and investment centers (Ewert and Wagenhofer, 2008). The department managers' salaries are often directly affected by their department's performance. Since the managers are therefore primarily concerned with their individual department's performance, the conflict potentials arising in inter- and intra-organizational supply chains can be very similar. As in inter-organizational supply chains, incongruent incentives amplified by information asymmetries between the various parties put the overall success at risk (Milgrom and Roberts, 1992). Sophisticated transfer prices (Martini, 2007) and other framework arrangements can become necessary to decentrally align the managers' actions with the head office's interests. Hence, from the intra-organizational perspective, transfer pricing and many other approaches known from management accounting and principal-agent literature can be interpreted as supply chain management instruments.

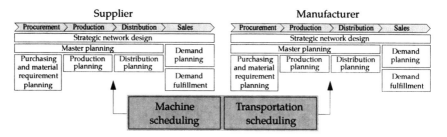

Figure 2.3: An inter-organizational Supply Chain Scheduling scenario

To conclude, an inter-organizational supply chain is a network of intra-organizational supply chains. Figure 2.3 depicts a supply chain consisting of a manufacturer that purchases components from a supplier. Both parties have to deal with an intra-organizational supply chain management problem as implied by the planning matrices. Furthermore, as indicated by the dark gray background, the supplier and the manufacturer are assumed to integrate and coordinate their machine and transportation schedules which, if the supplier and the manufacturer are independent companies, is inter-organizational Supply Chain Scheduling. Chapter 4 examines such a scenario. Highlighted in Figure 2.2, the focus of Chapter 3 is on integrated machine and transportation scheduling. According to the definitions discussed, this can be interpreted as intra-organizational Supply Chain Scheduling. However, if the delivery vehicles belonged to a third-party transporter, integrated machine and transportation scheduling would even constitute an example of inter-organizational Supply Chain Scheduling.

Chapter 3

Supply Chain Scheduling: Integrated machine scheduling and vehicle routing

3.1 Motivation

Increasing pressure on global markets forces companies as well as entire supply chains to capitalize rigorously on saving potentials.[1] For example, just-in-time and just-in-sequence concepts are widely used to reduce logistics expenditures which often represent over 30% of the total costs of a product (Thomas and Griffin, 1996). Such approaches, however, involve a need to comply with due dates since tardy deliveries may cause the recipients to struggle to meet their own due dates. Manufacturers of special purpose machines, for example, are not able to assemble a machine until their suppliers release the required components such as motors, cases, and control modules. A similar problem arises in modular construction. Warehouses or parking decks cannot be built until special industry doors, concrete modules, and steel components have been supplied. The tardiness of a single component can disrupt the entire supply chain. Rearrangement or interruption of production schedules, idle time, tardiness penalties, and unnecessarily high inventories sometimes drive up costs considerably. However, just-in-time approaches are pointless if they incur high transportation costs in an attempt to prevent such situations. Cost-efficient suppliers that rarely exceed due dates are hence essential in just-in-time environments and hold an enormous competitive advantage.

---

[1]Chapters 3–6 each begin with an introduction that provides specific motivations and background information regarding the respective chapter's line of argumentation. Since the issues covered in the three chapters on Supply Chain Scheduling are closely related, this approach does lead to some minor redundancies but at the same time allows the reader to digest each chapter separately without the risk of losing out on important information.

In order to reduce total logistics costs, production and delivery operations need to be well coordinated, first within intra- and then within inter-organizational supply chains (Manoj et al., 2008).

As illustrated in Figure 2.2 on page 13, this chapter deals with intra-organizational integration and coordination of production and distribution operations. The next sections take a scheduling-oriented perspective and assume the possibility of conflict-free integration of production and distribution operations, as do most of the papers introduced in the following literature survey. Note that Chapter 4's literature review discusses intra-organizational as well as the conflict-prone inter-organizational integration of production and delivery operations in the context of the entire research area of Supply Chain Scheduling.

A given set of jobs has to be processed on parallel machines and delivered to job-dependent destinations by a fleet of vehicles within distinct delivery time windows. Such settings often occur in the automotive industry. Suppliers of injection molded plastic components, for example, usually run many parallel machines and deliver to several manufacturers like BMW, Daimler, and VW. If they deliver late, suppliers may cause the above mentioned problems, damage their reputation, and incur contractual penalties. Hence, minimizing tardiness-based performance criteria such as the number of tardy jobs, maximum tardiness, and total (weighted) tardiness is frequently encountered in practice. Because of its widespread use (Koulamas, 1994), the objective criterion discussed in this chapter is the minimization of total tardiness.

To reduce complexity, classic decomposition approaches break down the overall problem, solve the production and delivery subproblems successively, and merge the subsolutions to form a solution to the overall problem. Such approaches are particularly appropriate when interdependencies between the two planning subproblems can be prevented by high buffer stocks. However, low or even zero buffer inventories are frequently encountered in practice. The popularity of the just-in-time philosophy, which serves to cut down on holding costs, is only one of several reasons for that. Make-to-order, perishable, and time-sensitive goods such as ready-mixed concrete (Garcia et al., 2002, 2004) simply cannot be kept in stock. Companies selling such products, in particular, see the coordination of production and distribution as one of the most important success factors (Dawande et al., 2006; Geismar et al., 2008; Akkerman et al., 2010; Huo et al., 2010; Geismar et al., 2011; Cakici et al., 2012). In order to be up-to-date, newspapers cannot be printed before midnight (Hurter and Van Buer, 1996; Van Buer et al., 1999). Drop-off points, however, have to be supplied with area-dependent editions by, say, 4:00 am so home delivery carriers can pick up the newspapers early enough to prevent tardy delivery and thus dissatisfied customers. The same applies to the customized computer and food catering industries where fierce competition causes the need to produce and deliver high quality goods within very narrow time windows (Chen and Vairaktarakis, 2005; Farahani et al., 2012). Wal-Mart and Amazon aim to provide same-day delivery for online orders placed before noon (Bhattarai, 2012; Clifford, 2012). Customers can select a four-hour time window during which they wish to receive the ordered items. The coordination of picking and delivery is a very demanding logistical task yet also the key success factor for same-day delivery strategies. Effective and efficient integrated planning approaches are indispensable for managers who work with such business models.

As will be shown, although they are often able to handle the subproblems successfully, classic decomposition approaches can cause poorly coordinated composite overall plans, resulting in high tardiness. Hence, two questions motivate this chapter. Are the results of integrating machine scheduling and vehicle routing significantly better than those of classic decomposition approaches? And if so, is it possible to capitalize on these potentials despite the complexity of the integrated problem? Both questions are addressed by means of a numerical study. A genetic algorithm that tackles the integrated problem as a whole is compared with two classic decomposition approaches.

The remainder is structured as follows. Section 3.2 surveys the related literature. In Section 3.3, the machine scheduling and vehicle routing subproblems as well as the integrated overall problem are described by mixed integer linear programs. The generation of test instances, needed for the numerical study, is explained in Section 3.4. Section 3.5 introduces the decomposition approaches and the genetic algorithm. The results of the numerical study are presented in Section 3.6. Section 3.7 concludes.

3.2 Literature survey

Sarmiento and Nagi (1999), Erengüç et al. (1999), and Fahimnia et al. (2013) survey the entire research area of integrated production and distribution systems. The authors address strategic, tactical, as well as operational issues. Chen (2004, 2010) extensively reviews papers that deal only with the operational subtopic of integrated scheduling of machines and outbound job delivery, which is the issue most relevant to this dissertation. The publications gathered by Chen (2004, 2010) can be divided into two main groups: While some studies deal with rather 'simple' delivery considerations, like direct or shuttle shipments, others allow for vehicle routing. Tables 3.1 and 3.2 provide an overview of the literature on these two problem types, subdividing the publications in question according to whether they account for due dates or not. The articles are also categorized by the number of job destinations. Some papers consider only a single job destination, like a distribution center or a warehouse, while others handle multiple destinations such as several customer locations. Since vehicle routing does not make sense in the case of a single job destination, there are only papers in Table 3.2 that take account of multiple destinations.

Table 3.1: Integrated scheduling of machines and 'simple' delivery operations

Problems	without due dates	with due dates
with a single job destination	Cheng and Kahlbacher (1993), Cheng and Gordon (1994), Cheng et al. (1996), Cheng et al. (1997), Wang and Cheng (2000), Lee and Chen (2001), Chang and Lee (2004), Li and Ou (2005), Soukhal et al. (2005), Chen and Pundoor (2006), Chen et al. (2007), Ji et al. (2007), Yuan et al. (2007), Wang and Cheng (2007), Zhong et al. (2007), Pan et al. (2009), Wang and Cheng (2009a), Wang and Cheng (2009b), Lee and Yoon (2010), Mazdeh et al. (2011), Ng and Lingfa (2012)	Matsuo (1988), Herrmann and Lee (1993), Chen (1996), Yuan (1996), Yang (2000), Hall et al. (2001), Hall and Potts (2005), Qi (2008), Chen and Pundoor (2009), Fu et al. (2012), Hamidinia et al. (2012)
with multiple job destinations	Potts (1980), Woeginger (1994), Zdrzalka (1995), Woeginger (1998), Gharbi and Haouari (2002), Liu and Cheng (2002), Hall and Potts (2003), Averbakh and Xue (2007), Li and Vairaktarakis (2007), Mazdeh et al. (2007), Chen and Lee (2008), Mazdeh et al. (2008), Li and Yuan (2009), Selvarajah and Steiner (2009), Averbakh (2010), Li et al. (2011), Averbakh and Baysan (2012)	Hall and Potts (2003), Pundoor and Chen (2005), Wang and Lee (2005), Qi (2006), Stecke and Zhao (2007), Steiner and Zhang (2009), Huo et al. (2010), Cakici et al. (2012), Farahani et al. (2012)

As they concern machine scheduling and vehicle routing, the publications listed in Table 3.2 are most closely related to this chapter. Chang and Lee (2004) examine a single machine scheduling and vehicle routing problem. Only one vehicle with a limited loading capacity is available for delivery. Each job requires a job-dependent loading capacity and is preassigned to one of only two possible destinations. A tailor-made heuristic is proposed to minimize the arrival time of the last job at its destination. Chen

Table 3.2: Integrated machine scheduling and vehicle routing

Problems	without due dates	with due dates
	Chang and Lee (2004), Chen and Vairaktarakis (2005), Li and Vairaktarakis (2007)	Garcia et al. (2002), Garcia et al. (2004)

and Vairaktarakis (2005) extend the problem to more destinations and an infinite number of vehicles with a loading capacity limited to a certain number of jobs. Single and parallel machine scheduling problems are addressed. The authors propose constructive algorithms to minimize convex combinations of the maximum arrival time (average arrival time) and the transportation costs which depend on the number of employed vehicles and the routes assigned to them. Their integrated production and delivery approaches are compared to classic decomposition approaches. Numerical experiments reveal that integration induces average relative improvements of between 12 and 40%. Li and Vairaktarakis (2007) focus on a similar problem with jobs that consist of two tasks. There is a special machine for each task. The tasks can be done at the same time. Tailor-made heuristics are developed to minimize the sum of the weighted total arrival time and transportation costs. Garcia et al. (2004) deal with several plants, each equipped with parallel machines, and a fleet of vehicles that can deliver no more than one job at a time. The jobs can be processed only in job-dependent subsets of the plants and must be delivered immediately after completion. Furthermore, the jobs are characterized by job-dependent due dates, destinations, and service times at the destinations. The author's problem-specific heuristic aims to maximize the total weighted number of just-in-time delivered jobs minus the transportation costs. Garcia et al. (2002) apply a genetic algorithm to a similar problem which is described below.

In recognition of its strong practical relevance, Pundoor and Chen (2005) and Soukhal et al. (2005) explicitly call for more research on integrated machine scheduling and vehicle routing which, as Table 3.2 reveals, is a rarely studied type of problem. Appeals are also made for more research including due dates (Chang and Lee, 2004) and time windows:

"While vehicle routing problems with time windows have been well studied in the vehicle routing literature, few papers have considered integrated production and outbound distribution scheduling problems with both routing decisions and time window constraints. Such problems are more challenging than any other class or

subclass of integrated production and outbound distribution scheduling problems. However, due to their practicality, such problems clearly deserve more research" Chen (2010), p. 145

Furthermore, there is a call for research dealing with a processing company that owns a fleet of vehicles (Chen and Vairaktarakis, 2005). The number of available vehicles limits the number of concurrent shipments in such a scenario. The next section introduces a practice-oriented problem setting that combines all of these requests.

Since genetic algorithms are the method of choice to approach this chapter's integrated problem, the second part of the literature survey covers publications that apply genetic algorithms to related problem types. For example, genetic algorithms have been successfully used to solve machine scheduling problems (Aytug et al., 2003; Reeves, 2010). Min and Cheng (1999) aim to minimize the makespan on parallel machines. Their genetic algorithm outperforms a simulated annealing approach and a priority rule based heuristic. Sivrikaya-Şerifoğlu and Ulusoy (1999) address a parallel machine scheduling problem with job-dependent due dates. The goal is to minimize the sum of earliness and tardiness penalties. For larger-size instances, a heuristic based on neighborhood exchange turns out to perform less well than a genetic algorithm. Moreover, Valente and Gonçalves (2009) develop a well-performing genetic algorithm for a single machine scheduling problem with linear earliness and quadratic tardiness penalties. Genetic algorithms have also been successfully applied to vehicle routing problems. Numerical studies with common benchmark instances for capacitated vehicle routing problems with total travel distance (time) and total travel cost objectives reveal that the hybrid genetic algorithms by Berger and Barkaoui (2003) and Prins (2004) can compete with the best known tailor-made heuristics. Ting and Huang (2005), Alvarenga et al. (2007), Vidal et al. (2013) and some earlier papers surveyed by Bräysy and Gendreau (2005) obtain similar results for vehicle routing problems with time windows.

Despite these successful applications of genetic algorithms to problems that are similar to the subproblems introduced in the next section, there are only very few genetic algorithm and other meta-heuristic approaches to integrated production and delivery scheduling problems. Hamidinia et al. (2012) apply a genetic algorithm to a single machine scheduling and batch delivery problem with the aim to minimize the sum of transportation, inventory holding, earliness, and tardiness costs. Cakici et al. (2012) combine genetic algorithms with simple dispatching rules to solve multi-objective single machine scheduling and batch delivery problems. Garcia et al. (2002) select jobs, assign them to one of several plants equipped with parallel machines, and schedule the production and delivery operations. A fleet of vehicles is available to deliver the jobs immediately after processing in single-job shipments to their respective customers. The objective is to maximize the profit associated with the selected jobs minus penalty payments incurred for deviations from job-dependent due dates. A comparison with an exact graph-based method reveals that the authors' genetic algorithm results in near-optimum solutions. To the best of my knowledge, this is the sole application of genetic algorithms to an integrated machine scheduling and vehicle routing problem so far.

3.3 Mixed integer linear programs

The integrated machine scheduling and vehicle routing problem examined in this chapter consists of two subproblems. The subproblems are described and modeled in Sections 3.3.1 and 3.3.2, respectively. Section 3.3.3 shows how the models of the subproblems can be linked to formalize the integrated problem. The following parameters and variables are employed:

Parameters

c_v	Loading capacity of vehicle v ($v = 1, ..., V$)
d_j	Processing due date of job j ($j = 1, ..., J$)
u_j	Size of job j ($j = 1, ..., J$)
p_j	Processing time of job j ($j = 1, ..., J$)
q	Sufficiently large number
r_m	Ready time of machine m ($m = 1, ..., M$)
$\hat{r}_v$	Ready time of vehicle v ($v = 1, ..., V$)
s_j	Service time at the destination of job j ($j = 0, ..., J$; the index 0 denotes the processing site)
t_{ij}	Travel time from the destination of job i to the destination of job j ($i, j = 0, ..., J$). Note that two or more jobs may belong to the same customer and destination. In this case holds $t_{ij} = 0$
$\underline{w}_j, \overline{w}_j$	Lower and upper bound of job j's delivery time window ($j = 1, ..., J$)

Variables

C_j	Completion time of job j ($j = 1, ..., J$; parameter in the vehicle routing model of Section 3.3.2)
D_j	Delivery time of job j ($j = 1, ..., J$)

S_{vt}	Start time of the tth tour of vehicle v $(v = 1, ..., V; t = 1, ..., J)$. Note that it may be optimal to employ only one vehicle that ships each job separately. Hence, the tour index t must go up to J
T_j	Tardiness of job j $(j = 1, ..., J)$
g_{jvt}	Binary variable which takes the value 1 if job j is delivered on the tth tour of vehicle v $(j = 1, ..., J; v = 1, ..., V; t = 1, ..., J)$
x_{ij}	Binary variable which takes the value 1 if job i is processed before job j and no other job is processed in between on that machine $(i, j = 1, ..., J; i \neq j)$
$x_{j,J+1}$	Binary variable which takes the value 1 if job j is the last job processed on a machine $(j = 1, ..., J)$. Job $J + 1$ is an artificial last job
y_{mj}	Binary variable which takes the value 1 if job j is the first job processed on machine m $(m = 1, ..., M; j = 1, ..., J)$
z_{ijvt}	Binary variable which takes the value 1 if job i is delivered before job j on the tth tour of vehicle v $(i, j = 0, ..., J; v = 1, ..., V; t = 1, ..., J)$

3.3.1 Parallel machine scheduling

Consider a set of J jobs with job-dependent processing times p_j and due dates d_j $(j = 1, ..., J)$. Subsection 3.3.2 explains how the due dates for processing are imposed by delivery planning. Each job j has to be assigned to one of M identical parallel machines and scheduled to fit the timetable of that machine. Preemption is not allowed. The point in time a machine finishes processing its last job is equal to the moment the machine is ready to process the next set of jobs. As these points in time generally differ between machines, each machine m has its own ready time r_m $(m = 1, ..., M)$.

Using the Three-Field-Notation by Graham et al. (1979), this problem can be described by $IP, r_m // \sum_j T_j$ where IP in conjunction with r_m is an abbreviation for identical parallel machines with differing machine ready times. $\sum_j T_j$ denotes the objective of minimizing total tardiness.

Theorem 1. *The problem $IP, r_m // \sum_j T_j$ is NP-hard.*

Proof. Du and Leung (1990) prove that minimizing total tardiness on a single machine $(1 // \sum_j T_j)$ is NP-hard (in the ordinary sense). Since $IP, r_m // \sum_j T_j$ contains $1 // \sum_j T_j$ as a special case, it must be NP-hard, too. □

The term 'NP-hard' (non-deterministic polynomial-time hard) refers to the complexity of a problem. For NP-hard problems, it is unlikely to find an algorithm that is guaranteed to result in global minima within an acceptable computation time. To tackle such problems, the development of fast heuristics that ensure near-optimum solutions is indispensable, especially when dealing with large-size instances. Small-size instances, however, can often still be solved using a commercial optimization software.

Based on a model by Biskup et al. (2008), the deterministic and static machine scheduling subproblem $IP, r_m//\sum_j T_j$ is formalized by the following mixed integer linear program. The model needs far fewer binary variables than the classic approaches by Bowman (1959), Wagner (1959), and Manne (1960), for example, which affects the computation time of commercial optimization software packages like CPLEX or LINDO.

$$\min_{T_j; j=1,\ldots,J} \left\{ \sum_{j=1}^{J} T_j \right\} \tag{3.1}$$

subject to

$$1 \geq \sum_{j=1}^{J} y_{mj} \qquad \forall\, m = 1, \ldots, M \tag{3.2}$$

$$y_{mj} \in \{0,1\} \qquad \forall\, m = 1, \ldots, M;\ j = 1, \ldots, J \tag{3.3}$$

$$1 = \sum_{i=1, i \neq j}^{J+1} x_{ji} \qquad \forall\, j = 1, \ldots, J \tag{3.4}$$

$$x_{ij} \in \{0,1\} \qquad \forall\, i = 1, \ldots, J;\ j = 1, \ldots, J+1;\ i \neq j \tag{3.5}$$

$$1 = \sum_{m=1}^{M} y_{mj} + \sum_{i=1, i \neq j}^{J} x_{ij} \qquad \forall\, j = 1, \ldots, J \tag{3.6}$$

$$C_j \geq y_{mj}(r_m + p_j) \qquad \forall\, j = 1, \ldots, J;\ m = 1, \ldots, M \tag{3.7}$$

$$C_j \geq C_i + p_j - q(1 - x_{ij}) \qquad \forall\, i,j = 1, \ldots, J;\ i \neq j \tag{3.8}$$

$$T_j \geq 0 \qquad \forall\, j = 1, \ldots, J \tag{3.9}$$

$$T_j \geq C_j - d_j \qquad \forall\, j = 1, \ldots, J \tag{3.10}$$

Explanation of the constraints. 3.2–3.3: Some of the M available machines may not be used for processing. For example, if there are fewer jobs than machines ($J < M$), it would be impossible to employ all machines. So there is at most one job that is the first to be processed on a certain machine m. 3.4–3.5: Each job either precedes another job or is the last to be processed on a machine. 3.6: Each job is either the first to be processed on a machine or succeeds another one. 3.7: The completion time of the first job in the sequence of a machine must be equal to or greater than the machine's ready time plus the job's processing time. 3.8: The completion time of a job that is not the first to be processed on a machine is equal to or greater than the completion time of its predecessor plus its processing time. 3.9–3.10: The tardiness of a job is calculated as the maximum of 0 and the difference between its completion time and its due date.

In order to explain the decomposition approaches, a second machine scheduling subproblem becomes necessary. The sole difference between this and the first is the objective of minimizing total completion time instead of total tardiness. It can hence be described by $IP, r_m // \sum_j C_j$. Since due dates and tardiness are no object, Restrictions 3.9 and 3.10 can be omitted in the second machine scheduling model.

$$\min_{C_j, j=1,...,J} \left\{ \sum_{j=1}^{J} C_j \right\} \tag{3.11}$$

subject to

$$(3.2) - (3.8)$$

If all machines are ready at the same time, a simple algorithm based on shortest processing time (SPT) priority leads to optimality (Baker, 1997). This algorithm has to be slightly modified to apply also to the case of different machine ready times. The job with the shortest processing time has to be assigned to the first machine that is ready. If there are several eligible jobs and/or machines, selection can be arbitrarily. The job is scheduled without idle time on that machine's timetable. The new ready time of the machine is given by the completion time of the job. The remaining jobs are successively scheduled accordingly.

3.3.2   Vehicle routing with time windows

The literature on machine scheduling usually defines a due date as the latest point in time a job should be completed or delivered. The literature on vehicle routing[2] additionally refers to earliest delivery dates, which are given by the opening time of the recipient's incoming goods department, for example. Earliest and latest delivery dates

---

[2]For a brief and recent introduction to the entire research area of vehicle routing and scheduling see Grunow and Stefánsdóttir (2012).

form the bounds of delivery time windows. A distinction is made between soft and hard time windows. Hard time window bounds may not be violated while soft ones allow for early or tardy deliveries but generally involve a penalty for any violation. In order to avoid reputational damage or contractual penalties, a supplier should endeavor to ensure that all jobs are delivered within their time windows. At the same time, it should accept enough jobs to maximize the utilization of its processing capacity. The trade-off between these two competing aims, plus other factors like small time windows and widely scattered customer locations, often means that even the best possible solution will include at least one tardy delivery. To achieve a feasible solution in the first place, upper time window bounds must be seen as soft in many real world applications. Hence, the job-dependent time windows in this chapter are confined by hard lower bounds $\underline{w}_j$ and soft upper bounds $\overline{w}_j$.

Such time windows can be encountered in the automotive industry. The strong bargaining power of large manufacturers enables them to impose small and restrictive time windows on their suppliers. If a job arrives early, it has to remain on the vehicle until its delivery time window opens. Tardiness occurs but is often severely penalized. Although they often claim to coordinate the operations of all involved parties when enforcing their rigid just-in-time regimes, strong focal companies actually put the entire supply chain's competitiveness at risk (Manoj et al., 2008). Even though this causes the dominating manufacturer's performance to improve, which by the way mostly seems to be the primary goal, the supply chain's overall performance can nevertheless worsen. Due to restrictive delivery time windows, the planning flexibility of the multiple smaller suppliers is drastically reduced, which at first only affects the suppliers' performances but sooner or later will likely have repercussions for the focal company and the entire supply chain's competitiveness. Only a joint coordination approach, such as inter-organizational Supply Chain Scheduling, allows for achieving global supply chain optima. By considering the current cross-company order, cost, and capacity situation in search for the overall optimum, Supply Chain Scheduling goes far beyond establishing a just-in-time supplier-buyer environment. The next chapter discusses inter-organizational optimization issues in detail.

Back to the intra-organizational planning problem of the company in focus of this chapter. A fleet of V heterogenous vehicles, which may differ in their loading capacities c_v and ready times $\hat{r}_v$ $(v = 1, ..., V)$, is available to deliver the jobs. Job-dependent physical sizes u_j, measured in the number of pallets or in weight, for example, determine the loading capacity the jobs require. Jobs cannot be split across several vehicles or different tours. Destination-dependent service times s_j, which correspond to the time needed for waiting, registering, quality inspection, unloading, and signing documents, must be taken into account. The time required to service the vehicles at the processing site is represented by the parameter s_0. The delivery time D_j denotes the point in time a job arrives at its destination and begins to be serviced. Each job has to be assigned to a certain tour t ($t = 1, ..., J$) of one of the vehicles. Simultaneously, the delivery routes of the tours must be defined and scheduled, considering the travel times between each pair of locations t_{ij} ($\forall\ i, j = 0, ..., J$).

Note that the start time of a tour S_{vt} minus the service time at the processing site denotes the latest point in time a job must be completed in order to be delivered on that tour. Hence, if the vehicle routing subproblem is solved first, this moment constitutes the due date for the machine scheduling subproblem. On the other hand, if the machine scheduling subproblem is solved first, the completion times of the jobs impose release dates on the vehicle routing subproblem.

According to Desrochers et al. (1990), this capacitated vehicle routing problem with time windows can be described by $1, s_j, twhs_j, C_j / V, c_v, \hat{r}_v, mT // \sum_j T_j$. A single depot, job-dependent service times, time windows with hard lower and soft upper bounds, and job release dates $(1, s_j, twhs_j, C_j)$ have to be accounted for. Furthermore, V vehicles, which may differ in their loading capacities and ready times, are each available for multiple tours $(V, c_v, \hat{r}_v, mT)$. The objective is to minimize total tardiness $\left(\sum_j T_j\right)$.

Theorem 2. *The problem* $1, s_j, twhs_j, C_j / V, c_v, \hat{r}_v, mT // \sum_j T_j$ *is NP-hard.*

Proof. It is an NP-complete problem to verify whether there is a solution to a single non-capacitated vehicle routing problem without tardy jobs (Savelsbergh, 1985). The more general optimization problem $1, s_j, twhs_j, C_j / V, c_v, \hat{r}_v, mT // \sum_j T_j$ must thus be NP-hard.   □

The following mixed integer linear program formalizes the deterministic and dynamic vehicle routing subproblem.

$$\min_{T_j; j=1,...,J} \left\{ \sum_{j=1}^{J} T_j \right\} \tag{3.12}$$

subject to

$$1 = \sum_{v=1}^{V} \sum_{t=1}^{J} g_{jvt} \qquad\qquad \forall\ j = 1, ..., J \tag{3.13}$$

$$g_{jvt} \in \{0,1\} \qquad \forall\, j = 0, ..., J;\ v = 1, ..., V;\ t = 1, ..., J \quad (3.14)$$

$$g_{0vt} \geq g_{jvt} \qquad \forall\, j = 1, ..., J;\ v = 1, ..., V;\ t = 1, ..., J \quad (3.15)$$

$$q \sum_{j=1}^{J} g_{jvt} \geq \sum_{j=1}^{J} g_{jv,t+1} \qquad \forall\, v = 1, ..., V;\ t = 1, ..., J-1 \quad (3.16)$$

$$g_{jvt} = \sum_{i=0, i \neq j}^{J} z_{ijvt} \qquad \forall\, j = 0, ..., J;\ v = 1, ..., V;\ t = 1, ..., J \quad (3.17)$$

$$g_{jvt} = \sum_{i=0, i \neq j}^{J} z_{jivt} \qquad \forall\, j = 0, ..., J;\ v = 1, ..., V;\ t = 1, ..., J \quad (3.18)$$

$$z_{ijvt} \in \{0,1\} \qquad \forall\, i,j = 0, ..., J;\ v = 1, ..., V;\ t = 1, ..., J \quad (3.19)$$

$$c_v \geq \sum_{j=1}^{J} u_j\, g_{jvt} \qquad \forall\, v = 1, ..., V;\ t = 1, ..., J \quad (3.20)$$

$$S_{v1} \geq \hat{r}_v + s_0 \qquad \forall\, v = 1, ..., V \quad (3.21)$$

$$S_{vt} \geq C_j + s_0 - q(1 - g_{jvt}) \qquad \forall\, j = 1, ..., J;\ v = 1, ..., V;\ t = 1, ..., J \quad (3.22)$$

$$S_{vt+1} \geq D_j + s_j + t_{j0} + s_0 - q(1 - g_{jvt}) \quad \forall\, j = 1, ..., J;\ v = 1, ...V;\ t = 1, ..., J-1 \quad (3.23)$$

$$D_j \geq \underline{w}_j \qquad \forall\, j = 1, ..., J \quad (3.24)$$

$$D_j \geq S_{vt} + t_{0j} - q(1 - g_{jvt}) \qquad \forall\, j = 1, ..., J;\ v = 1, ..., V;\ t = 1, ..., J \quad (3.25)$$

$$D_j \geq D_i + s_i + t_{ij} - q(1 - z_{ijvt}) \qquad \forall\, i,j = 1, ..., J;\ i \neq j;\ v = 1, ..., V;\ t = 1, ..., J \quad (3.26)$$

$$T_j \geq 0 \qquad \forall\, j = 1, ..., J \quad (3.27)$$

$$T_j \geq D_j - \overline{w}_j \qquad \forall\, j = 1, ..., J \quad (3.28)$$

Explanation of the constraints. 3.13–3.14: Each job is assigned to exactly one tour of one vehicle. 3.15: A tour is denoted 'empty' if there is no job assigned to it. Tours comprising at least one job are referred to as 'active' tours. The processing site must be be included in each active tour. 3.16: For each vehicle it is ensured that there is no empty tour before an active. 3.17–3.19: The vehicle, delivering job j on its tth tour, travels either from another customer or from the processing site to the destination of job j. After being serviced, the vehicle returns to the processing site or delivers another job. 3.20: The cumulated size of all jobs delivered on the same tour may not exceed the loading capacity of the vehicle. 3.21: The start time of the first tour of each vehicle is equal to or greater than its ready time plus the service time needed at the processing site. 3.22: The start time of a tour is equal to or greater than the latest completion time of the jobs assigned to it plus the service time needed at the processing site. 3.23: If it is not the first tour of a vehicle, the start time is equal to or greater than the delivery time of the last delivered job on the preceding tour plus the time needed for the service at the destination of that job, for returning to the processing site, and for servicing at the processing site. 3.24–3.25: The delivery time of the first job on a tour is equal to or greater than the lower time window bound and the start time of the tour plus the time needed to reach the destination. 3.26: If a job is not the first to be delivered on a certain tour, its delivery time is equal to or greater than the sum of the delivery time of the preceding job, the service time at the previous destination, and the travel time between the two destinations. 3.27–3.28: The tardiness of a job is calculated as the maximum of 0 and the difference between its delivery time and its upper time window bound.

3.3.3 Integrated machine scheduling and vehicle routing

The two subproblems are linked and integrated by the completion times of the jobs. Obviously, due dates for processing and thus Restrictions 3.9 and 3.10 can be omitted.

$$\min_{T_j;j=1,\dots,J} \left\{ \sum_{j=1}^{J} T_j \right\} \tag{3.29}$$

subject to

$$(3.2) - (3.8) \text{ and } (3.13) - (3.28)$$

Theorem 3. *The integrated problem is NP-hard.*

Proof. As the integrated problem is a generalization of the subproblems, the integrated problem must be NP-hard, too.   □

The NP-hard complexity implies that algorithms that ensure the identification of global optima in polynomial-bounded computation time are unlikely to exist unless $P = NP$ (Garey and Johnson, 1979). Hence, heuristics must be developed and applied to obtain acceptable solutions for larger-size instances within a reasonable computation time. After Section 3.4 introduces the instance generator, Section 3.5 presents two decomposition heuristics and a genetic algorithm.

3.4 Generation of test instances

The instance generator and the genetic algorithm make use of the linear congruential pseudo random numbers generator introduced by Lehmer (1951). Biskup and Feldmann (2001) provide a brief description.

The processing times p_j are generated as follows. *RD* is an abbreviation for rectangular distribution, which means that all integers of the interval $[1, \rho]$ are equally probable.

$$p_j \sim RD\,[1, \rho] \qquad\qquad \forall\, j = 1, ..., J \quad (3.30)$$

The job sizes u_j are assumed to depend on the processing times. The longer the processing time, the greater the probability that the job needs a lot of space. This relationship frequently holds true in practice, such as in beverage bottling, newspaper printing, and injection molding, for example.

$$u_j \sim RD\,\big[1, p_j\big] \qquad\qquad \forall\, j = 1, ..., J \quad (3.31)$$

To allow for the existence of a feasible solution in the first place, it is necessary for at least one vehicle to have enough capacity to deliver the job with the largest size: $\max_{j;j=1,...,J}\{u_j\}$. Real-world companies need to comply with this constraint, too. So, as in practice, the capacities of the vehicles c_v are matched with the job sizes. The smaller the adjustment parameter μ, the smaller the capacities of the vehicles in relation to the job sizes.

$$c_v := \max_{j;j=1,...,J}\{u_j\} + \tau_v \quad \text{with} \quad \tau_v \sim RD\left[0, \mu \max_{j;j=1,...,J}\{u_j\}\right] \qquad \forall\, v = 1, ..., V \quad (3.32)$$

In order to generate the matrix of travel times, the job destinations are randomly allocated in a two-dimensional area around the processing site, one destination for each job. As is common practice, the rounded integer values of the Euclidian distances can also be interpreted as travel times t_{ij} ($\forall\, i, j = 0, ..., J$) with $t_{ij} = t_{ji}$ and, for $i = j$, $t_{ij} = 0$. However, integrated planning is easy if the production and transportation capacities, suffice to immediately process and deliver all jobs. Since competition generally causes a need for efficient management, in practice the number of vehicles and machines is mostly reduced to a minimum and well-matched. Here, the capacities are balanced out by considering the number of vehicles (V), the number of machines (M), and the processing times (ρ) when generating travel times. When allocating the destinations around the processing site, it is ensured that the maximum travel time does not exceed $\lfloor \rho \left(V/M \right) \rfloor$. The floor function $\lfloor \cdot \rfloor$ denotes the largest integer value lower than or equal to $\rho \left(V/M \right)$.

The service times s_j are also matched to the processing times.

$$s_j \sim RD \left[1, \lfloor \lambda \, \rho \rfloor \right] \qquad\qquad \forall \, j = 0, ..., J \quad (3.33)$$

The first machine ready to process a new set of jobs is labeled machine 1. Its ready time is scaled to $r_1 = 0$. Since other machines may start processing their last jobs of the previous set only at this moment, the upper limit for the other machines' ready times is the maximum processing time ρ.

$$r_m \sim RD \left[0, \rho \right] \qquad\qquad \forall \, m = 2, ..., M \quad (3.34)$$

The latest machine ready time plus the service time at the processing site denotes the earliest moment at which the last job of the previous set can start to be delivered. The vehicle delivering that job is labeled vehicle 1. Since the last job of the previous set is assumed to be delivered in a one-job-shipment, vehicle 1 needs at least three and at most $\lfloor \rho \left(V/M \right) \rfloor + \lfloor \lambda \, \rho \rfloor$ time units[3] to travel to the destination, hand over the job, and return to the processing site, so its ready time for the new set of jobs is:

$$\hat{r}_1 := \max_{m; m = 1, ..., M} \{ r_m \} + s_0 + \gamma \quad \text{with} \quad \gamma \sim RD \left[3, \lfloor \rho \left(V/M \right) \rfloor + \lfloor \lambda \, \rho \rfloor \right] \qquad (3.35)$$

The other vehicles' ready times are drawn from an interval with the maximum ready time of vehicle 1 as limit:

$$\hat{r}_v \sim RD \left[0, \max_{m; m = 1, ..., M} \{ r_m \} + s_0 + \lfloor \rho \left(V/M \right) \rfloor + \lfloor \lambda \, \rho \rfloor \right] \qquad \forall \, v = 2, ..., V \quad (3.36)$$

Finally, the lower and upper time window bounds are generated. To avoid unsatisfiable cases, the earliest moment a job can be delivered, given by the processing time plus the service time at the processing site and the travel time from the processing site to the

---

[3]Remember that the job destinations are randomly allocated around the processing site and that the maximum travel time between any two destinations, $\max_{i,j;i,j=1,...,J} \{ t_{ij} \}$, does not exceed $\lfloor \rho \left(V/M \right) \rfloor$. Consequently, the maximum travel time from the processing site to a destination $\max_{j;j=1,...,J} \{ t_{0j} \}$ cannot exceed $1/2 \cdot \lfloor \rho \left(V/M \right) \rfloor$. Hence, at least $2 \cdot 1 = 2$ and at most $2 \cdot 1/2 \cdot \lfloor \rho \left(V/M \right) \rfloor = \lfloor \rho \left(V/M \right) \rfloor$ periods are needed to shuttle between the processing site and a destination. Furthermore, the service at the destination needs at least one and at most $\lfloor \lambda \, \rho \rfloor$ periods.

destination, is the minimum lower bound. These minimum lower bounds are enlarged by an integer drawn from an interval which is controlled by the adjustment parameter δ_1. Small values of δ_1 produce time windows close to the planning moment and to each other, so that there is little time to produce and deliver the jobs. Hence, the smaller the adjustment parameter, the tighter the lower bounds. By additionally considering the factor $J/(M+V)$ in the upper bound of the interval, the number of jobs J, machines M, and vehicles V can be varied without causing major changes to the relative tightness of the instances expressed by δ_1.

$$\underline{w}_j := p_j + s_0 + t_{0j} + \pi_j \quad \text{with} \quad \pi_j \sim RD\left[0, \lfloor \delta_1\, \rho\, J/(M+V) \rfloor \right] \qquad \forall\, j = 1, ..., J \quad (3.37)$$

By controlling the upper time window bounds $\overline{w}_j$ through the adjustment parameter δ_2 and the maximum processing ρ, the sizes of the time windows formed by their lower and upper bounds are adjusted to the other parameters.

$$\overline{w}_j := \underline{w}_j + \kappa_j \quad \text{with} \quad \kappa_j \sim RD\left[0, \lfloor \delta_2\, \rho \rfloor \right] \qquad\qquad\qquad \forall\, j = 1, ..., J \quad (3.38)$$

The following small-size instance with seven jobs, two machines, and two vehicles ($J = 7$, $M = 2$, $V = 2$) is obtained from the instance generator using the parameter settings $\rho = 100$, $\mu = 1$, $\lambda = 0.2$, $\delta_1 = 0.5$, and $\delta_2 = 0.5$. The vector notation is explained by the processing times: $p = (p_1, p_2, \ldots, p_J)$.

$$p = (48, 30, 54, 84, 95, 23, 46) \qquad u = (32, 15, 7, 42, 54, 18, 25)$$
$$\underline{w} = (133, 120, 142, 197, 194, 122, 94) \qquad \overline{w} = (152, 143, 176, 214, 225, 168, 131)$$
$$s = (1, 1, 7, 1, 11, 15, 5, 13) \qquad c = (77, 57)$$
$$r = (0, 28) \qquad \hat{r} = (58, 123)$$

$$(t) = \begin{pmatrix} t_{11} & t_{12} & \cdots & t_{1J} \\ t_{21} & & & \vdots \\ \vdots & & \ddots & \vdots \\ t_{J1} & & \cdots & t_{JJ} \end{pmatrix} \qquad (t) = \begin{pmatrix} 0 & 19 & 32 & 45 & 43 & 34 & 41 & 5 \\ 19 & 0 & 15 & 37 & 24 & 21 & 43 & 22 \\ 32 & 15 & 0 & 28 & 19 & 8 & 41 & 34 \\ 45 & 37 & 28 & 0 & 46 & 19 & 22 & 43 \\ 43 & 24 & 19 & 46 & 0 & 27 & 61 & 47 \\ 34 & 21 & 8 & 19 & 27 & 0 & 34 & 35 \\ 41 & 43 & 41 & 22 & 61 & 34 & 0 & 36 \\ 5 & 22 & 34 & 43 & 47 & 35 & 36 & 0 \end{pmatrix}$$

Via a Gantt chart, Figure 3.1 illustrates the optimal solution to the example computed

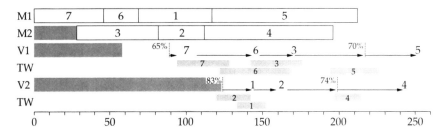

Figure 3.1: Optimal solution to the example

by a commercial optimization software. Dark gray rectangles visualize the intervals during which machine 2 (M2) and the vehicles (V1 and V2) are not available. Both vehicles are employed for two tours whose start times are indicated by dotted lines. The capacity utilization of the vehicles is quoted to the left of the dotted lines. Service times are scheduled between travel times symbolized by the arrows and to the left of the dotted lines. The pale gray rectangles represent the time windows (TW) of the jobs. Jobs 2, 4, and 5 are tardy causing a total tardiness of 70. This example shows that, using the proposed settings, the generator is able to provide reasonable instances.

3.5   Heuristics

Section 3.3 shows that the overall problem can be decomposed in a machine scheduling and a vehicle routing subproblem. Now, Section 3.5.1 introduces two decomposition approaches that tackle the subproblems one after the other and merge the resulting solutions into an overall solution to the integrated problem. Note that even solving the subproblems optimally does not guarantee to result in the overall optimum. Aiming to improve the overall solutions, Section 3.5.2 proposes a genetic algorithm to deal with the integrated problem as a whole.

3.5.1   Decomposition approaches

Approach 1: VMV. In brief, this approach consists of firstly vehicle routing, secondly machine scheduling, and thirdly vehicle routing, so it is referred to as VMV. It proceeds as follows:

1. Set: $C_j^{Step\ 1} := p_j \ (\forall j = 1, ..., J)$

   Since the moment at which processing begins is scaled to 0, no job can be completed earlier than its processing time.

2. Solve: $1, s_j, twhs_j, C_j^{Step\ 1} / V, c_v, \hat{r}_v, mT / / \sum_j T_j$ (Section 3.3.2)

   To obtain the best possible delivery schedule, solve the vehicle routing subproblem with respect to the completion times resulting from step 1.

3. Set: $d_j := S_{vt} - s_0$ for $g_{jvt} = 1 \ (\forall j = 1, ..., J)$

   Calculate the due dates for machine scheduling from the solution of step 2.

4. Solve: $IP, r_m / / \sum_j T_j$ (Section 3.3.1, machine subproblem 1)

   Search for the machine schedule that best meets the due dates calculated in step 3. If there is a feasible machine schedule that complies with all due dates, the optimum of the integrated problem is found and can be composed of the solutions produced in the second and fourth step. Otherwise $\rightarrow$ step 5.

5. Solve: $1, s_j, twhs_j, C_j^{Step\ 4} / V, c_v, \hat{r}_v, mT / / \sum_j T_j$ (Section 3.3.2)

   Solve the vehicle routing subproblem again, but now take account of the feasible completion times resulting from step 4.

6. Aggregate the solutions of step 4 and 5 to form a feasible solution to the integrated problem.

Applying this approach to the instance given in Section 3.4 leads to a total tardiness of 86, which is 23% above the optimum of 70. So although the subproblems are optimally solved, overall coordination is poor. Note that further computations reveal that more iterations (VMVMV, VMVMVMV, etc.) do not significantly improve the results.

Approach 2: MV. In brief, this approach consists of firstly machine scheduling and secondly vehicle routing, so it is referred to as MV. It proceeds as follows:

1. Solve: $IP, r_m / / \sum_j C_j$ (Section 3.3.1, machine subproblem 2)

   The aim of minimizing total completion time tends to cause as many jobs as possible to be completed at each point in time (Conway et al., 1967). The intention is to provide the subsequent vehicle routing subproblem with great degrees of freedom.

2. Solve: $1, s_j, twhs_j, C_j^{\text{Step 1}} / V, c_v, \hat{r}_v, mT // \sum_j T_j$ (Section 3.3.2)
   Solve the vehicle routing subproblem with respect to the feasible completion times resulting from step 1.

3. Aggregate the solutions of steps 1 and 2 to produce a solution to the integrated problem. Feasibility is ensured.

Applying this approach to the example also results in a total tardiness of 86.

3.5.2   Genetic algorithm approach

Genetic algorithms (Holland, 1975; Goldberg, 1989; Davis, 1991; Gendreau and Potvin, 2010) are stochastic search methods which are part of evolution-motivated meta-heuristics. A population of individuals, given by encoded solutions to the considered problem, is iteratively altered. Each new individual emerges from crossover, mutation, or reproduction of the current individuals. Genetic algorithms simulate the Darwinian principle of survival of the fittest. In the case of a minimization problem, the lower an individual's objective value, the better its fitness and in turn, the higher the probability it will influence the next generation of individuals. In this way, the population is intended to gradually converge towards the optimum.

The great advantages of genetic algorithms are that they have no need for continuity, differentiability, and convexity of the objective function, and that they are relatively easily adjustable to almost every linear and non-linear type of problem. Genetic algorithms with an elitist strategy have been proven to find the global optimum even if the restrictions or the objective function include non-smooth operators such as *IF, MIN, MAX,* and *ABS* functions (Suzuki, 1995; Lozano et al., 1999). However, the sun could explode before this happens (Albright and Winston, 2012) and, unless the optimum is verified by some other means, one never knows whether optimality is already reached. Hence, genetic algorithms are usually applied as heuristics, reporting the best solution found after a pre-defined runtime or a certain number of iterations without improving the solution, for example. Greenhalgh and Marshall (2000) deal with convergence criteria influencing the number of populations needed to find an acceptable solution.

Justified by the above mentioned advantages and the successful applications summarized in the literature review, this chapter's integrated problem is tackled by a genetic algorithm. Figure 3.2 illustrates the proposed genetic algorithm on a meta-level. First, a predefined number of arbitrary feasible solutions is generated in order to build the

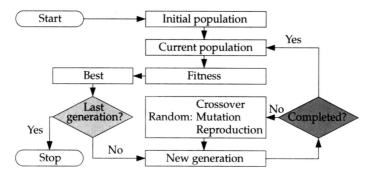

Figure 3.2: The major cycle of the genetic algorithm

initial population which is the first current population. How to generate arbitrary feasible solutions is explained later in conjunction with the mutation procedure. In the next step, the fitness of each individual is calculated. Aiming to minimize total tardiness, an individual with a low objective value obj_{ind} should have a high fitness. This is achieved by defining the fitness fit_{ind} of an individual ind by $fit_{ind} = 1/obj_{ind}$.[4] The fittest individual of a generation is compared to the best individual found before and saved if it is better. After a predefined number of new generations, the pale gray aborting criterion is answered with 'yes' and the genetic algorithm stops. The best individual found provides the solution. If the pale gray aborting criterion is answered with 'no,' a new generation is created.

The genetic algorithm applies an elitist strategy which means that the currently best individual is assigned to each new generation in order for it to change for the better. All other new individuals are successively created by either crossover, mutation, or reproduction of the current population's individuals. Predefined probabilities, summing up to 100%, influence the random choice between those three procedures. The dark gray aborting criterion is answered with 'yes' if both populations have the same number of individuals. At this moment, the new generation replaces the current population, a process referred to as general replacement. Now, the next major cycle of the genetic algorithm begins again with the calculation of the individuals' fitness values.

The individuals are implemented by permutation coding with path representation

---

[4]It must be ensured that the genetic algorithm stops when an individual with an objective value of 0 is found.

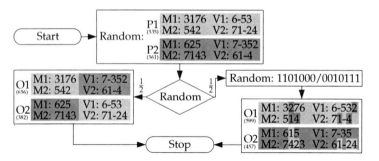

Figure 3.3: The crossover procedure explained by an example

which is generally assumed to be the method of choice for sequencing problems. This kind of phenotype coding[5] and the way an individual's fitness can be determined from its code is explained by parent 1 (P1) in Figure 3.3. The instance introduced in Section 3.4 again provides the data. Jobs 3, 1, 7, and 6 (5, 4, and 2) are processed in sequence on M1 (M2). Obviously, only active machine schedules, without idle time, need to be considered when minimizing total tardiness. Therefore, taking account of the machine ready times and the processing times of the jobs, the following completion times can be easily obtained from the code of P1: $C = (102, 237, 54, 207, 123, 171, 148)$. The part of the code that relates to the vehicles is similarly interpretable. V1 (V2) delivers job 6 (7 and 1) on its first tour and jobs 5 and 3 (2 and 4) in sequence on its second tour. The earliest possible delivery dates, which are of interest when minimizing total tardiness, unambiguously result from the vehicle ready times, the completion times of the jobs, the travel times, the lower time window bounds, and the service times: $D = (189, 270, 328, 296, 294, 213, 154)$. The tardiness of a job is determined by the maximum of 0 and the difference between its earliest possible delivery date and its upper time window bound: $T = (37, 127, 152, 82, 69, 45, 23)$. Accordingly, P1 has a total tardiness of 535 and a fitness of $1/535$.

The rectangle in Figure 3.2 that encloses the procedures 'crossover,' 'mutation,' and 'reproduction' represents the core of the genetic algorithm. The crossover procedure is explained by Figure 3.3. Initially, two parents are chosen from the current population using the commonly applied roulette wheel selection method (Iba et al., 2009). A certain

---

[5]Phenotype representation is commonly said to be more appropriate than genotype representation when dealing with sequencing and other combinatorial problems.

individual's probability to be a parent is determined by its relative fitness: fit_{ind}/Fit. Fit denotes the cumulated fitness of the current population: $Fit = \sum_{ind} fit_{ind}$. The two parents are altered using one of two different crossover methods. Both methods are assumed to be equally probable. As visualized by the pale and the dark gray rectangles, the machine and vehicle codes of the two parents are rearranged en bloc if the left-hand method is chosen. In doing so, promising machine codes get the chance of being matched up with better fitting vehicle codes and vice versa. Offspring 1 (O1) receives the machine code of P1 and the vehicle code of P2, leading to a greater total tardiness (656) than either of its parents (535 and 561). However, O2 (382), which receives the remaining codes, is better than both parents. Note that crossover is the only one of the three core procedures that generates two offspring at once.[6]

The right-hand crossover method starts with randomly generating a sequence of J equally probable ones and zeros. The resulting binary mask (Reeves, 2010) serves as an instruction for combining O1 from the parents' codes. For example, in Figure 3.3 the third value of the left-hand binary mask 1101000 is 0 which means that job 3 is assigned to the machine and vehicle position of P1. Hence, O1 inherits from P1 that job 3 is the first job processed on M1 and the second job delivered on the second tour of V1. If the third value was 1, job 3 would be assigned to the machine and vehicle position of P2. The machine position comprises the number of the machine processing the job and the position of the job in the sequence of that machine. The vehicle position reflects the number of the vehicle the job is assigned to, the number of the tour, and the job's position in the delivery sequence of that tour. The jobs are placed successively on their new positions in ascending order according to their indices. The right-hand binary mask 0010111, which is the 'inverse' of the left, serves as an instruction for combining O2. The pale gray (P1) and dark gray (P2) backgrounds illustrate which elements of an offspring originate from which parent. O2 (457) outperforms both parents. Using the right-hand crossover method, jobs with good matching machine and vehicle positions may be combined with other promising ones. However, this method could cause two jobs to be assigned to the same machine or vehicle position, for machine or vehicle positions to remain free although the following positions are occupied, and for jobs batched to one tour to exceed the loading capacity of the vehicle. In these cases, fixing mechanisms take effect:

- If the machine position of a job is already occupied, the job is passed onto the next

---

[6]If only one individual is needed to complete a new generation and if this individual is chosen to be generated by crossover, only the first of the two offspring is assigned to the new generation.

free position in front. If all positions in front are occupied, it is assigned to the next free position following.

- If the remaining capacity of a vehicle is insufficient for accommodating the next job assigned to a certain tour, the job is passed onto the next possible tour in front. The position in the delivery sequence remains unchanged. If there is no tour in front with enough remaining capacity, it is assigned to the next possible tour following.

- If the vehicle position of a job is already occupied, the job is passed onto the tour's next free position in front. If all positions in front are occupied, it is assigned to the tour's next free position following.

- If there are free machine and vehicle positions in front of occupied ones after all jobs are placed, the free positions are deleted.

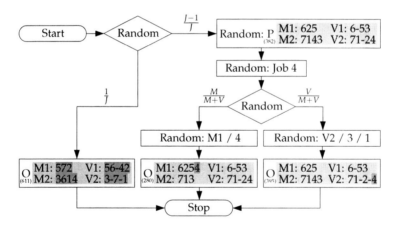

Figure 3.4: The mutation procedure explained by an example

Figure 3.4 exemplifies the mutation procedure. Again, two different methods take effect. The left-hand mutation method, which randomly creates completely new individuals, is also used to generate the initial population. Its purpose is to bring new chromosomes into the population and thus to avoid premature convergence. Since the right-hand method, comprising mutation in its proper meaning, is more important, the left-hand method is applied with a probability of only $\frac{1}{J}$, decreasing in the number of jobs J. The left-hand mutation method randomly chooses a job and places that job in the queue of an also randomly chosen machine. This is repeated until all jobs occupy a certain machine position. A similar approach is applied to generate the vehicle code. First, a job and a vehicle are randomly selected. It needs to be ensured that the capacity of the vehicle suffices to carry out the job. Then, the job is randomly assigned to one of the vehicle's already active tours with enough remaining capacity or an empty last tour. The job is placed at the first free position in the queue of that tour. Note that if no job was assigned to this vehicle before, the job is put in the first position in the first tour's delivery sequence. This is repeated until all jobs occupy a certain vehicle position. In Figure 3.4, the individual generated by the left-hand mutation method gains a total tardiness of 611. The dark gray background indicates that each machine and vehicle position is newly generated.

The right-hand mutation method starts with the random selection of a parent from the current population. In the example, the chosen parent is the second offspring obtained from the left-hand crossover method in Figure 3.3. Then, it is decided whether to mutate the machine or the vehicle code of a randomly chosen job (here job 4). The probabilities $\frac{M}{M+V}$ and $\frac{V}{M+V}$ depend on the numbers of machines and vehicles. If there are many machines in relation to the number of vehicles, meaning that there is a relatively large number of possible machine-job permutations, the machine code is expected to be more often mutated. The same consideration, but vice versa, holds for the case of many vehicles in relation to machines.

In order to mutate the machine code, the selected job first needs to be deleted from the machine code. Here, job 4 and the resulting empty position have been deleted from the sequence of M2. Then the job needs to be randomly re-allocated to a possible position in the sequence of an also randomly chosen machine. In the example, job 4 now occupies the fourth of four possible positions in the sequence of M1. The offspring achieves a total tardiness of 280. If job 4 was assigned to the second position, it would displace job 2 to the third and job 5 to the fourth position.

The mutation of the vehicle code proceeds in a similar manner. The selected job is deleted from the vehicle code, one of the vehicles that are large enough to carry the job is randomly chosen, then the job is randomly assigned to a possible position in one of the active tours with enough remaining capacity or an empty last tour. Here, job 4 has been re-allocated to the first and sole possible position in the sequence of the empty third tour, causing a total tardiness of 395.

Reproduction is the third and last procedure of the genetic algorithm. Reproduction means that the chosen parent is passed onto the new generation without modification. Note that an individual can be assigned twice or more often to the new generation. Since this is expected to happen more with individuals having high fitness values, data redundancy is accepted as part of convergence.

3.6   Computational results

Although there has been a lot of research on genetic algorithms, there is no standardized way of adjusting the parameters (Aytug et al., 2003). Suitable parameter adjustments for certain applications must still be found by trial and error (Pongcharoen et al., 2002). For this reason, a commercial optimization software is used to calculated optimal solutions to small-size instances. By comparing the results of the optimization software with the solutions obtained for varying parameter adjustments, an appropriate adjustment for the genetic algorithm is identified. Subsection 3.6.1 describes this approach in detail and furthermore compares the genetic algorithm to the decomposition approaches introduced in Section 3.5. Subsection 3.6.2 investigates the performance and computation time of the genetic algorithm for large-size instances.

3.6.1   Small-size instances

90 instances with seven jobs $(J = 7)$, two machines $(M = 2)$, and two vehicles $(V = 2)$ are examined $(\rho = 100, \mu = 1, \lambda = 0.2, \delta_1 = 0.5, \delta_2 = 0.5)$. All computations are performed on one core of an Intel Core 2 Duo CPU with 2.33 GHz and 2048 MB RAM. The mean computation time of the optimization software is 28.306 hours whereas the genetic algorithm, implemented in Turbo Delphi, needs only seconds for 10^5 generations. Commercial optimization software is rarely able to find optima for more jobs, machines, or vehicles within an acceptable time. The study on small-size instances is hence limited to these relatively low numbers.

Figure 3.5 illustrates the relative deviations from the optimum for the decomposition approaches (VMV and MV) and for different parameter adjustments of the genetic algorithm. The first entry in the parentheses below the boxplots shows the probability of crossover, the second of mutation, and the third of reproduction. The four probability constellations (45, 45, 10), (60, 30, 10), (30, 60, 10), and (0, 90, 10) are tested with 10^2, 10^3, 10^4, and 10^5 generations, each generation consisting of 100 individuals. Since the

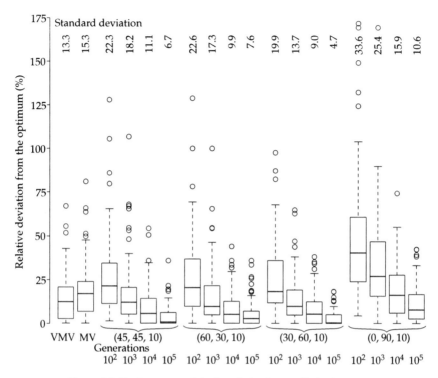

Figure 3.5: Performance of the heuristics for small-size instances

subproblems arising in connection with the decomposition approaches are optimally solved, deviations from the overall optimum can be unambiguously ascribed to decomposition. Possible distorting influences caused by the application of heuristics to the subproblems are avoided.

The boxplots suggest that VMV outperforms MV. Both the median and the standard deviation are lower. However, compared to the genetic algorithm, both decomposition approaches produce poor results. The probability constellation (30, 60, 10) seems to perform best, especially for large numbers of generations where around half of the 90 instances are optimally solved and the standard deviation is only 4.7. Remember that in contrast to mutation and reproduction, each time crossover is chosen, not only one but two offspring are generated. So the constellation (30, 60, 10) is expected to generate as many offspring by crossover as by mutation. To deflect any criticism that this constellation only performs well due to its high mutation-probability[7] (60%), the results of the constellation (0, 90, 10), which are the poorest results by far, are also presented. Accordingly, mutation as well as crossover need to be applied to achieve good performance. Note that (30, 60, 10) is not necessarily the optimal constellation, but the best of all those investigated.

Table 3.3: Performance results for varying numbers of machines and vehicles

Number of machines and number of vehicles	Mean relative deviation from the optimum (%)		
	VMV	MV	Genetic algorithm
$M = 1, V = 1$	7.9	18	0.7
$M = 1, V = 2$	13	13.8	2.2
$M = 2, V = 1$	8.9	17.1	2.2
$M = 2, V = 2$	13.8	18	3.2

Table 3.3 presents the average results for three other small-size combinations of the number of machines and vehicles: $(M = 1, V = 1)$, $(M = 1, V = 2)$, and $(M = 2, V = 1)$. Using the above mentioned generator setting, 30 instances are created and solved for each combination. The column headed 'Genetic algorithm' contains the average deviations from the optimum after 10^5 generations with the probability constellation (30, 60, 10). Note that this constellation turns out to perform best during the whole numerical study. For the sake of clarity and to save space, the following section discusses only the solutions after 10^5 generations with the probability constellation (30, 60, 10). Comparing the results for $(M = 1, V = 1)$ to $(M = 2, V = 1)$ and for $(M = 1, V = 2)$ to $(M = 2, V = 2)$ suggests that an increasing number of machines and thus a larger search space ceteris paribus causes a deterioration in the solutions obtained by the decomposition approaches and in the solutions of the genetic algorithm. The same generally applies to the number of vehicles. An attempt was made to find other factors that influence the hardness of the instances. Except for the parameter δ_1, which indicates the tightness of the instances, all investigated factors turned out to be non-significant. The investigation of large-size instances therefore mainly focuses on δ_1 and the number of machines, vehicles, and jobs.

---

[7]For many types of problem, the genetic algorithm implemented in Microsoft Excel 2010, for example, is also found to perform best with a high probability of mutation (Albright and Winston, 2012).

3.6.2 Large-size instances

Due to the NP-hard nature of this chapter's integrated problem, the optimization software is not able to solve large-size instances within a reasonable time. Moreover, since the specific integrated problem has not been investigated so far, there is no benchmark heuristic that can be compared with the genetic algorithm. For lack of a suitable heuristic approach to this chapter's vehicle routing subproblem, the decomposition approaches cannot be applied either. Instead, the integrated problem is reduced to two simpler integrated problems which already have been successfully tackled by heuristics. For a given instance, these problems and the respective heuristics can be used to approximate a lower and an upper bound for the optimum. With the help of these bounds, it becomes possible to assess the accuracy of the genetic algorithm for large-size instances.

- **The lower bound problem and heuristic:** Suppose there is a sufficiently large number of vehicles so that each job can be delivered to its destination immediately after its completion. Furthermore, let the due date of a job be given by its upper time window bound minus the service time at the processing site and the travel time to its destination: $d_j := \overline{w}_j - s_0 - t_{0j}$ ($\forall\, j = 1, ..., J$). If the completion time of a job is equal to or before that due date, it is ensured that the job meets its time window. The integrated problem is thereby reduced to the first machine scheduling problem of Section 3.3.1: $IP, r_m // \sum_j T_j$. It is obvious that optimal solutions to this problem provide lower bounds for the optimal solutions to the original problem.

  Since this and the following upper bound problem are still NP-hard, heuristics must be applied to solve large-size instances. Biskup et al. (2008) provide the currently best heuristic for the problem $IP // \sum_j T_j$ which is $IP, r_m // \sum_j T_j$ with $r_m = 0$ ($m = 1, ..., M$). Their heuristic is used to approximate the lower bounds.

- **The upper bound problem and heuristic:** Now suppose that, as in the original problem, there are V vehicles, however, the vehicles again deliver only one job at a time. This assumption leads to shuttle shipments with job-dependent durations comprising the service time at the processing site, the travel time to the destination, the service time at the destination, and the travel time back to the processing site: $s_0 + 2\, t_{0j} + s_j$ ($\forall\, j = 1, ..., J$). The reduced problem can be interpreted as a hybrid flow shop (Linn and Zhang, 1999; Ribas et al., 2010; Ruiz and Vázquez-Rodriguez, 2010) with M identical parallel machines at the first and V identical parallel machines at the second stage. Each machine m and v has its own ready time r_m and $\hat{r}_v$, respectively ($m = 1, ..., M, v = 1, ..., V$). The processing times at the first and the second stage are $p_{1j} := p_j$ and $p_{2j} := s_0 + 2 t_{0j} + s_j$, respectively ($\forall j = 1, ..., J$). The completion time at the second stage C_{2j}, which describes the moment a vehicle arrives at the processing site after having delivered a job, must be greater than or equal to the lower time window bound plus the service time at the destination and the travel time back to the processing site: $\underline{w}_j + s_j + t_{0j} \leq C_{2j}$ ($j = 1, ..., J$). This restriction ensures that the delivery time of job j, $D_j = C_{2j} - s_j - t_{0j}$, is equal to or greater than the lower time window bound: $\underline{w}_j \leq D_j$ ($j = 1, ..., J$). Let the tardiness of a job be $T_j = \max\{0, D_j - \overline{w}_j\}$ ($\forall j = 1, ..., J$) then the problem can be described by $HFS, IP^{1,2}, r_m, \hat{r}_v / \underline{w}_j \leq D_j / \sum_j T_j$ where HFS is an abbreviation for hybrid flow shop scheduling. $IP^{1,2}$ means that there are identical parallel machines at stage 1 as well as at stage 2. Optimal solutions to this problem provide upper bounds for the optima of the original problem.

Brah (1996) compares some dispatching rules for a multiple stage hybrid flow shop problem with due dates. It turns out that a rule based on modified due dates performs very well. Hence, the two-stage hybrid flow shop upper bound problem is tackled by the following dispatching rule. Schedule the job with the currently smallest modified due date in such a way that the job is delivered as early as possible. The modified due date is calculated as the maximum of the earliest possible delivery date and the upper time window bound. When scheduling a job, ensure that the availability of the machines, which changes with each job that is added to the schedule, and the restriction $\underline{w}_j \leq D_j$ are taken into account. It may be necessary to insert idle time at the second stage. If two or more machines are eligible, choose one arbitrarily. The same holds if two or more jobs have the same modified due date. Apply this rule successively until all jobs are scheduled. Note that, unlike the lower bound solutions, the upper bound solutions are feasible with regard to the original problem.

The lower bound, the upper bound, and the genetic algorithm's solution can be aggregated to the following performance ratio.

$$\frac{\text{Solution of the genetic algorithm} - \text{Lower bound}}{\text{Upper bound} - \text{Lower bound}} \qquad (3.39)$$

A ratio of 0.50, for example, means that the solution of the genetic algorithm is exactly in the middle of the interval defined by the lower and the upper bound. Note that the upper bound solutions are henceforth assigned to the initial population of the genetic algorithm so the genetic algorithm is at least as good as the upper bound. Consequently, the worst possible performance ratio is 1.[8]

Table 3.4: Mean performance ratios calculated for small-size instances

	Optimal solution	Genetic algorithm
Optimal bounds	0.43	0.45
Heuristic bounds	0.48	0.50

The 90 small-size instances of the previous section ($J = 7$, $M = 2$, and $V = 2$) are again investigated in order to calculate benchmark performance ratios. Without benchmark ratios it would be impossible to assess whether a performance ratio of, say, 0.75 is good or bad. Remember that the optimization software is able to optimally solve small-size instances, so the lower and upper bound problems can be tackled by the heuristics described in this section as well as by the optimization software. This provides the additional opportunity to validate the accuracy of the lower and upper bound heuristics. Both the solutions of the genetic algorithm and the overall optimum obtained by the optimization software are inserted in Formula 3.39. Table 3.4 presents the mean ratios for each of the four possible combinations. The optimal solutions to the original problem together with the optimal solutions to the lower and upper bound problems result in an exact mean performance ratio of 0.43. Note that calculating the ratio with the solutions of the genetic algorithm and the bounds obtained by optimization software lead to an average ratio of 0.45 which comes very close to the exact ratio. The row 'Heuristic bounds' reveals that the mean performance ratios are generally around 0.05 higher if the lower and upper bound problems are solved with the above proposed lower and upper bound heuristics, respectively. This may be partly due the heuristics' inaccuracy, but also due to the fact that the lower bound heuristic does not consider the machine ready times. The optimization software is able to take the ready times into account which causes higher lower bounds and thus lower performance ratios. To sum up, the results for small-size instances recommend a performance ratio of 0.50 as a benchmark for the following investigations.

---

[8]Due to the inaccuracy of heuristics, the lower bound heuristic can theoretically result in worse solutions than the genetic algorithm and even the upper bound heuristic. However, for the instances investigated here, this case never occurred.

Table 3.5: The genetic algorithm's performance for large-size instances

V	δ_1	M = 3		M = 4		M = 5	
		J = 30	J = 50	J = 30	J = 50	J = 30	J = 50
4	1	0.51	0.57	0.51	0.57	0.50	0.58
	0.5	0.58	0.57	0.59	0.59	0.61	0.60
6	1	0.54	0.58	0.55	0.58	0.54	0.59
	0.5	0.63	0.62	0.64	0.63	0.64	0.64
8	1	0.55	0.61	0.57	0.60	0.58	0.61
	0.5	0.65	0.65	0.66	0.65	0.68	0.67
10	1	0.58	0.61	0.57	0.63	0.59	0.64
	0.5	0.64	0.67	0.68	0.69	0.69	0.71

Table 3.5 presents the mean performance ratios for various values of the number of machines M (3, 4, 5), the number of vehicles V (4, 6, 8, 10), the number of jobs J (30, 50), and the tightness parameter δ_1 (1, 0.5). 100 instances are investigated for each combination, resulting in 4 800 large-size instances in total. The main observations are summarized below.

- The worst average ratio in Table 3.5 is 0.71 ($J = 50$, $M = 5$, $V = 10$, $\delta_1 = 0.5$), a just about acceptable figure, which suggests that the genetic algorithm provides relatively good solutions for instances with up to 50 jobs, 5 machines, and 10 vehicles.

- Comparing the columns for $J = 30$ and $J = 50$ indicates that an increasing number of jobs generally has a negative impact on performance. Note that the performance ratios for 70 job-instances, which are not reported here for the sake of clarity and to save space, are often close to 1, meaning that the genetic algorithm is no longer able to yield good solutions. The average ratio for the hardest examined problem setting with 70 jobs, 5 machines, 10 vehicles, and $\delta_1 = 0.5$, for example, is even 0.99.

Table 3.6 aggregates the results of Table 3.5. For example, half of the 4 800 instances deal with 30 jobs. The average performance ratio of these 2 400 instances is 0.595 which is recorded in the last column. As a second example, the mean ratio of the 1 200 instances with 8 vehicles is 0.623.

Table 3.6: Aggregated average performance ratios for large-size instances

Vehicles	∅ ratio	δ_1	∅ ratio	Machines	∅ ratio	Jobs	∅ ratio
4	0.565	1	0.573	3	0.598	30	0.595
6	0.598	0.5	0.641	4	0.607	50	0.619
8	0.623			5	0.617		
10	0.642						

- Checking the mean ratio of the 30 job instances against the mean ratio of the 50 job instances confirms that an increasing number of jobs negatively affects performance. The same generally holds for the number of vehicles and machines.

- Moreover, comparing the aggregated results for $\delta_1 = 0.5$ and $\delta_1 = 1$ suggests that the genetic algorithm produces better results if the time windows are less close to the planning moment and to each other.

Table 3.7: Impact of the number of job destinations on the performance ratio

Number of job destinations	1	2	5	10	25	50
Genetic algorithm	0.34	0.45	0.56	0.64	0.68	0.71

In the default setting, the instance generator creates an individual destination for each job. Table 3.7 deals with the special case that several jobs must be shipped to the same destination. 50 jobs are assigned to either 1, 2, 5, 10, 25, or 50 different job destinations. For example, in the scenario dealing with 25 destinations, each destination belongs to two jobs $(50/25 = 2)$. The other generator settings are held constant at $\delta_1 = 0.5$, $M = 5$, and $V = 10$. For each scenario, 100 instances are investigated. Note that the results for 50 job destinations are taken from Table 3.5 since this is the default scenario where each job has its own destination.

- Table 3.7 reveals that an increasing number of job destinations has a negative impact on the performance of the genetic algorithm.

- An investigation of 100 instances with $J = 70$, $M = 5$, $V = 10$, $\delta_1 = 0.5$, and only one destination results in a mean performance ratio of 0.72 (not reported in Table

3.7), showing that the genetic algorithm can handle instances with up to 70 jobs in this special case.

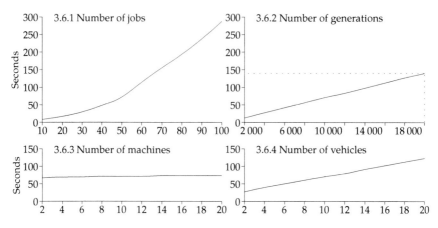

Figure 3.6: Computation time of the genetic algorithm

Finally, Figure 3.6 examines the influence of the number of jobs, generations, machines, and vehicles on the genetic algorithm's computation time. While one of these factors is varied, the others are held constant on $J = 50$, $10\,000$ generations, $M = 5$, and $V = 10$. All mean computation times depicted in Figure 3.6 hold for the probability constellation $(30, 60, 10)$ which, as already mentioned, performs best throughout the whole numerical study. For example, given instances with 50 jobs, 5 machines, and 10 vehicles, the algorithm on average needs about 140 seconds to carry out $20\,000$ generations. This is indicated by the dotted lines in Figure 3.6.2.

- Figure 3.6.1 reveals that the major driver of computation time is the number of jobs.

- A growing number of generations causes an approximatively linear increase in computation time (see Figure 3.6.2). The same holds for the number of vehicles (see Figure 3.6.4).

- The number of machines has almost no impact on computation time (see Figure 3.6.3).

- Further investigations show that the number of different job destinations, the parameter δ_1, and other parameters of the instance generator do not affect computation time.

While the probabilities of reproduction and mutation do not have a significant influence on computation time, the probability of crossover does. The second crossover method needs $O(n^2)$ time in the worst case, which is also the upper bound for the genetic algorithm's computation time if crossover is applied.

3.7 Summary and outlook

This chapter tackles a practice-oriented integrated machine scheduling and vehicle routing problem using a genetic algorithm and two classic decomposition approaches. The decomposition approaches, which break down the overall problem, successively solve the subproblems, and aggregate the solutions to the subproblems, yet yield relatively poor results. The mean relative deviations from the optimum for 90 small-size instances is 13.8 and 18%, respectively. This answers the first question that motivates this chapter. For many instances, integrating machine scheduling and vehicle routing holds significant potential for performance improvements. The second and more interesting question about the possibility of capitalizing on these potentials despite the complexity of the integrated problem is also answered. Around half of the 90 small-size instances are optimally solved by the proposed genetic algorithm. The mean relative deviation from the optimum of 3.2% is close to 0. Moreover, an investigation of large-size instances shows that the genetic algorithm is able to provide relatively good results for instances with up to 50 jobs, 5 machines, and 10 vehicles within an acceptable computation time. In the special case of only one job destination, the performance for instances with up to 70 jobs, 5 machines, and 10 vehicles is acceptable.

As reasoned in this chapter's motivation, especially companies selling time-sensitive goods and companies embedded in just-in-time supply chain environments should seriously consider integrating production and distribution planning to improve their competitiveness. Unfortunately, as seen in the previous sections the resulting planning problems can be extremely challenging. When handling integrated problems, managers are dependent on effective and efficient decision support tools and on progress in research. Indeed, Tables 3.1 and 3.2 reveal that this topic has already attracted a lot of attention. There are nevertheless many problems of practical relevance that have not yet been addressed. This applies particularly to problems involving vehicle routing decisions. For example, Miele, a German manufacturer of high quality domestic appliances and commercial equipment, picks up several of the required components and materials from regional suppliers using its own vehicles and a subcontracted third-party logistics provider. Taking account of deadlines imposed by production schedules, routes and schedules have to be determined for inbound milk-runs. Due to low buffer inventories and the danger of production breakdowns, this is especially important for materials sourced just-in-time. Apart from genetic algorithms, there are many other promising meta-heuristic approaches, such as simulated annealing, ant colony optimization, and tabu search that could be also examined as to their ability to deal with integrated problems.

Besides developing effective and efficient planning approaches to mainly intra-organizational integrated production and delivery problems, the inter-organizational coordination of several production and transportation stages clearly requires more research, too. Hence, focusing on the overall logistic expenditures of a supplier and a subsequent manufacturer, the next chapter endeavors to trade-off inventory holding, transportation, earliness, and tardiness costs so as to find cost-minimal cross-company schedules.

To conclude, this chapter shows that it is possible to improve overall performance by integrating machine scheduling and vehicle routing. Future research on this topic to bridge the gap between theory and practical application is likely to be highly worthwhile.

Chapter 4

Supply Chain Scheduling: Cost-cutting potential

4.1 Motivation

Increasing pressure on competitive global markets means companies have to rigorously capitalize on any cost-cutting potential. It has thus become common practice to introduce logistics practices that aim to cut costs, such as just-in-time and just-in-sequence material flows. However, innovative approaches should also be considered as a proactive way to generate advantages in competitive markets and build barriers to entry in monopolistic or duopolistic markets. Supply Chain Scheduling is such a new approach. The pioneers of this field of study, who include Hall and Potts (2003), Kreipl and Pinedo (2004), and Agnetis et al. (2006), define Supply Chain Scheduling as the coordination of the machine and delivery schedules of two or more supply chain stages. For example, a manufacturer of special-purpose machines cannot assemble its machines until its suppliers release the required components like customized motors, cases, and control modules. A modular constructor cannot build warehouses or car parks until special industry doors, concrete modules, and steel components are supplied. Schedules that result from a separate planning approach of the involved companies do not necessarily match up to produce an efficient overall schedule. By focusing on the coordination of several stages' operations, Supply Chain Scheduling aims to improve overall performance criteria, such as total logistics costs or the supply chain makespan, in order to improve the entire supply chain's competitiveness. Empirical investigations reveal that logistics costs constitute over 30% of many products' overall costs (Thomas and

Griffin, 1996) which indicates that there actually may be a significant savings potential. However, the potential for improvement through Supply Chain Scheduling has never been properly quantified, so this relatively new and ambitious field of study has not yet been justified. If performance improvements were unable to compensate for the cost incurred by the joint coordination approach, Supply Chain Scheduling would be unprofitable and therefore expendable.

As depicted in Figure 2.3 on page 15, this chapter focusses on two frequently interacting companies at consecutive supply chain stages that are considering a close collaboration in operations scheduling. The two companies, referred to as 'supplier' and 'manufacturer,' are embedded in a larger supply chain environment, meaning that the manufacturer is not the supplier's only customer and the supplier is not the manufacturer's only source. At their respective inter-organizational supply chain stage, both the supplier and the manufacturer face an intra-organizational machine and delivery scheduling problem similar to the integrated problem of the previous chapter. To quantify the profitability of Supply Chain Scheduling in this inter-organizational scenario, the sum of earliness, tardiness, inventory holding, and transportation costs that results if the two companies schedule on their own, is compared to the total cost incurred by synchronized cross-company schedules. Note that the cost factors in focus can compete with each other. For example, grouping of jobs to form delivery batches reduces transportation costs but may increase inventory holding and tardiness costs. Completed jobs may need to be stored until the processing of the last job assigned to the same delivery batch is finished and transportation can finally start. Here, the task of Supply Chain Scheduling is to find an optimal or at least good trade-off between

- improving compliance with contractual or promised due dates to prevent earliness/tardiness penalties,

- grouping jobs into delivery batches to reduce transportation costs,

- and the reduction or cost-optimized positioning of inventories along the supply chain.

Other cost factors generally remain unaffected by classic scheduling decisions[1] and are therefore neglected here. For example, decisions on machine processing intensities and lot sizes, which have direct impacts on production and set-up costs, are already made in

---

[1]Note that there are some exceptions. For example, the *discrete lot-sizing and scheduling problem* (Dinkelbach, 1964; Fleischmann, 1990) and scheduling problems, concerning sequence-dependent set-up times and costs (White and Wilson, 1977), additionally take set-up times/costs into account.

the preceding 'production planning' phase of the intra-organizational planning matrix (see Figure 2.2 on page 13). Consequently, set-up and production costs are predetermined, constant, and thus irrelevant to classic scheduling decisions.

As discussed in Section 2.2, supply chain stages are not necessarily under the control of several independent companies. For example, Zara, a popular chain of fashion stores, is characterized by almost fully vertical supplier integration (Mihm, 2010b). Fabric-weaving, dyeing, tailoring, and printing production stages are all owned by the same holding company, Inditex, a setting that can be seen as an intra-organizational supply chain (Stadtler, 2005). If the central head office is able to enforce information interchange and collaboration between the different production stages, the implementation and application of supply chain management instruments such as Supply Chain Scheduling is relatively easy. However, in recent decades there has been a tendency towards globally operating inter-organizational supply chains consisting of independent companies, each highly focused on its core competence (Prahalad and Hamel, 1990). Due to the lack of a joint head office, introducing and carrying out methods aiming at coordinating the various decentralized stages is much more difficult. Data interchange, which is inevitable when scheduling jointly, can be a major problem in terms of trade secrets and bargaining positions, for example. So there is a need to design suitable contracts with effective profit or cost sharing mechanisms that prevent strategic data distortions. At the same time, these contracts must ensure fair Pareto improvements for all parties involved. As implied by Cachon (2003) in the quote on page 4, companies that do not benefit or even suffer from collaboration have no incentive to participate. For example, shipping each component as soon as possible increases the supplier's transportation costs, but may also allow the manufacturer to substantially cut its tardiness costs since it becomes able to start processing earlier. Only the appropriate sharing of the collaboration surplus allows for a win-win situation. Hence, thoughtful preparation is necessary when intending to implement Supply Chain Scheduling in inter-organizational supply chains and also in decentralized intra-organizational supply chains that consist of self-contained cost, profit, or investment centers.

Hofmann (2000), Chen and Hall (2007), Manoj et al. (2008), and Aydinliyim and Vairaktarakis (2013) deal especially with contracting, conflict, and cooperation issues at operational supply chain planning level. However, this is not the focus here. Neither is assessing the costs incurred by contracting, information sharing, new soft- and hardware, and carrying out Supply Chain Scheduling, which must be traded off against the benefits. The primary aim of this chapter is to assess the cost-cutting potential of inter-organizational Supply Chain Scheduling. This aim is justified by the following simple and rational questions. Why develop sophisticated channel coordination schemes and put money in new soft- and hardware when it is not yet clear whether there is enough potential to compensate for the effort and expense? And even if there is enough potential, is it possible at all to exploit it in spite of the arising problem complexity?

In preparation for the numerical study, this chapter develops an Excel-based heuristic to deal with real-world-size problem instances of NP-hard Supply Chain Scheduling problems. Note that, without additional coordination measures, the heuristic already enables centrally controlled intra-organizational supply chains to align the channel. As a by-product, the spreadsheet approach is shown to be easily transferable to many classic batching, sequencing, scheduling, and routing problems. Since Excel is an omnipresent software and such problems occur almost everywhere, the proposed approach provides enormous opportunities for practice. To the best of my knowledge, no such approach has existed until now.

The remainder is structured as follows. Section 4.2 surveys the literature on Supply Chain Scheduling. Using mixed integer linear programs, Section 4.3 introduces and formulates the scheduling problems handled in the following sections. The methodology and the assumptions underlying the numerical study are discussed in Section 4.4. Section 4.5 explains and motivates the generation of the benchmark instances needed for the numerical study. The heuristic spreadsheet approach that is able to deal with real-world-size Supply Chain Scheduling instances is explained in Section 4.6. Finally, Sections 4.7 and 4.8 present the results of the numerical study and conclude, respectively. In the Appendix, a first idea for a simple cost-sharing mechanism is discussed.

4.2   Literature survey

Steiner and Zhang (2009), Potts and Strusevich (2009), and Hall (2011) have already reviewed the literature on Supply Chain Scheduling. Therefore, only the most important publications with regard to this chapter's approach and research question need to be discussed here. However, before dealing with these articles, the hybrid field of Supply Chain Scheduling in general is linked to closely related research areas. In doing so, this relatively new field of study is for the first time properly embedded into the all-encompassing operations research and management literature.

As already motivated above, especially when dealing with inter-organizational supply chains, game-theory based Supply Chain Contracting literature aiming at channel coordination must not be ignored. There are many publications such as Tsay et al. (2003) and Cachon (2003) that focus in particular on contracting issues. Most of these studies, however, study strategic cooperations rather than problems at an operational level. Thomas and Griffin (1996) were the first to recognize the general lack of research on operational planning approaches in supply chain management literature. Aware of the need to improve coordination of logistics operations along supply chains, Hall and Potts (2003) coin the term 'Supply Chain Scheduling.' Primarily dealing with scheduling issues, Hall and Potts (2003) consider the machine scheduling and delivery costs incurred by a supply chain consisting of a supplier, several manufacturers, and several customers. Conflict potentials and channel alignment measures are only addressed in passing on the basis of some examples. However, subsequent papers such as Chen and Hall (2007) and Manoj et al. (2008) demonstrate that Supply Chain Scheduling research often implies the need to combine elements of classic scheduling and game-theory.

Integrated production and transportation scheduling, which is extensively discussed in the previous chapter, is another closely related research area. The emphasis here is on coordinating production and delivery operations such as machine scheduling and vehicle routing. Especially in industrial manufacturing, materials, parts, and components normally must be supplied to factories, further processed, and then delivered to subsequent production stages or customers. So an individual factory's problem mostly consists of coordinating inbound deliveries, processing operations, and outbound deliveries. A smooth and swift process flow is particularly essential when manufacturing products with a short shelf life, such as food and newspapers,[2] that can hardly be held in inventory. Chen (2004, 2010) reviews publications dealing with integrated production and distribution scheduling approaches. Most of the literature focusses on the coordination of production and outbound deliveries. Some papers, however, address integrated inbound delivery and production planning (Qi, 2005; Selvarajah and Steiner, 2006; Chung et al., 2010; Zhu, 2012). To the best of my knowledge, there are no articles that analyze attempts to schedule inbound deliveries, production operations, and outbound deliveries at the same time.

Integrated production and transportation scheduling is related to Supply Chain Scheduling for several reasons. Firstly, since transportation of goods between processing sites is mostly inevitable, it is unreasonable to aim to synchronize the operations of entire supply chains before one is able to deal with the integrated production and transportation scheduling problem of a single factory embedded in the supply chain. Note

---

[2]Remember the discussion on perishable goods on page 18.

that many Supply Chain Scheduling papers reduce intermediate transportation considerations to a minimum. Secondly, some authors adopt a activity-based perspective (Handfield and Nichols, 1999). As explained in Section 2.2.2, they interpret subsequent activities, such as procurement, production, and delivery as supply chain stages. From this perspective, a single company that executes only a few activities already represents an intra-organizational supply chain. Authors following this perspective consequently see integrated production and transportation scheduling as Supply Chain Scheduling (Dawande et al., 2006; Averbakh and Xue, 2007; Potts and Strusevich, 2009). Thirdly, delivery operations can be either carried out by a proprietary fleet of vehicles, vehicles of business partners, or a third-party logistics provider. If transportation is not undertaken by the same company that owns the processing facilities, a classic inter-organizational coordination problem arises, including the possibility of conflicts of interest (Manoj et al., 2008). Hence, using the term 'Supply Chain Scheduling' here is appropriate as well.

Classic flow shop scheduling deals with several consecutive productions stages, each equipped with a single machine. This structure suggests interpreting flow shops as simple linear supply chains. By incorporating transportation considerations and other elements, such as parallel machines, hybrid flow shops are an even more realistic reproduction of the supply chains encountered in practice. However, primarily addressing scheduling issues, conflict and cooperation problems between the stages are generally disregarded in hybrid flow shop scheduling literature. Nevertheless, it is worthwhile screening this research area especially with regard to its application to centrally controlled intra-organizational supply chains where conflict issues are sometimes negligible. For reviews on hybrid flow shop scheduling see Linn and Zhang (1999), Ribas et al. (2010), and Ruiz and Vázquez-Rodriguez (2010).

This section concludes with a review of papers that take a narrower perspective of the topic and provide numerical evidence of the savings potential of Supply Chain Scheduling. Note that these articles examine very specific settings and objective functions. The following sections introduce and investigate a much more general supply chain environment.

The first paper on Supply Chain Scheduling by Hall and Potts (2003) indicates the savings potential using three simple numerical examples. The first example is a setting with a supplier, a manufacturer, and two customers, both of whom order one job. It is analytically shown that total system costs, consisting of processing and transportation costs, can be reduced by up to 20% if both companies cooperate. The second example reveals that cooperation can cut total system costs by up to 25% if the objective is to minimize the sum of maximum tardiness and transportation costs. In the third example, cooperation reduces total system costs by as much as up to 100%. Here, the goal is to minimize the number of tardy jobs plus transportation costs.

Manoj et al. (2008) carry out a computational study on the basis of randomly generated test instances. Two different products are alternately processed at a production stage. Lot-sizes and processing sequences need to be determined. At a subsequent transportation stage, finished units are consolidated into batches and delivered to several customers. Since the schedule that minimizes the production stage's costs may produce high inventory holding costs for the transportation stage and vice versa, a conflict arises that incurs costs. For all test instances, the authors find that Supply Chain Scheduling results in win-win situations.

Manoj et al. (2012) consider a two-stage production system with an intermediate buffer storage in which the first stage's job processing sequence is rearranged according to the production plan of the second stage. While the first stage aims to minimize inventory holding costs, the second stage focuses on the sum of tardiness and re-sequencing costs. Integrating both stages' problems and then tackling the overall problem by a genetic algorithm is numerically shown to result in significantly lower overall costs than a separate planning scenario.

4.3 Mixed integer linear programs

Subsection 4.3.1 formalizes the problem, both the supplier and the manufacturer face at their respective supply chain stage. As explained in Sections 2.2.2 and 4.2, from an activity-based perspective, the process of dealing with this integrated machine and delivery scheduling problem can already be interpreted as intra-organizational Supply Chain Scheduling. The inter-organizational Supply Chain Scheduling problem that is introduced in Subsection 4.3.2 combines both companies' individual problems to form a joint cross-company problem. Note that for convenience, in this chapter the term 'Supply Chain Scheduling' is used to refer only to inter-organizational coordination.

4.3.1 Integrated machine and delivery scheduling

There is a set of J jobs with job-dependent release dates r_j, processing times p_j, and due dates d_j $(j = 1, ..., J)$. Each job has to be non-preemptively processed on one of

M homogenous identical parallel machines. If a job is not processed immediately after release, the required materials and parts need to be held in inventory, causing holding costs of $\underline{h}_j$ per time unit. The same applies if the start time of delivery S_j is later than the completion time of the job C_j. Due to changes in the cost of tied-up capital or in technical warehousing requirements, for example, the storage costs of a completed job $\overline{h}_j$ can differ from the holding costs of the parts and materials $\underline{h}_j$ (Lee and Yoon, 2010).

Jobs destined for the same customer are consolidated to form customer-specific de-livery batches, but job-dependent physical sizes u_j need to be taken into account. Fur-thermore, a job may not be divided into different delivery batches. The batches, limited to a maximum capacity measured in the number of pallets or by weight, for example, can be interpreted as containers or truck loads. Each batch incurs a fixed charge b_{fix} and variable costs per unit b_{var} of travel time (Chen and Vairaktarakis, 2005; Li and Vairaktarakis, 2007). The travel time to the customer k is t_k ($k = 1, ..., K$). Accordingly, customer k causes delivery costs of $b_{fix} + b_{var}t_k$ per batch.[3] There is a flexible forward-ing agent or a sufficiently large fleet of vehicles, so batches can be delivered at each point in time. As is common practice, a tardy job arrival T_j incurs a penalty of $\beta_j T_j$. If a job arrives E_j periods before its due date, an earliness penalty of $\alpha_j E_j$ is payable. Apart from monetary payments, earliness and tardiness often also lead to reputational dam-ages that result in costs manifested as loss of future profits, for example. Indeed, such costs are also relevant for decision-making and thus should be incorporated into α_j and β_j although they are generally hard to quantify (Anderson et al., 2006). Furthermore, it is questionable whether such costs linearly depend on a job's tardiness T_j.

Using the Three-Field Notation by Graham et al. (1979), this integrated machine and delivery scheduling problem can be described by $IP/r_j, u_j, \overline{b}/ETP + IC + TC$. The jobs are processed on identical parallel machines (IP), taking job release dates r_j into account. Considering job-dependent physical sizes u_j, customer-specific transportation batches with a maximum size of $\overline{b}$ are formed. The objective is to minimize the sum of earliness/tardiness penalties (ETP), inventory holding costs (IC), and transportation costs (TC).

Theorem 4. *The problem $IP/r_j, u_j, \overline{b}/ETP + IC + TC$ is NP-hard.*

Proof. Du and Leung (1990) prove that minimizing total tardiness on a single machine ($1//\sum_j T_j$) is NP-hard (in the ordinary sense). Since $IP/r_j, u_j, \overline{b}/ETP + IC + TC$ is a

---

[3]Note that, technically, the term $b_{fix} + b_{var}t_k$ can be summarized into a single customer-dependent parameter symbolizing the costs per transportation batch. Nevertheless, for didactic and interpretive reasons, the extensive form is chosen.

generalization of $1//\sum_j T_j$, it must be NP-hard, too.   □

The NP-hard nature implies that, unless $P = NP$, algorithms ensuring the identification of global optima in polynomial-bounded computation time are unlikely to exist
(Garey and Johnson, 1979). Hence, heuristics are needed to tackle larger-size instances
within a reasonable computation time. Section 4.6 therefore proposes a suitable Excel-
based genetic algorithm.

After a list of the applied parameters and variables, the integrated machine and
delivery scheduling problem is formalized by a mixed integer linear program.[4]

Parameters

α_j	Job j's earliness penalty per time unit $(j = 1, ..., J)$
b_{fix}	Fixed batch delivery costs
b_{var}	Variable batch delivery costs per time unit
B_k	Maximum number of delivery batches for customer k $(k = 1, ..., K; B_k = \sum_{j=1}^{J} w_{jk}, \forall k = 1, ..., K)$
$\bar{b}$	Batch capacity (there is no feasible solution if $\bar{b} < \max_{j;j=1,...,J}\{u_j\}$)
β_j	Job j's tardiness penalty per time unit $(j = 1, ..., J)$
d_j	Due date of job j $(j = 1, ..., J)$
$\underline{h}_j$	Job j's inventory holding costs per time unit before processing $(i = 1, ..., J)$
$\bar{h}_j$	Job j's inventory holding costs per time unit after processing $(j = 1, ..., J)$
M	Number of identical parallel machines
p_j	Processing time of job j $(j = 1, ..., J)$
q	Sufficiently large number
r_j	Release date of job j $(j = 1, ..., J)$
t_k	Travel time to customer k $(k = 1, ..., K)$
u_j	Size of job j $(j = 1, ..., J)$
w_{jk}	Binary parameter which has the value 1 if job j is ordered by customer k $(j = 1, ..., J; k = 1, ..., K; \sum_{k=1}^{K} w_{jk} = 1, \forall j = 1, ..., J)$

Variables

C_j	Completion time of job j $(j = 1, ..., J)$
E_j	Earliness of job j $(j = 1, ..., J)$

---

[4]Constraints 4.1–4.6, which determine the job sequences on the machines, come from Biskup et al.
(2008). Remember that this approach needs far fewer binary variables than classic models (Bowman,
1959; Wagner, 1959; Manne, 1960), affecting the computation time of commercial optimization software
packages like CPLEX and LINDO.

g_{jkb} Binary variable which takes the value 1 if job j is delivered within the bth batch to customer k ($j = 1, ..., J$; $k = 1, ..., K$; $b = 1, ..., B_k$)

T_j Tardiness of job j ($j = 1, ..., J$)

S_j Start time of the delivery of job j ($j = 1, ..., J$)

x_{ij} Binary variable which takes the value 1 if job i is processed before job j and no other job is processed in between on that machine ($i, j = 1, ..., J$; $i \neq j$)

$x_{j,J+1}$ Binary variable which takes the value 1 if job j is the last job processed on a machine ($j = 1, ..., J$). Job $J + 1$ is an artificial last job

x_{0j} Binary variable which takes the value 1 if job j is the first job processed on a machine ($j = 1, ..., J$)

Z_{kb} Variable which takes the value 1 if at least one job is delivered within the bth batch shipped to customer k ($k = 1, ..., K$; $b = 1, ..., B_k$)

The objective is to minimize the sum of earliness/tardiness, inventory holding, and transportation costs.

$$\min_{\substack{E_j,T_j,C_j,S_j,Z_{kb} \\ j=1,...,J;k=1,...,K;b=1,...,B_k}} \left\{ \sum_{j=1}^{J} \left(\alpha_j E_j + \beta_j T_j + \underline{h}_j(C_j - p_j - r_j) + \overline{h}_j(S_j - C_j) \right) + \sum_{k=1}^{K} \sum_{b=1}^{B_k} Z_{kb}(b_{fix} + b_{var}t_k) \right\}$$

subject to

$$M \geq \sum_{j=1}^{J} x_{0j} \tag{4.1}$$

$$\sum_{i=1,i\neq j}^{J+1} x_{ji} = 1 \qquad\qquad \forall\, j = 1, ..., J \tag{4.2}$$

$$x_{ij} \in \{0,1\} \qquad\qquad \forall\, i = 0, ..., J;\ j = 1, ...J + 1;\ i \neq J \tag{4.3}$$

$$\sum_{i=0,i\neq j}^{J} x_{ij} = 1 \qquad\qquad \forall\, j = 1, ..., J \tag{4.4}$$

$$C_j \geq r_j + p_j \qquad\qquad \forall\, j = 1, ..., J \tag{4.5}$$

$$C_j \geq C_i + p_j - q(1 - x_{ij}) \qquad\qquad \forall\, i, j = 1, ..., J;\ i \neq j \tag{4.6}$$

$$\sum_{b=1}^{B_k} g_{jkb} = w_{jk} \qquad\qquad \forall\, j = 1, ..., J;\ k = 1, ..., K \tag{4.7}$$

$$g_{jkb} \in \{0,1\} \qquad\qquad \forall\, j = 1, ..., J;\ k = 1, ..., K;\ b = 1, ..., B_k \tag{4.8}$$

$$Z_{kb} \geq g_{jkb} \qquad \forall j = 1, ..., J; \ k = 1, ..., K; \ b = 1, ..., B_k \qquad (4.9)$$

$$\bar{b} \geq \sum_{j=1}^{J} u_j g_{jkb} \qquad \forall k = 1, ..., K, \ b = 1, ..., B_k \qquad (4.10)$$

$$S_j \geq C_i - q(2 - g_{ikb} - g_{jkb}) \qquad \forall i, j = 1, ..., J; \ k = 1, ..., K; \ b = 1, ..., B_k \qquad (4.11)$$

$$S_j \geq S_i - q(2 - g_{ikb} - g_{jkb}) \qquad \forall i, j = 1, ..., J; \ i \neq j; \ k = 1, ..., K; \ b = 1, ..., B_k \qquad (4.12)$$

$$E_j \geq d_j - S_j - \sum_{k=1}^{K} w_{jk} t_k \qquad \forall j = 1, ..., J \qquad (4.13)$$

$$T_j \geq S_j + \sum_{k=1}^{K} w_{jk} t_k - d_j \qquad \forall j = 1, ..., J \qquad (4.14)$$

$$E_j, T_j \geq 0 \qquad \forall j = 1, ..., J \qquad (4.15)$$

Explanation of the constraints. 4.1: Obviously, there are at most M jobs which can occupy the first position in one of the M machine processing sequences. 4.2–4.3: Each job either precedes another job or is the last one in a machine's processing sequence. 4.4: At the same time, each job is either the first to be processed on a machine or succeeds another job. 4.5–4.6: The completion time must be equal to or greater than the release date plus the processing time, and equal to or greater than the completion time of the preceding job plus the processing time. 4.7–4.8: Each job is assigned to exactly one batch destined for its respective customer. 4.9: Z_{kb} takes the value 1 if at least one job is delivered within the bth batch shipped to customer k. In optimum, the objective functions forces Z_{kb} to be 0 if there is no job assigned to the bth batch for customer k. 4.10: The maximum batch capacity may not be exceeded. 4.11: A job cannot be delivered until all jobs assigned to the same batch are completed. 4.12: All jobs within the same batch have the same delivery start time. 4.13–4.15: Earliness and tardiness can be concluded from the jobs' due dates and arrival times at the destinations. A job's arrival time at the destination is calculated as the start time of delivery plus the travel time $S_j + \sum_{,k-1}^{K} w_{jk} t_k$.

4.3.2 Supply Chain Scheduling

One of the most often mentioned reasons for favoring a dual or multiple sourcing strategy is that relying on only one source bears the risk of a supply shortage due to capacity problems or insolvency on the part of the supplier. Also, multiple sourcing is expected to encourage price competition between suppliers, to maintain suppliers' capability of processing and developing specific components, and in turn, to prevent a single supplier from occupying a monopoly position with strong bargaining power. There are similar reasons for maintaining business relationships with several customers. Restricting oneself to just one customer can lead to dependence. If the customer becomes insolvent, the supplier's business may be affected, too. Moreover, a single customer may exploit its strong position when negotiating prices, due dates, and penalties. Despite these disadvantages and risks there is an observable trend towards fewer supplier/customer relationships (Monczka et al., 2009). Long-term relationships with a small number of trustworthy partners or even just one are expected to reduce negotiation periods and costs, to enable close cooperation when developing innovative high-quality products, and to allow for joint optimization approaches such as just-in-time or just-in-sequence material flows and, of course, Supply Chain Scheduling (Berger and Zeng, 2006). Nevertheless, many companies still do business with more than one supplier and one customer, which the following model takes into account. The focus, however, is on the supplier-manufacturer relationship.

The manufacturer is one of several customers of the supplier and the supplier is one of several sources of the manufacturer. Both companies face the intra-organizational machine and delivery scheduling problem described in the previous section. Each of the manufacturer's jobs is assumed to require a customized component that is provided either by the supplier or by another source. The manufacturer cannot process a job until the job-specific component has been provided. Consider the German steel manufacturer Salzgitter Flachstahl GmbH, which coats steel coils according to customer preferences and usage requirements such as color, eco-efficiency, anti-corrosion coating, and scratch resistance (Höhn et al., 2011). These preferences and requirements result in the need to source job-specific paints and coatings. Akzo Nobel, DuPont Performance Coatings, and BASF Coatings, for example, are globally operating suppliers of paints and coatings that cooperate closely with their customers when developing innovative and tailor-made products.

In the Supply Chain Scheduling model, both companies' relationships with other supply chain partners are taken into account. Jobs that are not destined for the manufacturer leave the cross-company system after the first stage, while jobs that are not provided by the supplier enter it only at the second stage. As explained in Section 4.2, this structure is interpretable as a specific hybrid flow shop. The Supply Chain Scheduling problem investigated in this chapter can thus be described by $asymHF2, IP^{1,2}/r_j, u_j, \bar{b}/$

$\sum_{1,2}(ETP + IC + TC)$. $HF2, IP^{1,2}$ denotes a hybrid flow shop with two stages, both equipped with identical parallel machines. Asymmetric ($asym$) means that some jobs may have to be processed at only one of the two stages, so the stages may differ in the number of jobs to be scheduled.

Theorem 5. *The problem* $asym HF2, IP^{1,2}/r_j, u_j, \bar{b}/\sum_{1,2}(ETP + IC + TC)$ *is NP-hard.*

Proof. Since $asym HF2, IP^{1,2}/r_j, u_j, \bar{b}/\sum_{1,2}(ETP + IC + TC)$ is a generalization of the NP-hard integrated machine and delivery scheduling problem introduced in the previous section, it must be NP-hard, too. $\square$

The notation of the mixed integer linear Supply Chain Scheduling program differs only slightly from that introduced in the previous section. The sole difference is that an additional company index c ($c = s, m$) is needed here (see the dissertation's List of Symbols). This index separates symbols according to whether they belong to the supplier s or the manufacturer m. For example, the supplier's (manufacturer's) number of jobs is J_s (J_m).

The objective is to minimize the sum of the supplier's and the manufacturer's earliness/tardiness, inventory holding, and delivery costs.

$$\min_{\substack{E_{cj},T_{cj},C_{cj},S_{cj},Z_{ckb} \\ c=s,m;j=1,...,J_c;k=1,...,K_c;b=1,...,B_{ck}}} \left\{ \sum_{j=B_{s1}+1}^{J_s} (\alpha_{sj}E_{sj} + \beta_{sj}T_{sj}) + \sum_{j=1}^{J_m}(\alpha_{mj}E_{mj} + \beta_{mj}T_{mj}) + \right.$$

$$\left. \sum_{c=s,m} \left(\sum_{j=1}^{J_c} \left(\underline{h}_{cj} \left(C_{cj} - p_{cj} - r_{cj} \right) + \overline{h}_{cj} \left(S_{cj} - C_{cj} \right) \right) + \sum_{k=1}^{K_c} \sum_{b=1}^{B_{ck}} Z_{ckb} \left(b_{fix_c} + b_{var_c} t_{ck} \right) \right) \right\}$$

subject to

$$M_c \geq \sum_{j=1}^{J_c} x_{c0j} \qquad\qquad\qquad \forall\, c = s, m \quad (4.16)$$

$$\sum_{i=0, i \neq j}^{J_c} x_{cij} = 1 \qquad\qquad\qquad \forall\, c = s, m;\ j = 1, ..., J_c \quad (4.17)$$

$$\sum_{i=1, i \neq j}^{J_c+1} x_{cji} = 1 \qquad\qquad\qquad \forall\, c = s, m;\ j = 1, ..., J_c \quad (4.18)$$

$$x_{cij} \in \{0, 1\} \qquad\qquad \forall\, c = s, m;\ i = 0, ..., J_c;\ j = 1, ... J_c + 1;\ i \neq j \quad (4.19)$$

$$C_{cj} \geq r_{cj} + p_{cj} \qquad\qquad\qquad \forall\, c = s, m;\ j = 1, ..., J_c \quad (4.20)$$

$$C_{cj} \geq C_{ci} + p_{cj} - q(1 - x_{cij}) \qquad\qquad \forall c = s, m; \ i,j = 1, ..., J_c; \ i \neq j \quad (4.21)$$

$$r_{mj} = S_{sj} + t_{s1} \qquad\qquad\qquad\qquad\qquad \forall j = 1, ..., B_{s1} \quad (4.22)$$

$$\sum_{b=1}^{B_{ck}} g_{cjkb} = w_{cjk} \qquad\qquad \forall c = s, m; \ j = 1, ..., J_c; \ k = 1, ..., K_c \quad (4.23)$$

$$g_{cjkb} \in \{0,1\} \qquad\qquad \forall c = s, m; \ j = 1, ..., J_c; \ k = 1, ..., K_c; \ b = 1, ..., B_{ck} \quad (4.24)$$

$$\bar{b}_c \geq \sum_{j=1}^{J_c} u_{cj} g_{cjkb} \qquad\qquad \forall c = s, m; \ k = 1, ..., K_c; \ b = 1, ..., B_{ck} \quad (4.25)$$

$$S_{cj} \geq C_{ci} - q(2 - g_{cikb} - g_{cjkb}) \quad \forall c = s, m; \ i,j = 1, ..., J_c; \ k = 1, ..., K_c; \ b = 1, ..., B_{ck} \quad (4.26)$$

$$S_{cj} \geq S_{ci} - q(2 - g_{cikb} - g_{cjkb}) \quad \forall c = s, m; \ i,j = 1, ..., J_c; \ i \neq j; \ k = 1, ..., K_c; \ b = 1, ..., B_{ck} \quad (4.27)$$

$$E_{sj} \geq d_{sj} - S_{sj} - \sum_{k=2}^{K_s}(w_{sjk}t_{sk}) \qquad\qquad \forall j = B_{s1} + 1, ..., J_s \quad (4.28)$$

$$T_{sj} \geq S_{sj} + \sum_{k=2}^{K_s}(w_{sjk}t_{sk}) - d_{sj} \qquad\qquad \forall j = B_{s1} + 1, ..., J_s \quad (4.29)$$

$$E_{mj} \geq d_{mj} - S_{mj} - \sum_{k=1}^{K_m}(w_{mjk}t_{mk}) \qquad\qquad \forall j = 1, ..., J_m \quad (4.30)$$

$$T_{mi} \geq S_{mi} + \sum_{k=1}^{K_m}(w_{mik}t_{mk}) - d_{mi} \qquad\qquad \forall j = 1, ..., J_m \quad (4.31)$$

$$E_{sj}, T_{sj} \geq 0 \qquad\qquad\qquad\qquad\qquad \forall j = B_{s1} + 1, ..., J_s \quad (4.32)$$

$$E_{mj}, T_{mj} \geq 0 \qquad\qquad\qquad\qquad\qquad \forall j = 1, ..., J_m \quad (4.33)$$

$$Z_{ckb} \geq g_{cjkb} \qquad\qquad \forall c = s, m; \ j = 1, ..., J_c; \ k = 1, ..., K_c; \ b = 1, ..., B_{ck} \quad (4.34)$$

Explanation of the constraints. Restrictions 4.16–4.34 are generally analogous to the constraints of the previous section's integrated machine and delivery scheduling model. The additional index c ($c = s, m$) implies that they hold for the supplier's as well as the manufacturer's supply chain stage. It is necessary to clarify the interface between the supplier and the manufacturer. The first of the supplier's K_s customers is the manufacturer. The jobs $j = 1, ..., B_{s1}$ in the supplier's set of jobs represent the components the manufacturer ordered for its jobs $j = 1, ..., B_{s1}$. For example, the first job of the supplier is the component required for the first job of the manufacturer. The arrival times of the components provided by the supplier impose job release dates on the manufacturer's processing. These release dates are decision variables in the Supply Chain Scheduling program (Constraint 4.22). Note that the release dates of the supplier's jobs remain parameters. The same holds for the release dates of the manufacturer's jobs that do not rely on components provided by the supplier. There is no need for due dates and earliness/tardiness penalties between the supplier and manufacturer because of the joint objective (objective function and Constraints 4.28, 4.29, and 4.32). Penalty payments imposed by the manufacturer on the supplier would reduce the manufacturer's costs to the same extent they would increase the supplier's costs. Hence, the relevant overall costs would remain unaffected.

4.4 Design of the numerical study

The separate scheduling scenario presented in Subsection 4.4.1 describes the status quo planning process. Separate scheduling means that the supplier and the manufacturer solve their problems individually and successively, each on the basis of private information only. The schedules resulting from this planning scenario are compared with the schedules yielded by cross-company Supply Chain Scheduling. The Supply Chain Scheduling scenario is introduced in Subsection 4.4.2.

4.4.1 The separate scheduling scenario

Figure 4.1 shows the sequence of events in the separate scheduling scenario.

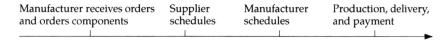

Figure 4.1: Timeline for separate scheduling

Initially, the manufacturer receives orders from its customers and orders the required components from its providers. The parties agree on due dates and earliness/ tardiness penalties. It is virtually impossible for due dates and penalties between the supplier and the manufacturer to be negotiated and set in such a way that they already optimally coordinate the schedules. Negotiations on due dates and penalties are generally affected by other factors such as product price, for example, which are not considered in the model. Sales representatives are likely to accept even very tight due dates and high penalties, if the product price a customer is willing to pay overcompensates for the strict requirements. Imagine a billionaire determined to order a new yacht for his next vacation. He may be willing to pay an enormous price but only if the boat is completed in time. Tardy completion may induce the Draconian penalty of a withdrawal from the purchase. There are many other practical factors that make it extremely hard to achieve perfect coordination simply by agreeing on appropriate due dates and penalties. For example, while negotiating with a customer, a sales representative is unable to know the terms and conditions other sales representatives have agreed with their key customers in parallel negotiations. Also, they cannot precisely anticipate the results of their own future negotiations with other customers. Only ex post, when aware of the whole set of jobs to be scheduled and having shared the information with supply chain partners, as is done in the Supply Chain Scheduling scenario, does it become possible to calculate the optimal overall schedule. Due dates and penalties can express the characteristics and the importance of a single job yet for the above reasons they are unsuitable for coordinating whole sets of jobs. Given a set of jobs, the purpose of scheduling is to trade off these characteristics so as to minimize total costs or other objective criteria.

Having received the component orders, the supplier and the other providers separately schedule their processing and delivery operations. The resulting schedules determine the arrival times of the components at the manufacturer. Due to scarce capacity, delivery batching, and other reasons, these arrival times may deviate from the stipulated due dates. The manufacturer hence cannot schedule its set of jobs until he is aware of all component arrival times.

The last step of the timeline comprises production, delivery, and payment of the earliness/tardiness penalties. Note that product price payments are irrelevant to decision making since they do not affect scheduling decisions, and price reductions due to tardy completions, for example, are incorporated in the tardiness penalties.

Figure 4.2: Supply chain structure in the example

In the following explanatory example both the supplier and the manufacturer have to process a set of six jobs ($J_s = J_m = 6$) on two parallel machines ($M_s = M_m = 2$). The number of customers is $K_s = 3$ and $K_m = 2$, respectively. The manufacturer sources four components from the supplier ($B_{s1} = 4$) and two from other providers. Figure 4.2 summarizes the supply chain structure. Note that the providers and customers, represented by empty rectangles, may also maintain relationships with further companies.

It is assumed that the supplier's processing does not rely on specific components, so its release dates and storage cost before processing are $r_s = (0,0,0,0,0,0)$ and $\underline{h}_s = (0,0,0,0,0,0)$, respectively. The four question marks in the vector of the manufacturer's job release dates denote the arrival times of the components sourced from the supplier. These dates result from the supplier's schedule.

$$p_s = (70, 31, 100, 24, 50, 54) \qquad p_m = (40, 42, 31, 45, 45, 75)$$
$$u_s = (8, 4, 10, 2, 6, 7) \qquad u_m = (6, 4, 9, 9, 6, 2)$$
$$d_s = (124, 77, 128, 78, 96, 117) \qquad d_m = (179, 152, 203, 133, 209, 219)$$
$$r_s = (0, 0, 0, 0, 0, 0) \qquad r_m = (?, ?, ?, ?, 122, 126)$$
$$\underline{h}_s = (0, 0, 0, 0, 0, 0) \qquad \underline{h}_m = (8, 1, 1, 5, 2, 1)$$
$$\overline{h}_s = (8, 5, 5, 10, 2, 4) \qquad \overline{h}_m = (1, 9, 5, 1, 6, 5)$$
$$\alpha_s = (9, 2, 4, 3, 6, 10) \qquad \alpha_m = (3, 1, 5, 8, 4, 2)$$
$$\beta_s = (36, 18, 12, 27, 18, 80) \qquad \beta_m = (18, 1, 35, 72, 24, 14)$$

Remember that the binary parameter w_{cjk} links jobs and customers. For example, the second, the third, and the sixth job of the manufacturer are destined for its second customer.

$$(w_c) = \begin{pmatrix} w_{c11} & w_{c12} & \cdots & w_{c1K_c} \\ & w_{c21} & & \\ \vdots & & \ddots & \vdots \\ w_{cJ1} & & \cdots & w_{cJK_c} \end{pmatrix} \quad (w_s) = \begin{pmatrix} 1 & 0 & 0 \\ 1 & 0 & 0 \\ 1 & 0 & 0 \\ 1 & 0 & 0 \\ 0 & 1 & 0 \\ 0 & 0 & 1 \end{pmatrix} \quad (w_m) = \begin{pmatrix} 1 & 0 \\ 0 & 1 \\ 0 & 1 \\ 1 & 0 \\ 1 & 0 \\ 0 & 1 \end{pmatrix}$$

The transportation related parameters are as follows: $t_s = (8, 9, 5)$, $t_m = (4, 2)$, $\overline{b}_s = 14$, $\overline{b}_m = 15$, $b_{var_s} = 4$, $b_{var_m} = 9$, $b_{fix_s} = 268$, and $b_{fix_m} = 135$.

Optimizing the supplier's integrated machine and delivery scheduling problem results in the schedule shown in Figure 4.3. For example, the supplier's first transportation batch, which consists of jobs 2 and 4, reaches the manufacturer at moment 63. Both

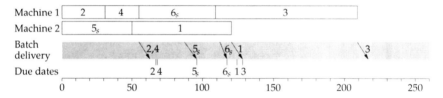

Figure 4.3: Optimal schedule of the supplier

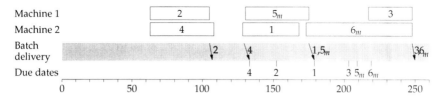

Figure 4.4: Optimal schedule of the manufacturer

jobs arrive ahead of their due dates. Remember that the arrival times of the supplier's jobs 1–4 correspond to the previously unknown release dates for the processing of the manufacturer's jobs 1–4. Taking the component release dates into account, the manufacturer schedules its operations. The result is illustrated in Figure 4.4. Aggregating Figures 4.3 and 4.4 leads to an overall schedule that incurs total costs of 4 681. The supplier and the manufacturer account for 2 983 and 1 698, respectively. Note that indices s and m indicate that the jobs leave the system after processing at the first stage or enter the system at the second stage, respectively.

4.4.2   The Supply Chain Scheduling scenario

In the Supply Chain Scheduling scenario, the supplier and the manufacturer jointly aim to minimize the overall costs. To this end, they integrate the intra-organizational planning problems and tackle the arising cross-company problem, sharing all relevant information. The sequence of events is illustrated in Figure 4.5.

As in the separate scheduling scenario, the manufacturer initially receives orders from its customers, places the orders for the required components, and agrees on due dates and penalties. Once aware of the arrival times/release dates of components 5 and

Figure 4.5: Timeline for Supply Chain Scheduling

6, which are provided by competitors of the supplier, the supplier and the manufacturer approach their joint Supply Chain Scheduling problem. Finally, production, delivery, and penalty payments to other supply chain parties take place.

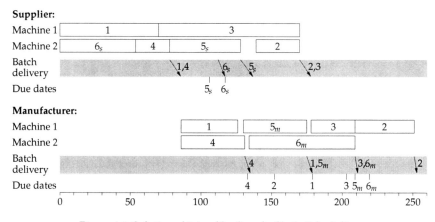

Figure 4.6: Solution obtained by Supply Chain Scheduling

Comparing the composite solution that results from separate scheduling (Figures 4.3 and 4.4) with the solution obtained by Supply Chain Scheduling (Figure 4.6) reveals fundamental differences. For example, in the Supply Chain Scheduling scenario, the supplier deploys other and fewer transportation batches, cutting transportation costs. This delays the manufacturer's processing but at the same time allows him to tighten up its production schedule. So the processing delay is compensated for by a reduction in intermediate idle time included in the manufacturer's machine schedule. As a result, although the supplier deploys fewer batches, there are no negative effects on the manufacturer's tardiness costs. The Supply Chain Scheduling solution incurs total costs of only 3 639, an overall saving of around 22% compared to the composite solution of separate scheduling. Here, the supplier and the manufacturer account for 2 218 and 1 421, respectively. The Appendix to this chapter discusses an idea for a simple mechanism that allows for varying the cost shares and thus the relative savings depending on the companies' bargaining powers.

Chapter 3 shows that integrated production and distribution schedules often deliver substantial intra-organizational optimization potential. Since the integrated production and distribution problems of the supplier and the manufacturer are optimally solved here, this potential is completely exploited and hence does not influence this chapter's results. The potential revealed in the above example and in the next sections can be unambiguously ascribed to inter-organizational coordination. However, a legitimate question for future research is: What is the potential of synchronizing intra- and inter-organizational operations at the same time?

4.5 Generation of test instances

This section describes the generation of the test instances on which the comparison between separate scheduling and Supply Chain Scheduling is based. Note that the previous section's example was also produced in the following manner.

During the first part of the numerical study, both the supplier and the manufacturer face a set of six jobs ($J_s = J_m = 6$). Despite the NP-hard nature of the investigated problems, instances of such a small size can still be optimally solved using the introduced mixed integer linear programs and a commercial optimization software. The second part of the numerical investigation concerns large-size instances which make the use of heuristics unavoidable, however, this involves the risk of distortions induced by solution inaccuracies. For simplicity, the generation of instances is explained with the help of the small-size setting only. The approach is straightforward for more jobs, machines, etc., as needed for the second part.

The numerical study is based on the relationship intensity between the supplier and the manufacturer. Relationship intensity is calculated as the number of common jobs divided by the total number of jobs in the system. For example, if the manufacturer sources the components for two of its six jobs from the supplier ($B_{s1} = 2$) the relationship intensity of both companies is $2/6 = 1/3$. The average relationship intensity thus is $1/2 \cdot (1/3 + 1/3) = 1/3$, too. Later on, the number of common jobs is varied from 1 to 6. This leads to growing relationship intensities of $1/6, 1/3, 1/2, 2/3, 5/6$, and 1 if the supplier is the sole provider of the manufacturer and the manufacturer the sole customer of the supplier.

Some restrictions have to be taken into account when generating the numbers of customers K_m and K_s. Both companies can have 6 different customers at most, each ordering one job. Furthermore, as long as the number of jobs the supplier produces for the manufacturer is smaller than 6 ($B_{s1} < 6$), the supplier must have at least one other customer besides the manufacturer.[5] So the numbers of customers are drawn according to the rules:

$$K_m \sim RD\,[1,6] \tag{4.35}$$

$$K_s := 1 + \tau \quad \text{with} \quad \tau \sim RD\,[\min\{1, 6 - B_{s1}\}, 6 - B_{s1}] \tag{4.36}$$

Then, each of the manufacturer's K_m customers is randomly assigned to at least one of the manufacturer's 6 jobs. Also, the supplier's $K_s - 1$ other customers get at least one of the $6 - B_{s1}$ jobs the supplier does not produce for the manufacturer. As shown on page 69, the binary parameters w_{cjk} that result from the job-customer assignment can be aggregated to two matrices, one for the supplier and one for the manufacturer.

In line with common practice, the processing times p_{cj} and the travel times t_{ck} are drawn from the following intervals.

$$p_{cj} \sim RD\,[1, 100] \qquad\qquad \forall\, c = s, m;\ j = 1, ..., 6 \tag{4.37}$$

$$t_{ck} \sim RD\,[1, 10] \qquad\qquad \forall\, c = s, m;\ k = 1, ..., K_c \tag{4.38}$$

As already explained, negotiations on due dates are influenced by many factors such as product price, the sales representative's negotiating skills, and capacity utilization. However, sales representatives do not usually agree on due dates that cannot be met at all. Accordingly, due dates that do not allow for a job's processing time plus travel time to the customer should not be generated (Hariri and Potts, 1989; Biskup et al., 2008). Also, due dates should not be scattered too widely since this makes no sense in terms of capacity utilization. It is unlikely that companies with sets of jobs that involve production on, say, only one day per month will survive on the market. Capacity utilization, measured in mean processing time, is therefore incorporated in the generation formula so as to create realistic due dates that can vary from between very tight to relatively relaxed.

$$d_{sj} := p_{sj} + 10 + \gamma_j \quad \text{with} \quad \gamma_j \sim RD\left[0, \left\lfloor \frac{1}{6} \sum_{j=1}^{6} p_{sj} \right\rfloor\right] \qquad \forall\, j = 1, ..., 6 \tag{4.39}$$

---

[5]Again, Lehmer's (1951) congruential pseudo random numbers generator is applied.

The manufacturer's due dates are created in analogy to the supplier's. However, unlike the supplier's job release dates ($r_{sj} := 0 \; \forall \; j = 1,...,6$), the manufacturer's release dates are not equal to 0 but depend on the arrival times of the ordered components. The supplier's due dates, which represent the expected arrival times, must thus also be taken into account to ensure that the manufacturer generally can meet its due dates.

$$d_{mj} := d_{sj} + p_{mj} + 10 + \kappa_j \quad \text{with} \quad \kappa_j \sim RD \left[0, \left\lfloor \frac{1}{6} \sum_{j=1}^{6} p_{mj} \right\rfloor \right] \qquad \forall \; j = 1,...,B_{s1} \quad (4.40)$$

The release dates r_{mj} of the jobs $j = B_{s1} + 1,...,6$ whose components are not sourced from the supplier, are generated in the same manner as the due dates for the supplier. They can hence be used to create the related due dates for the manufacturer without involving distorting influences on the results of the numerical study. Remember that the manufacturer's release dates r_{mj} for the components $j = 1,...,B_{s1}$ result from the supplier's schedule.

$$r_{mj} := \pi_j + 10 + \epsilon_j \qquad \forall \; j = B_{s1} + 1,...,6 \quad (4.41)$$

$$\text{with} \quad \pi_j \sim RD \, [1, 100] \quad \text{and} \quad \epsilon_j \sim RD \left[0, \left\lfloor \frac{1}{6} \sum_{j=1}^{6} p_{sj} \right\rfloor \right]$$

$$d_{mj} := r_{mj} + p_{mj} + 10 + \kappa_j \quad \text{with} \quad \kappa_j \sim RD \left[0, \left\lfloor \frac{1}{6} \sum_{j=1}^{6} p_{mj} \right\rfloor \right] \qquad \forall \; j = B_{s1} + 1,...,6 \quad (4.42)$$

A necessary condition for the existence of a feasible solution is that even the job with the largest size fits in the batches. Real-world companies also need to comply with this constraint. Hence, the physical job sizes u_{cj} and batch capacities $\bar{b}_c$ are created so that this condition is met.

$$u_{cj} \sim RD \, [1, 10] \qquad \qquad \forall \; c = s, m; \; j = 1,...,6 \quad (4.43)$$
$$\bar{b}_c \sim RD \, [10, 20] \qquad \qquad \forall \; c = s, m \quad (4.44)$$

Intending realistic proportions, the fixed transportation costs per batch b_{fix_c} are generated as a multiple of the variable transportation costs b_{var_c} per time unit. Justified by empirical findings (Thomas and Griffin, 1996; Swenseth and Godfrey, 2002), the intervals for b_{var_c} and σ_c are chosen such that the transportation costs on average account for around 50% of the total costs in the separate scheduling scenario.

$$b_{var_c} \sim RD[1,10] \qquad\qquad \forall\, c = s, m \quad (4.45)$$

$$b_{fix_c} := \sigma_c\, b_{var_c} \quad \text{with} \quad \sigma_c \sim RD\,[1,100] \qquad\qquad \forall\, c = s, m \quad (4.46)$$

The earliness penalties α_{cj} are henceforth attributed to the storage costs since their main purpose is to compensate customers for storage costs caused by early deliveries. The intervals for the inventory holding parameters are chosen such that the sum of the supplier's and the manufacturer's storage costs on average make up around 25% of the composite schedule's total costs. Remember that $\underline{h}_{sj} := 0$ ($\forall\, j = 1, ..., 6$).

$$\underline{h}_{mj} \sim RD\,[1,10] \qquad\qquad \forall\, j = 1, ..., 6 \quad (4.47)$$

$$\overline{h}_{cj} \sim RD\,[1,10] \qquad\qquad \forall\, c = s, m;\; j = 1, ..., 6 \quad (4.48)$$

$$\alpha_{cj} \sim RD\,[1,10] \qquad\qquad \forall\, c = s, m;\; j = 1, ..., 6 \quad (4.49)$$

In a just-in-time supply chain environment, tardiness can cause major problems and incur enormous costs since the customer's production is put at risk of a total breakdown. By contrast, earliness mostly only involves inventory holding, incurring rather modest costs. To ensure that these parameters are also in realistic proportion to each other, the tardiness penalties β_{cj} are generated as a multiple of the earliness penalties (Wan and Yen, 2002). The tardiness costs on average account for the remaining 25% of the total costs.

$$\beta_{cj} := v_{cj}\, \alpha_{cj} \quad \text{with} \quad v_{cj} \sim RD\,[1,10] \qquad\qquad \forall\, c = s, m;\; j = 1, ..., 6 \quad (4.50)$$

4.6 Applying Excel to scheduling problems

First, this section shows that Microsoft Excel's evolutionary algorithm is generally able to produce good solutions to larger-size instances of classic scheduling problems. Then, the approach is applied to the problems introduced in Section 4.3. Once the spreadsheet approach developed in this chapter is understood, transferring it to many types of batching, sequencing, scheduling, and routing problems is easy.

In the tenth edition of their famous textbook *Management Science Modeling* Albright and Winston (2012) tackle a vast number of problems occurring in business administration and economics using Excel spreadsheets. However, despite their enormous practical relevance, Excel has barely been applied to any of the sequencing and scheduling problems studied in an uncounted number of papers for more than 50 years (Potts and Strusevich, 2009). Many machine scheduling and vehicle routing problems are formulated by mixed integer linear and non-linear models which can be transferred to Excel. So why not use this obvious approach to solve sequencing and scheduling problems? The reason is that implementing such programs in Excel is laborious. But more importantly, if Excel results in a feasible solution at all, the quality of the solutions is mostly very poor. Binary and integer variables, discontinuities of the objective functions, and the NP-hardness of many scheduling problems make it impossible to use the simplex and the non-linear solver included in Excel's free solver add-in. Only the evolutionary algorithm is applicable. Unfortunately, this algorithm is found to be poor at handling constraints (Albright and Winston, 2012). So approaching large mixed integer programs by Excel is generally pointless.

However, unlike expensive commercial optimization software packages like LINGO and CPLEX, Microsoft Excel does not need to be purchased and integrated in the computer system since almost every company around the world already uses it. So developing an efficient and effective way to solve batching, sequencing, scheduling, and routing problems with spreadsheets is highly worthwhile.

4.6.1   Minimizing total tardiness on parallel machines

Before dealing with this chapter's problems, Excel's ability to solve scheduling problems is generally proven by comparing it with an established tailor-made heuristic for the commonly known problem of minimizing total tardiness on parallel machines. A set of jobs with job-dependent processing times and due dates has to be scheduled on M identical parallel machines, aiming to minimize total tardiness. This problem is proven to be NP-hard by Du and Leung (1990) which brings about the necessity for heuristics. Biskup et al. (2008) propose an up-to-date tailor-made heuristic that outperforms most other approaches to that problem. So benchmark instances and solutions are generated according to Biskup et al. (2008).

Excel's solver add-in includes the option to apply an evolutionary algorithm. The collective term 'evolutionary algorithm' comprises all evolution-motivated meta-heuristic approaches. Excel makes use of the most popular one, a genetic algorithm (Holland, 1975; Goldberg, 1989; Davis, 1991; Gendreau and Potvin, 2010). Extensively covered in the previous chapter, genetic algorithms simulate the Darwinian principle of survival of the fittest. Encoded solutions to the considered problem, which are referred to as individuals, are iteratively altered by crossover, mutation, or reproduction. In doing so, the population is expected to gradually converge towards the optimum. The crossover mechanism first selects two individuals, or parents, and then recombines the parents' structures to create new individuals, or offspring. The mutation mechanism selects only one parent that is altered in a randomly chosen element of its code structure to produce offspring. Reproduction assigns a parent without modification to the next generation of individuals. When dealing with a minimization problem, individuals with low objective values are more likely to be chosen as parents. The following steps enable Excel's evolutionary algorithm to cope with the total tardiness benchmark problem. The instances are coded using a modified form of the random keys approach by Bean (1994).

1. Allow Excel's solver to manipulate as many cells as there are jobs and restrict the numbers Excel can assign to the cells to integers within a sufficiently large interval, say, $[1, 1\,000\,000]$. Note that this kind of restriction poses no problem to the evolutionary algorithm. Let job 1 be represented by cell 1, job 2 by cell 2,..., and job J by cell J. Then, diminish each of the J integers by an index-dependent number $\frac{(J-j+1)}{J}$ between 0 and 1. The resulting real values y_j $(j = 1, ..., J)$ need to be saved in another J cells. In doing so, it is ensured that no two jobs are characterized by the same number: $y_j \neq y_i \quad \forall j, i = 1, ..., J; \ i \neq j$.

2. Divide the upper limit of the interval, here $1\,000\,000$, by the number of available parallel machines M. All jobs with a number y_j that satisfies

$$\frac{1\,000\,000(m-1)}{M} \leq y_j < \frac{1\,000\,000\,m}{M} \qquad (4.51)$$

are assigned to machine m $(m = 1, ..., M)$. For example, if the number of job 6 is $y_6 = 673\,198.5$ and there are $M = 5$ parallel machines, job 6 is processed on machine $m = 4$ $(600\,000 <= 673\,198.5 < 800\,000)$.

3. Finally, order all jobs assigned to machine m in increasing order of their numbers y_j so as to determine job-processing sequences for each machine m $(m = 1, ..., M)$.

Inserting machine idle time between the production of two jobs makes no sense when aiming to minimize total tardiness. So the completion times of all jobs can be unambiguously obtained from the machines' processing sequences and the jobs' processing times. Total tardiness results from adding up the tardiness of all jobs completed after their due dates. Hence, there is a unique total tardiness value that follows straight from the integers which Excel's evolutionary algorithm assigns to the cells.

Before it can handle the benchmark problem, Excel must be prepared. First of all, the described steps need to be implemented in a spreadsheet. Then, in the solver options menu, Excel must be permitted to manipulate the J target cells, restricted to integers within the chosen interval. Furthermore, the cell containing the total tardiness value has to be marked as the objective cell to be minimized. Finally, in the evolutionary algorithm's options menu, the settings should be specified to scheduling problems in order to enhance performance. Albright and Winston (2012) mention that for some problem types, the evolutionary solver performs best with a high probability of mutation. Revealing that high mutation probabilities prevent premature convergence towards local optima, own numerical examinations confirm this finding. The options menu furthermore allows for adjusting the convergence rate,[6] the number of coexistent individuals (population size), the start seed of the random number generator (Biskup and Feldmann, 2001), and the maximum computation time without improvement before Excel stops. The following settings turn out to be suitable when approaching scheduling problems: convergence rate $\to$ 0.0001, mutation rate $\to$ 0.9, population size individuals $\to$ 200, random seed[7] $\to$ 0, maximum time without improvement of the solution $\to$ 6 000 seconds. Note that Excel's solver does not apply reproduction. Since the mutation probability is set to 90% ($0.9 \hat{=} 90\%$), the probability of crossover is 10%.

Table 4.1: Improvements achieved by Excel's evolutionary algorithm

Benchmark	Mean	Maximum	Minimum	Median	Standard deviation
BHG heuristic	8.6%	55.7%	-22.7%	2.7%	14.9%
Scheduling-specific genetic algorithm	-2.5%	34.6%	-47.6%	-0.5%	12.5%

On the basis of 100 benchmark instances[8] with 50 jobs and 5 machines, Excel's evolutionary algorithm is tested against the tailor-made BHG (Biskup, Herrmann, Gupta) heuristic (Biskup et al., 2008). Table 4.1 summarizes the results in the row 'BHG heuristic.' First of all, note that Excel's solutions are on average 8.6% better than BHG's. Recorded in the column 'Maximum,' the total tardiness is at most 55.7% lower. The

---

[6]Take the top 99% of the individuals in a given population and calculate the relative deviations of their objective values from the best solution found so far. A convergence rate of 0.0001 means that if the maximum relative deviation is below 0.01%, the evolutionary solver stops.

[7]When choosing option 0, Excel uses its own seeds.

[8]Ten instances are generated for each combination of the due date parameters α_{BHG} and β_{BHG} proposed by Biskup et al. (2008). The job's processing times are randomly drawn from the interval $[1, 100]$.

negative improvement percentage quoted in the column 'Minimum' (-22.7%), however, reveals that there are also instances BHG copes better with (43 of 100 instances). All in all, Excel nevertheless clearly outperforms BHG in the instances examined. Indeed, to some extent, the comparison is unfair since Excel's computation time, on average about 2 hours, is much longer than BHG's. But with the computer hardware industry's rapid progress in terms of computation speed, and meta-heuristics becoming ever more powerful, these results indicate that the future may belong to easily adjustable and commonly available meta-heuristics rather than elaborately developed problem-specific approaches.

In a second investigation, which is based based on the same 100 benchmark instances, Excel is compared with a scheduling-specific genetic algorithm on the basis of the approach developed in the previous section.[9] The row 'Scheduling-specific genetic algorithm' reveals that Excel is outperformed on average by 2.5%. Note that the specific genetic algorithm needs only a few minutes, supporting the above made surmise that in some years, meta-heuristics may be able to compete in terms of computation time.

Note that in scheduling research, model parameters are mostly considered to be deterministic. However, this assumption often does not hold true in reality, so practitioners rightly complain about the disregard of stochastic influences on parameters such as processing times, for example. Using Excel add-ins like @RISK and the genetic algorithm-based risk optimizer included in that software package, this chapter's approach also allows for dealing with stochastic influences on any kind of model parameter.

4.6.2 Integrated machine and delivery scheduling

With the help of a well-known benchmark problem and heuristic, it has been shown that, using the proposed approach, Excel's evolutionary algorithm becomes able to successfully handle scheduling problems. Motivated by these findings, the problems introduced in Section 4.3 are now transferred into similar spreadsheet models.

The integrated machine and delivery scheduling problem can be implemented by extending the parallel machine scheduling spreadsheet by a further element. The jobs also need to be assigned to transportation batches.

---

[9]By skipping the vehicle routing part and reducing the time windows to due dates, Chapter 3's genetic algorithm can be easily adapted to the total tardiness problem.

Remember that all jobs with a number y_j that satisfies the condition

$$\frac{1\,000\,000(m-1)}{M} \leq y_j < \frac{1\,000\,000\,m}{M} \tag{4.52}$$

are assigned to machine m. Now modify y_j according to Formula 4.53.

$$y_j^* := y_j - \frac{1\,000\,000(m-1)}{M} \tag{4.53}$$

Obviously, the maximum number of J batches is applied if each job is shipped separately. Job j is assigned to the δth ($\delta = \{1, 2, ..., J\}$) batch if its modified number y_j^* satisfies Condition 4.54.

$$\frac{1\,000\,000(\delta-1)}{J} \leq y_j^* < \frac{1\,000\,000\,\delta}{J} \tag{4.54}$$

Resuming the example, the number $y_6 = 673\,198.5$ leads to $m = 4$ and $y_6^* := 673\,198.5 - 600\,000 = 73\,198.5$. Now assume the set of jobs contains 10 jobs ($J = 10$), then, job 6 is allocated to batch $\delta = 3$ ($60\,000 <= 73\,198.5 < 80\,000$). Figure 4.7 depicts all intervals that arise. It becomes apparent that jobs processed on different machines can nevertheless be assigned to the same delivery batch.

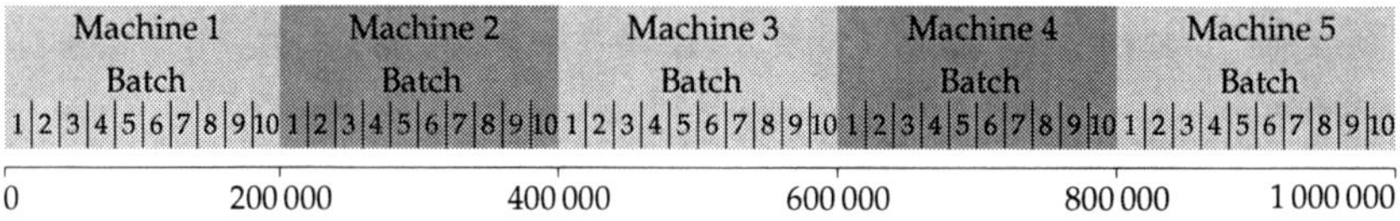

Figure 4.7: Assignment intervals used in the example

To obtain the machine's processing sequences, the number y_j^* needs to be further modified following Formula 4.55.

$$y_j^{**} := y_j^* - \frac{1\,000\,000\,\delta}{M \cdot J} \tag{4.55}$$

Order all jobs allocated to machine m in increasing order of their twice modified numbers y_j^{**} so as to determine machine m's job-processing sequence ($m = 1, ..., M$). For example, if the number of job 9 is $y_9 = 709\,428.8$, both job 6 and 9 are within the range of machine 4. Job 9's modified number is $y_9^* = 109\,428.8$, which implies that job 9 is shipped within batch 6. Comparing the two-times modified numbers $y_9^{**} = 9\,428.8 <$ $13\,198.5 = y_6^{**}$ reveals that job 9 comes before job 6 in the processing sequence although its initial number y_9 is much higher than that of job 6.

No matter to which batch a job is assigned, it can be processed on any machine and occupy any position in the machine's processing sequence. Without limiting the so-lution and search space, machine assignments, job-processing sequences, and delivery batches unambiguously result from the J integer numbers determined by the evolution-ary algorithm. However, this approach can produce too many jobs in a batch so that the maximum batch capacity is exceeded. Moreover, jobs ordered by different customers can be put in the same delivery batch. Neither is allowed according to the problems examined in this chapter. Since Excel's evolutionary algorithm is found to be poor at handling constraints, infeasible batch compilations are only penalized by adding a suf-ficiently high penalty per improper batch constellation to the objective cell (Albright and Winston, 2012).

In Section 4.4's example, the optimal schedules illustrated in Figures 4.3–4.6 include idle time prior to the processing and shipment of some jobs in order to cut inventory holding and earliness costs. Since there are J jobs and J batches at most, Excel needs to be allowed to manipulate another $2 \cdot J$ cells that contain the idle time inserted prior to the jobs' processing and the batches' deliveries, respectively. These cells have to be restricted to positive values including 0, which poses no problem for the evolutionary algorithm. To enhance computation time, it is helpful to define a reasonable maximum value, the maximum processing time p_{max}, for example. Also, these cells should be restricted to integers. However, note that such constraints limit the search space and thus should be well-considered. The numbers y_j and the idle times, together, result in an unique schedule and objective value.

It is also helpful to provide a feasible initial solution to Excel. This usually results in improvements in computation time and solution quality. Giving the J variable assign-ment cells initial numbers following the rule $\left\lfloor \frac{1\,000\,000(j-1)}{M \cdot J} \right\rfloor$ $(j = 1, ..., J)$, for example, implies that the jobs are processed in sequence according to their index number all on the first machine and shipped in J one-job batches to their respective customers. Fur-thermore, all idle time cells are initially set to 0, inducing that jobs and batches are processed and delivered as early as possible. If the infeasibility penalty per improper batch compilation is set to a value higher than the objective value of the initial solution, the ultimate solution is guaranteed to be feasible since it cannot be worse than the initial solution.

4.6.3   Supply Chain Scheduling

Using the described approach, Excel's evolutionary algorithm is able to handle the integrated machine and delivery scheduling problem of Section 4.3.1. Since the supplier and the manufacturer face the same problem, transferring the approach to the Supply Chain Scheduling problem of Section 4.3.2 is straightforward. The model only needs to be implemented twice and interlinked through the arrival times of the supplier's deliveries at the manufacturer.

4.7   Computational results

This section presents the results of the numerical investigation carried out on the basis of the models, the timelines, the instance generator, and the heuristics, all introduced in the previous sections. Subsection 4.7.1 deals with optimally solvable small-size instances. The heuristic-based investigation of real-world-size instances follows in Subsection 4.7.2.

4.7.1   Small-size instances

Remember that in the small-size scenario, both the supplier and the manufacturer have to cope with a set of 6 jobs. This allows for solving all arising problems with the mixed integer linear program formulated in Section 4.3.1 and a commercial optimization software. So, there is definitively no distorting influence caused by the need to apply a heuristic. The computations on one core of a Pentium Core 2 Duo processor (1.7 GHz) with 2 048 MB RAM usually take only minutes when dealing with the integrated machine and delivery scheduling problem. The computation times of the Supply Chain Scheduling program, however, often run to several hours, showing that larger-size instances cannot be tackled with the optimization software. Note that computation time increases as relationship intensity rises. 30 instances are generated and investigated for each relationship intensity, leading to 180 $(= 6 \cdot 30)$ small-size instances in total.

Figure 4.8 presents the average relative savings achieved by Supply Chain Scheduling, given the benchmark solutions of the separate scheduling scenario. For each relationship intensity, the standard deviation, the minimum saving, and the maximum saving are quoted in parentheses. The linear regression line, calculated for all 180 savings, indicates a correlation between relative savings and increasing relationship intensities.

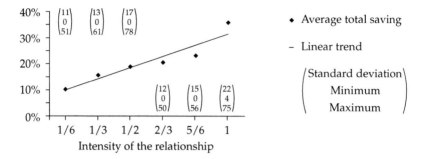

Figure 4.8: Overall savings (%) achieved by Supply Chain Scheduling

Due to the high level of variance in the relative savings, the regression line's $R^2 = 0.2$ is quite low. Hence, the linear trend should be only considered as an additional imaging element supporting the interpretation.

For the low relationship intensity of 1/6, an average relative saving of only around 10% results. Note that it is highly questionable whether a 10% saving can compensate for the contracting, labor input, and software costs associated with Supply Chain Scheduling. Average relative savings of around 20% are yielded for medium-range relationship intensities, so Supply Chain Scheduling may already make sense. For the maximum relationship intensity of 1, the average relative saving is around 35%, and for some instances savings amount to more than 75%. However, the minimum saving of only 4% shows that even for a relationship intensity of 1, Supply Chain Scheduling does not guarantee significant savings.

Now the cost-cutting potential is investigated in detail by breaking down total costs into the individual factors tardiness, inventory holding, and transportation costs.

Figure 4.9 illustrates the massive impact of Supply Chain Scheduling on tardiness costs. On average, Supply Chain Scheduling cuts these costs by around 60% for a relationship intensity of 1. The maximum saving of 100% means that tardiness is completely eliminated in some cases. The linear regression line again indicates the positive correlation between savings and relationship intensity. However, here as well, the high standard deviations and the large ranges between the minima and maxima reveal the unreliability of this trend.

Note that the average reduction in tardiness costs is higher for 1/3 than for 5/6. On the other hand, the mean reduction in inventory holding costs, which are discussed in

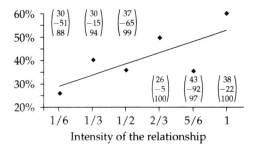

Figure 4.9: Relative reductions in tardiness costs

the next paragraph, is particularly low for 1/3 and high for 5/6. In total, these two cost factors compensate for each other, confirmed by the relatively steadily increasing total savings (Figure 4.8). The wide variations in the single cost factors' savings and thus the low R^2-values of their regression lines are due to reasonable trade-offs. Finding the global optimum often involves having to increase one cost factor in order to minimize the others. For example, assume that two jobs are waiting for processing on the same machine. Minimizing inventory holding costs requires processing the job that causes the higher storage costs first. But the reverse processing sequence may be more appropriate if the goal is to reduce tardiness costs. Consequently, reductions in tardiness, inventory holding, and transportation costs can vary widely.

By the way, the strong interrelation between the individual cost factors intimates a major problem with classic just-in-time approaches. Especially transportation and set-up costs are disregarded when striving for lot size 1. Primarily focusing on inventory holding costs, just-in-time approaches are only reasonable if transportation and set-up costs are negligible or can be drastically reduced which, indeed, is implied by the Japanese expression *kaizen* (change for the better), an integral part of the just-in-time philosophy. Nonetheless, given the ubiquitous application, this fundamental condition for the profitability of just-in-time approaches sometimes does not seem to be heeded.

Sharing crucial information enables Supply Chain Scheduling to eliminate inventory holding inefficiencies along the entire supply chain. For example, assume a job can be either shipped so that it arrives just-in-time, making intermediate storage necessary, or so that it arrives early, causing a penalty payment. In the separate scheduling scenario, the supplier delivers the job just-in-time if the storage costs are lower than the earliness

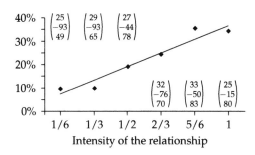

Figure 4.10: Relative reductions in inventory holding costs

penalty. Early delivery, however, would provide the manufacturer the flexibility to start its processing earlier which in turn reduces the system's storage costs and may enable him to avoid tardiness penalties. In contrast to separate scheduling, Supply Chain Scheduling takes these option into account.

Figure 4.10 shows the average relative reductions in storage costs, the positive linear trend, and the descriptive statistics. On average, Supply Chain Scheduling cuts up to around 35% of inventory holding costs. The negative minima again reveal that a worsening of one cost factor sometimes must be accepted in order to achieve improvements in the others. Note that, since the Supply Chain Scheduling solution cannot be worse than the composite separate scheduling solution, the minima of the total savings (Figure 4.8) is never lower than 0; at least as long as the optimization software can be applied.

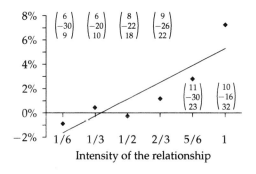

Figure 4.11: Relative reductions in the transportation costs

In Section 4.4's example, Supply Chain Scheduling results in fewer and different transportation batches than separate scheduling. The supplier's jobs are shipped in four instead of five batches. Fewer batches lead to lower transportation costs since the number of batches is the sole decision variable that determines transportation costs. Furthermore, cutting the inventory holding and tardiness costs, the modified batch compositions allow for improved coordination of the supplier's and the manufacturer's schedules.

Figure 4.11 depicts the average relative reductions in transportation costs. These savings are not as high as the reductions in tardiness and inventory holding costs. For low relationship intensities, there is almost no effect on the transportation costs and thus on the number of batches. The average relative reduction in transportation costs is even negative for the relationship intensities of 1/6 and 1/2, meaning that Supply Chain Scheduling sometimes produces even more batches than separate scheduling. The reason is again the trade-off consideration between tardiness, inventory holding, and transportation costs. Indeed, transportation costs can be reduced by delivering two jobs together in one batch, but joint deliveries can impact negatively on the schedules of the supplier and the manufacturer. For example, since one job must wait until the other is completed before the batch can be shipped, joint delivery can increase inventory holding and tardiness costs. However, for higher relationship intensities, Supply Chain Scheduling on average clearly reduces the transportation costs and therefore also the number of batch shipments.

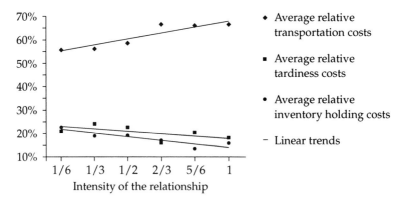

Figure 4.12: Breakdown of cost factors

Remember that the instance generator is calibrated to produce a mean breakdown of 50% transportation costs, 25% inventory holding costs, and 25% tardiness costs. In the separate scheduling scenario, these percentages remain unaffected by the relationship intensity between the supplier and the manufacturer. Figure 4.12 illustrates the proportions of the three cost factors for the Supply Chain Scheduling scenario. The average transportation cost share increases in step with growing relationship intensities since the reductions in tardiness and inventory holding costs are much greater than in transportation costs.

4.7.2 Large-size instances

Section 4.6's Excel-based spreadsheet approach allows for investigating larger-size instances, so the cost-cutting potential of Supply Chain Scheduling can be approximated for instance sizes that occur in practice. Here, both the supplier and the manufacturer have to schedule 50 jobs on 10 parallel machines. Two settings are dealt with. First, half of the supplier's 50 jobs are destined for the manufacturer and half for other customers. Then, the supplier's whole set of jobs is for the manufacturer. Thirty instances are examined for each setting, producing $60 \ (= 2 \cdot 30)$ benchmark instances. Apart from that, the generation of instances and the numerical study are carried out analogously to the investigation of small-size instances.

In a test run on the same small-size instances that are examined in the previous section, it turns out that Excel's solution quality is significantly better when first only optimizing the J assignment cells. The $2 \cdot J$ idle time cells should meanwhile be held constant at 0. Then, given the resulting assignment integers, Excel should be applied to the idle time cells. Although this reduces the search space, Excel finds the optimal solution to most of the small-size instances. This implies that the solution space's parts that are cut away are generally likely to contain only inferior solutions. This procedure is therefore also applied to the large-size instances.

For both the integrated machine and delivery scheduling problem and the Supply Chain Scheduling problem, the evolutionary algorithm is run until there are 6 000 seconds without improvement to the objective cell, or the convergence rate is below 0.0001 Indeed, this can lead to computation times of up to several hours, far too long for most practitioners. However, ceteris paribus, the solution quality increases with computation time, so distortions produced by heuristics can be minimized. And since the primary purpose of this investigation is to accurately assess cost-cutting potential, long computation times are reasonable here. However, note that the objective values obtained after some minutes are for the most part already very close to the values yielded after several hours, meaning that the marginal improvement rate is very low after, say, 10 minutes. Practitioners should thus not reject the spreadsheet approach from the outset.

Table 4.2: Results for a relationship intensity of 1/2 (25 common jobs)

		Monetary saving in		
	total	tardiness	inventory holding	transportation
Mean	17.3%	33.4%	14.4%	-1.4%
Standard deviation	11.5%	25.1%	9.2%	3.9%
Minimum	-5.5%	-45.6%	-2.7%	-9.4%
Maximum	44.2%	76.7%	34.4%	7.3%

Table 4.2 summarizes the results for 25 common jobs and hence a relationship intensity of $1/2$ ($= 25/50$). In the small-size scenario, the average saving achieved by Supply Chain Scheduling for this relationship intensity is about 17% (Figure 4.8). The mean saving for large-size instances in Table 4.2 is almost the same. For the individual cost factors, the investigations of small-size and large-size instances also lead to similar results.

These findings disprove an often mentioned argument against Supply Chain Scheduling and other integrated approaches. Many researchers fear that applying heuristics to a large integrated problem may produce worse overall solutions than applying heuristics successively to substantially smaller subproblems. The argument is that heuristics generally tend to be the worse the larger the instances. So they expect that merging near-optimum solutions to subproblems leads to better solutions than using a holistic heuristic approach to solve the overall problem. However, given the Supply Chain Scheduling problem of this chapter and instances with up to 50 jobs, the holistic heuristic on average finds significantly better solutions than the successive approach. But note that the values recorded in the row 'Minimum' reveal that for some instances, the successive approach indeed leads to better results.

The disadvantage of decomposition approaches is that they only account to a limited extent for the interactions of the subproblems. When a solution to the supplier's subproblem is already determined, it is no longer possible to achieve all feasible solutions to the integrated overall problem. The manufacturer's subproblem is substantially influ-

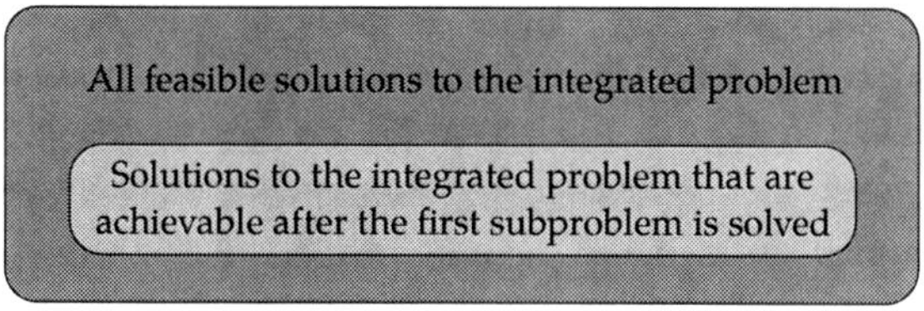

Figure 4.13: Solution space of the integrated problem

enced by the job release dates arising from the arrival times of the components sourced from the supplier. So the supplier's scheduling decisions can already lead to a situation where the supply chain optimum and many near-optimal overall solutions are no longer achievable by a composite solution that consists of the solutions to the supplier's and the manufacturer's subproblems. Figure 4.13 illustrates this problem. The location of the pale gray solution subspace depends on the supplier's planning decisions. Like a person with a flashlight, the supplier decides which area in the dark gray space is illuminated. Its planning decisions can cause many superior overall solutions to lie in the unreachable dark gray area. Hence, the much larger search space of integrated approaches, such as Supply Chain Scheduling, is a disadvantage and an advantage at the same time. The increased hardness of integrated problems is partially compensated by a higher number of reachable satisfactory solutions. By the way, analogous considerations apply to the integrated machine scheduling and vehicle problem investigated in the previous chapter.

Table 4.3: Results for a relationship intensity of 1 (50 common jobs)

	Monetary saving in			
	total	tardiness	inventory holding	transportation
Mean	24.1%	40.2%	24.9%	-0.3%
Standard deviation	14.0%	30.6%	10.3%	9.4%
Minimum	-0.4%	-41.2%	-5.0%	-25.9%
Maximum	46.4%	83.2%	42.1%	24.5%

The results for a relationship intensity of 1 stated in Table 4.3 differ from those for small-size instances. While the average total saving is around 35% for small-size instances, here it is only about 24%. However, the linear trend depicted in Figure 4.8 suggests that the average saving for small-size instances is an upward outlier, meaning that the real average saving may be closer to 25 than 35%. Since only 30 instances are investigated for each relationship intensity, such an outlier is not unlikely to occur.

It is notable that, in their initial Supply Chain Scheduling paper, Hall and Potts (2003) conclude from a numerical example a savings potential of 25% given an objective function consisting of transportation and tardiness costs. Since their example deals with only one supplier and one manufacturer, the relationship intensity is 1, as in Table 4.3. Although their model is not really comparable to this chapter's model, the similarity of the results is striking.

4.8   Summary and outlook

This chapter describes a numerical study that is carried out to compare the sum of a supplier's and a manufacturer's costs produced by a successive and separate scheduling approach with the costs resulting from joint Supply Chain Scheduling. In focus are tardiness, inventory holding, and transportation costs. Since a reduction in one of these cost factors can lead to an increase in the others, the challenge of Supply Chain Scheduling is to find a schedule with a cost-optimal trade-off between all three. While Supply Chain Scheduling is found to greatly reduce tardiness and inventory holding costs, the reductions in transportation costs are moderate at best. The total cost-cutting potential of Supply Chain Scheduling increases with the relationship intensity between the supply chain partners. Given a very close business relationship, the numerical investigation reveals a mean potential of up to 24% (35% for small-size instances). Since logistics expenditures constitute over 30% of many products' overall costs (Thomas and Griffin, 1996), inter-organizational Supply Chain Scheduling of only two stages may reduce such products' costs by around 10%. However, keep in mind, that the results are partly driven by the settings of the instance generator and the underlying assumptions. Indeed, the settings are reasonably chosen but do not hold for all practical cases.

This chapter also contributes to scheduling research in general. The developed Excel-based heuristic spreadsheet approach is proven to be able to compete with a tailor-made state-of-the-art heuristic for a classic NP-hard scheduling problem. Since the approach can be easily adjusted to many problem types, it provides a powerful benchmark heuristic to compare with new algorithms designed to solve vehicle rout-

ing, machine scheduling, and many other problem types including batching, sequencing, scheduling, and routing decisions.

Finally, bear in mind that there are still obstacles that make it difficult to apply Supply Chain Scheduling in practice. First of all, it requires sharing confidential information on processing times, due dates, costs, etc. Joint scheduling should therefore be
only done with trustworthy and reliable business partners. Furthermore, a profit or
cost sharing contract needs to be drawn up in order to ensure a win-win situation for all
involved stages. Hall and Potts (2003), Dudek and Stadtler (2005), Manoj et al. (2008),
and Schenkenbach (2009) discuss some promising ideas. Special consideration should
be given to Nash bargaining (Nash, 1950, 1953) on the benefit of Supply Chain Scheduling, using the separate planning scenario as status quo (see this chapter's Appendix).
However, keep in mind that contracting, information sharing, new soft- and hardware,
running the Supply Chain Scheduling, etc. can incur substantial costs that may exceed
the joint approach's benefits. Also, the question of who runs the operational Supply
Chain Scheduling must be resolved. Should it be done by a team consisting of members from all involved companies, should an autonomous computer system confiden-
tially handel the data and produce the schedules, or should one company take the lead?
'Vendor managed scheduling' may be an option. Future research should also be undertaken into whether the savings potential of Supply Chain Scheduling is affected if one
company is significantly bigger than the other in terms of the number of jobs. However, since all these subjects cannot be handled within a single dissertation, a selection
needed to be made. The next Chapter assesses the potential of a collaboration between
more than two supply chain stages.

4.9 Appendix. Cost sharing mechanism

Table 4.4: Comparison of the scheduling scenarios given Section 4.4's example

	Separate scheduling	Supply Chain Scheduling	Saving
Supplier:	2 983	2 218	765
Manufacturer:	1 698	1 421	277
Sum:	4 681	3 639	1042

Table 4.4 summarizes the results of Section 4.4's example. Without further coordination both parties benefit from Supply Chain Scheduling. The costs of both companies are lower in the Supply Chain Scheduling scenario than in the separate scheduling scenario. However, the two parties' individual shares of the overall saving are a random outcome of the integrated optimization approach. In the example, the supplier's costs decrease much more than the manufacturer's. As mentioned before, it can even occur that one party suffers from joint Supply Chain Scheduling, so there is clearly the need for a coordinating cost sharing mechanism in order to prevent conflicts. In the following, such a mechanism is discussed using the symbols introduced in Table 4.5.

Table 4.5: Basic scenario for the coordination approach

	Separate scheduling	Supply Chain Scheduling
Supplier:	$K_s(\omega_{sep})$	$K_s(\omega_{SCS}) + A_s + L$
Manufacturer:	$K_m(\omega_{sep})$	$K_m(\omega_{SCS}) + A_m - L$

Let ω_{sep} and ω_{SCS} denote the overall schedules that emerge from separate scheduling (sep) and Supply Chain Scheduling (SCS), respectively. Then, $K_c(\cdot)$ symbolizes company c's $(c = s, m)$ logistics costs resulting from separate scheduling and Supply Chain Scheduling, respectively. The costs incurred by contracting, information sharing, and running the Supply Chain Scheduling are taken into account by the parameter A_c. A_c is positive if these additional Supply Chain Scheduling costs are higher than the separate scheduling costs that cease to exist in the Supply Chain Scheduling scenario, such as the costs of bargaining for the due dates and penalties between the supplier and the manufacturer. Otherwise, A_c is negative. This section's coordination approach is based on a lump sum payment L. A positive L means that the supplier pays the manufacturer a counterbalancing sum. By contrast, a negative L implies a compensating payment from the manufacturer to the supplier.

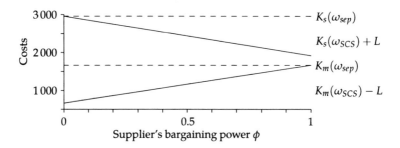

Figure 4.14: The companies's costs as a function of ϕ

For the scenario described in Table 4.5 the fairness principle introduced by Nash (1950, 1953) leads to the bargaining solution[10]

$$L(\phi) = \underbrace{K_s(\omega_{sep}) - K_s(\omega_{SCS}) - A_s}_{\text{supplier's saving}} - \phi \underbrace{\sum_{c=s,m} \left[K_c(\omega_{sep}) - K_c(\omega_{SCS}) - A_c \right]}_{\text{overall saving}} \quad (4.56)$$

where $\phi \in [0,1]$ symbolizes the supplier's bargaining power. The first term of the supplier's lump sum payment L to the manufacturer is the reduction in the supplier's costs achieved by Supply Chain Scheduling. In the example is $K_s(\omega_{sep}) = 2\,983$, $K_s(\omega_{SCS}) = 2\,218$, and $A_s = 0$, so the supplier's saving is 765. If the supplier has no bargaining power ($\phi = 0$), it passes its entire saving on to the strong manufacturer. Hence, the supplier neither benefits nor suffers from Supply Chain Scheduling. Note that if the supplier's saving is negative (and $\phi = 0$), the lump sum L is also negative, which means that the manufacturer pays the supplier compensation. In this case, the negative L is balanced exactly such that the supplier again neither suffers nor benefits from Supply Chain Scheduling. In the other extreme, the manufacturer has no bargaining power ($\phi = 1$), so the supplier benefits from the entire overall saving. In the example, this scenario results in a payment from the manufacturer to the supplier ($L = -277$)

---

[10]For a discussion of common bargaining solutions see Rosenmüller (2000).

which is balanced such that the manufacturer neither benefits nor suffers from Supply Chain Scheduling. Given that both parties hold at least a little bargaining power $(0 < \phi < 1)$, which is a more realistic scenario, the side payment L from the supplier to the manufacturer is reduced by a fraction ϕ of the overall saving achieved by Supply Chain Scheduling. For example, in the case where both companies hold a similar bargaining position $(\phi = 0.5)$, the lump sum is $L = 765 - \phi \cdot 1\,042 = 244$. Figure 4.14 depicts the run of both parties' costs as a function of the supplier's bargaining power $(A_s = A_m = 0)$. Since the lump sum L decreases in the supplier's bargaining power ϕ, the manufacturer's (supplier's) total costs resulting from a joint Supply Chain Scheduling approach with the proposed cost sharing mechanism increase (decrease) in ϕ.

But what happens if one or both parties are not honest when sharing the required information? Assume the supplier and the manufacturer agree on a joint Supply Chain Scheduling approach with the supplier being tasked to gather information and carry out the computations (vendor managed scheduling), leading to additional Supply Chain Scheduling costs of $A_s = 100$ and $A_m = 0$, respectively. In the Supply Chain Scheduling scenario of Section 4.4 this leads to costs of $2\,512$ (supplier) and $1\,227$ (manufacturer). However, if the Supply Chain Scheduling efforts are not observable, the supplier may claim that A_s is higher than 100, say, 200. As a consequence, the supplier's and the manufacturer's costs after the lump sum payment are $2\,462$ and $1\,277$, respectively. Hence, in lying when it comes to A_s, the supplier can cut its costs by 50 $(2\,512 - 2\,462)$ while the manufacturer's costs consequently increase by 50 $(1\,227 - 1\,277)$. However, when sharing relevant information with the manufacturer, the supplier does not yet know the overall cost-cutting potential inherent in the joint Supply Chain Scheduling approach. Ex ante, the supplier therefore cannot calculate the level of A_s that leads to a situation in which the manufacturer's costs are not reduced and the supplier exploits the entire cost-cutting potential held in Supply Chain Scheduling. If the supplier exaggerates its strategic behavior regarding A_s, the computations may reveal Supply Chain Scheduling to be inferior to separate scheduling although there is actually a cost-cutting potential which is more than fully consumed by the supplier. Since the manufacturer will reconsider Supply Chain Scheduling if it barely benefits or even suffers from it, the partnership with the supplier is likely to end soon and thus neither of the parties profits from Supply Chain Scheduling any longer. Furthermore, anticipating strategic behavior on the part of the supplier, the manufacturer may also try to benefit from strategic manipulation of its inventory holding costs, due dates, or earliness-tardiness penalties. However, such a reaction is likely to affect the overall schedule. When using manipulated input, the optimality of the schedule resulting from Supply Chain Scheduling is no longer guaranteed. A suboptimal schedule means a lower overall saving to be shared by the parties. These considerations highlight that choosing trustworthy and honest business partners is of utmost importance for the success and profitability of Supply Chain Scheduling.

Chapter 5

Supply Chain Scheduling: Makespan reduction potential

5.1 Motivation and literature survey

Specialization, concentration on core competencies, and increasing globalization lead to a situation where competition between big national companies is increasingly replaced by competition between globally operating supply chains (Christopher, 1992; Cooper et al., 1997; Handfield and Nichols, 1999; Barnes, 2006; Vandaele et al., 2007; Stadtler, 2008). However, sophisticated business relationships between multiple supply chain partners and the lack of a centralized management can create problems such as the bullwhip effect or double marginalization. Supply chain management has thus become a very important topic in the literature ever since the term was first mentioned by Oliver and Webber (1982). Globally operating supply chains that need efficient supply chain management can be found in many industries such as in automotive, computer, and apparel manufacturing (Bruce et al., 2004; Chopra and Meindl, 2012; Bruce and Daly, 2011).

For example, Zara, a popular chain of fashion stores, maintains a global dual-sourcing strategy. Products with highly uncertain demand are sourced from quick European suppliers, whereas slower but low-cost Asian suppliers satisfy the demand for products with more predictable demand. Since, nowadays, a new collection can only be considered up-to-date for a few weeks in a given retail season, it is vital for both European and Asian suppliers that production and delivery operations are swift and reliable (Caro et al., 2010; Mihm, 2010a; Cachon and Swinney, 2011). Note that in the

1980s, the average duration from the beginning of production to the market launch of a new fashion collection was still 66 weeks (Kurt Salmon Associates, author unknown, 1988). However, production and delivery operations needed only around 11 weeks. Poorly coordinated schedules between the fabric-weaving, dyeing, tailoring, and printing production stages caused idle and waiting times that summed up to the remaining 55 weeks. This delay became unacceptable when many companies changed their business model and begun to adopt the currently prevalent fast fashion strategy. Involving enhanced design and quick response to new trends, fast fashion means increasing numbers of articles and collections per year, each with a very short shelf life (Tokatli, 2008; Tokatli et al., 2008; Caro and Gallien, 2010). Well-known companies that pursue this strategy are Marks & Spencer, World Co., Mango, H&M, Primark, and Zara. Zara, for example, endeavors to design, produce, and launch a new collection all within only 2 weeks (Tiplady, 2006). Since this is very demanding in terms of process coordination, efficient supply chain management is crucial to success.

This chapter again focuses on Supply Chain Scheduling as a coordinating supply chain management instrument. As shown in the previous chapters, specific schedules for individual supply chain stages do not necessarily combine to form a good solution from the perspective of the whole supply chain. Supply Chain Scheduling therefore deals with the coordination of the machine and delivery schedules of two or more supply chain stages. The aim is to improve the supply chain's competitiveness measured in, for example, total logistics costs or the supply chain makespan which is especially important for companies like Zara that sell products with a short shelf life (Thomas and Griffin, 1996). Remember, supply chain stages can consist of several processing sites belonging to either one single company or to different companies. In the case of Zara, which has almost fully vertical supplier integration, the consecutive production stages have to be seen as an intra-organizational supply chain. Note that there are also inter-organizational supply chains in the apparel industry. For example, the US general merchandiser Kohl's and its suppliers successfully sell Vera Wang lines (Mihm, 2010a).

The following sections investigate a supply chain with four consecutive stages, each consisting of a processing site. For convenience, it is assumed that each processing site is owned by a different company so that company 1–4 means stage 1–4 and vice versa. Note that the following ideas and results also hold for the case where all processing sites are self-contained areas of responsibility that schedule on their own but belong to one company. Remember the discussion in the previous chapter. A joint head office facilitates Supply Chain Scheduling since information interchange and collaboration can be enforced, which for independent companies may be a problem in terms of trade secrets or bargaining positions. A set of J jobs has to be processed successively at each stage. The objective is to minimize the supply chain makespan which is the completion time of the last finished job at the fourth stage. For example, in the apparel industry, the makespan describes the moment in which a given set of items in a new collection is ready to be shipped to an (overseas) distribution center.

The performances of eight different scheduling scenarios are compared by means of a numerical study. The simplest scenario, which represents the benchmark, is characterized by separate scheduling of all four companies. Planning separately combined with asymmetric information on the processing times at the other stages can lead to poorly coordinated overall supply chain schedules, resulting in unnecessarily long makespans. The most promising scenario is the joint scheduling approach involving all stages. The question is whether it leads to significantly better results than the benchmark scenario and the other scenarios in which only subsets of companies coordinate their schedules.

Some scheduling problems emerging out of the four-stage supply chain environment are NP-hard. Since using heuristics is likely to distort the results, the numerical study is thus limited to small-size instances that can still be solved using a commercial optimization software. However, a second study investigates a simpler two-stage supply chain with only one machine at each stage. All problems arising in this modified environment can be optimally solved in polynomial-bounded time which enables us to deal with large-size instances as well.

Minimizing the makespan allows the use of production capacity as soon as possible for the next set of jobs, leading to high overall capacity utilization. Hence, it is one of the most important and most often encountered objective criteria in practice and theory (Framinan et al., 2004; Hejazi and Saghafian, 2005). Short makespans are of high importance for single companies as well as for whole supply chains. Note that, as explained in the previous chapters, there are other important objectives in the context of Supply Chain Scheduling. In the build-to-order industry such as the production of special-purpose machines, supply chains are organized as pull systems. End customers trigger production by placing specific orders. Since the orders often include due dates and earliness-tardiness penalties, the supply chain makespan is an unsuitable objective criterion. Compliance with due dates and minimization of total costs are of much greater importance. Chapters 3 and 4 examine such pull systems. By focusing on the makespan, this chapter now suggests a multi-stage supply chain that operates as a push system.

The next sections are organized as follows. Section 5.2 describes and classifies the optimization problems arising during the subsequent sections. The scheduling scenarios, the experimental settings, and the assumptions of the numerical studies are introduced in Section 5.3. Results and conclusions follow in Section 5.4 and 5.5, respectively.

5.2   Mixed integer linear program

This section introduces and classifies the scheduling problems to be solved in the numerical study. The main problem is introduced in detail while several related and simpler problems are briefly summarized at the end of this section. Again, the close relationship between Supply Chain Scheduling and hybrid flow shop scheduling becomes apparent.

Figure 5.1: Supply chain structure

A supply chain consisting of S stages is investigated. Each stage s $(s = 1, ..., S)$ supplies the adjacent downstream stage so that a linear supply chain structure arises (see Figure 5.1). There are M_s identical parallel machines at stage s. Each job j $(j = 1, ..., J)$ entails a non-preemptive processing operation with the duration p_{sj} on one machine at each stage. The processing of a job cannot begin until the job is completed at the adjacent upstream stage. Furthermore, the processing of job j at the first stage must not begin before a given job release date r_j. The transportation time of job j from stage s to $s + 1$ $(s = 1, ..., S - 1)$ is t_s. Each job is assumed to be shipped immediately after completion. Grouping of jobs into transportation batches is not considered here.

Since the transportation times between two stages are equal for all jobs the optimal makespan increases by $\sum_{s=1}^{S-1} t_s$ through this simple kind of delivery modeling. The optimal machine schedules, however, are not affected by the actual values of t_s which means that the lengths of the makespans can be unambiguously traced back to machine scheduling decisions. Hence, without loss of generality, the travel times are set to 0 in the subsequent numerical studies.

In literature, flow shop scheduling with parallel machines is referred to as hybrid flow shop scheduling. According to the Three-Field Notation by Graham et al. (1979), the introduced overall problem can thus be denoted by $HFS, (IP^s)_{s=1}^{S} / r_j, t_s / C_{max}$ where

HFS is an abbreviation for hybrid flow shop. $(IP^s)_{s=1}^S$ means that there are homogenous identical parallel machines at each of S stages. Since the transportation times are assumed to be 0 later on, the problem reduces to $HFS, (IP^s)_{s=1}^S/r_j/C_{max}$.

Theorem 6. *The deterministic problem* $HFS, (IP^s)_{s=1}^S/r_j, t_s/C_{max}$ *is NP-hard in the strong sense. The same holds for* $HFS, (IP^s)_{s=1}^S/r_j/C_{max}$ *where* t_s *is 0* $(\forall\, s = 1, .., S - 1)$.

Proof. The flow shop problem $F2/r_j/C_{max}$ with job release dates at the first stage is NP-hard in the strong sense (Lenstra et al., 1977). Since $HFS, (IP^s)_{s=1}^S/r_j, t_s/C_{max}$ as well as $HFS, (IP^s)_{s=1}^S/r_j/C_{max}$ are generalizations of $F2/r_j/C_{max}$, these problems must be NP-hard in the strong sense, too. $\qquad\square$

When dealing with large-size instances of NP-hard problems, the development of fast heuristics that ensure near-optimum solutions is indispensable. Section 4.6's Excel-based approach provides a straightforward basis.[1] Small-size instances, however, can often still be solved using a commercial optimization software.

After the applied symbols are listed, the problem $HFS, (IP^s)_{s=1}^S/r_j, t_s/C_{max}$ is formulated by a mixed integer linear program.

Parameters

M_s	Number of identical parallel machines at stage s $(s = 1, ..., S)$
p_{sj}	Job j's processing time at stage s $(s = 1, ..., S; j = 1, ..., J)$
q	Sufficiently large number
r_j	Job j's release date at the first stage $(j = 1, ..., J)$
t_s	Travel time from stage s to stage $s + 1$ $(s = 1, ..., S - 1)$

Variables

C_{sj}	Completion time of job j at stage s $(s = 1, ..., S; j = 1, ..., J)$
C_{max}	Maximum completion time at the last stage
x_{sij}	Binary variable that takes the value 1 if job i is processed before job j on the same machine of stage s and no other job is processed in between $(s = 1, ..., S; i, j = 1, ..., J; i \neq j)$

---

[1]According to Section 4.6.1, J cells need to be addressed for each supply chain stage. Always considering the previous stage's dates, the start dates of processing and transportation at a given stage unambiguously result from these cells. Note that for the sake of feasibility it may be necessary to insert idle time in the stages' schedules. But in contrast to the previous chapter's integrated machine and delivery scheduling heuristic, extra idle time cells that delay the the jobs' earliest possible processing and transportation start dates are unnecessary.

$x_{j,J+1}$ Binary variable that takes the value 1 if job j is the last job processed on a machine at stage s ($s = 1, ..., S; j = 1, ..., J$). Job $J + 1$ is an artificial last job

x_{s0j} Binary variable that takes the value 1 if job j is the first job processed on a machine at stage s ($s = 1, ..., S; j = 1, ..., J$)

The objective is to minimize the maximum completion time at the last stage S which is equivalent to the supply chain makespan.

$$\min C_{max}$$

subject to

$$M_s \geq \sum_{j=1}^{J} x_{s0j} \qquad\qquad \forall s = 1, ..., S \qquad (5.1)$$

$$\sum_{i=0,i\neq j}^{J} x_{sij} = 1 \qquad\qquad \forall s = 1, ..., S; \; j = 1, ..., J \qquad (5.2)$$

$$\sum_{i=1,i\neq j}^{J+1} x_{sji} = 1 \qquad\qquad \forall s = 1, ..., S; \; j = 1, ..., J \qquad (5.3)$$

$$x_{sij} \in \{0,1\} \qquad \forall s = 1, ..., S; \; i = 0, ..., J; \; j = 1, ..., J+1; \; i \neq j \qquad (5.4)$$

$$C_{sj} \geq C_{si} + p_{sj} - q(1 - x_{sij}) \qquad \forall s = 1, ..., S; \; i,j = 1, ..., J; \; i \neq j \qquad (5.5)$$

$$C_{1j} \geq r_j + p_{1j} \qquad\qquad \forall j = 1, ..., J \qquad (5.6)$$

$$C_{sj} \geq C_{s-1j} + t_{s-1} + p_{sj} \qquad \forall s = 2, ..., S; \; j = 1, ..., J \qquad (5.7)$$

$$C_{max} \geq C_{Sj} \qquad\qquad \forall j = 1, ..., J \qquad (5.8)$$

Explanation of the constraints. 5.1: Since there are M_s machines at stage s, no more than M_s jobs can be first in the job-processing sequence of a machine at that stage. 5.2: Each job is either the first to be processed on a machine or succeeds another. 5.3–5.4: Each job either precedes another job or is the last to be processed on a machine. 5.5: The completion time of a job must be equal to or greater than the completion time of its predecessor plus its processing time. 5.6: At the first stage, the completion time of a job must be equal to or greater than its release date plus its processing time. 5.7: At every other stage, the completion time of a job must be equal to or greater than its completion time at the previous stage plus the travel time between the stages and its processing time. 5.8: This restriction ensures that the variable C_{max} is equal to or greater than all completion times at stage S. Since the goal is to minimize C_{max}, the objective function forces C_{max} to be equal to the completion time of the last finished job at stage S.

Some of the following calculations can refer to simpler special cases of the described problem, such as the classic two-stage flow shop problem $F2//C_{max}$ which can be optimally solved in polynomial-bounded time by Johnson's algorithm (Johnson, 1954). The flow shop problem becomes NP-hard if there are more than two stages (Garey et al., 1976). The related single stage and single machine problems $1//C_{max}$ and $1/r_j/C_{max}$ are trivial (Tadei et al., 1998), whereas the single stage and parallel machine scheduling problems $IP//C_{max}$ and thus the generalization $IP/r_j/C_{max}$ are NP-hard (Garey and Johnson, 1979). Finally, since $HFS, (IP^s)_{s=1}^S //C_{max}$ is a generalization of $IP//C_{max}$ it must also be NP-hard.

5.3 Design of the numerical studies

Two numerical studies are carried out in this chapter. Subsection 5.3.1 describes the first study that deals with four supply chain stages ($S = 4$). The design of the second study, investigating a two-stage supply chain environment ($S = 2$), is introduced in Subsection 5.3.2.

5.3.1 Four-stage supply chain environment

Given a linear supply chain consisting of four stages, various Supply Chain Scheduling scenarios are imaginable, each entailing certain scheduling problems. These problems are either solved by an algorithm ensuring optimality of the solutions or, in the case of NP-hard problems, by a commercial optimization software. The results of the first numerical study are thus prevented from distortions that may occur when using heuristics. Differences in the makespans can therefore be unambiguously traced back to the different characteristics of the scheduling scenarios. However, due to the long computation times the optimization software needs to solve NP-hard problems, the first study is limited to five jobs ($J = 5$) only.

Figure 5.2 illustrates all scheduling scenarios examined in the first study (gray colored stages schedule jointly). Scenario 0 describes the completely uncoordinated benchmark scenario. Since no stage has any information about the processing times at the other stages, minimizing its own makespan is the most obvious and suitable objective when intending to help minimize the supply chain makespan. Denoting the point

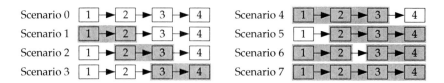

Figure 5.2: Supply Chain Scheduling scenarios

in time a new set of jobs can be processed, to minimize the makespan also means to maximize capacity utilization. Hence, this frequently encountered objective is also reasonable for companies that are primarily concerned with their own profits rather than supply chain performance (see the quote by Cachon (2003) on page 4). The gray rectangle in scenario 1 expresses that stages 1 and 2 jointly minimize the makespan at the second stage while stages 3 and 4 minimize their individual makespan separately. Treating the supply chain as a flow shop, scenario 7 describes the case of a joint Supply Chain Scheduling approach involving all four stages.

In each scenario, the whole set of jobs is simultaneously available for processing at the first stage. Since all transportation times are 0, the completion time at the current stage is the release date of the respective job at the following stage. The processing times are drawn from the interval $p_{sj} \sim RD[1, 100]$ ($\forall s = 1, ..., 4; j = 1, ..., 5$) where each unit may be a minute or an hour, for example.[2] The first numerical study conducts two experiments, only differing in the number of available machines. While there is exactly one machine at each stage in experiment 1, there are two in experiment 2. Both experiments examine the same 30 instances so that differences in the results can be directly ascribed to the number of machines.

All problems arising in experiment 1 are summarized in Table 5.1. For example, the uncoordinated benchmark scenario 0 consists of four problems, one at each stage. Stages 2, 3, and 4 have to process a set of jobs on one machine, considering job release dates that depend on the previous stage's completion times. Stage 1 faces a similar problem, however, all jobs are released at the same time. Obviously, each schedule without idle time results in the same makespan in this special case, so the following rule is applied: If two or more jobs can change their positions in the processing sequence of a machine without influencing the makespan, the jobs are ordered according to shortest

---

[2]Future research should investigate the impact of processing times that correlate with the other stages' processing times.

Table 5.1: Problems arising in experiment 1

| | Stage | | | |
Scenario	1	2	3	4
0	$1//C_{max}$	$1/r_j/C_{max}$	$1/r_j/C_{max}$	$1/r_j/C_{max}$
1	$F2//C_{max}$		$1/r_j/C_{max}$	$1/r_j/C_{max}$
2	$1//C_{max}$	$F2/r_j/C_{max}$		$1/r_j/C_{max}$
3	$1//C_{max}$	$1/r_j/C_{max}$	$F2/r_j/C_{max}$	
4	$F3//C_{max}$			$1/r_j/C_{max}$
5	$1//C_{max}$	$F3/r_j/C_{max}$		
6	$F2//C_{max}$		$F2/r_j/C_{max}$	
7	$F4//C_{max}$			

processing time priority. An experimental study by Conway et al. (1960) shows that this simple dispatching rule is generally most appropriate when trying to minimize the makespan. In doing so, processing at the next stage can begin as early as possible.

As a second example see scenario 6. As they jointly aim to minimize the makespan, stages 1 and 2 together deal with a classic two-stage flow shop problem. Then, given the job release dates determined by the schedule of stages 1 and 2, stages 3 and 4 cooperate to minimize their makespan.

Table 5.2: Problems arising in experiment 2

| | Stage | | | |
Scenario	1	2	3	4
0	$IP2//C_{max}$	$IP2/r_j/C_{max}$	$IP2/r_j/C_{max}$	$IP2/r_j/C_{max}$
1	$HF2,(IP2^s)_{s=1}^2//C_{max}$		$IP2/r_j/C_{max}$	$IP2/r_j/C_{max}$
2	$IP2//C_{max}$	$HF2,(IP2^s)_{s=1}^2/r_j/C_{max}$		$IP2/r_j/C_{max}$
3	$IP2//C_{max}$	$IP2/r_j/C_{max}$	$HF2,(IP2^s)_{s=1}^2/r_j/C_{max}$	
4	$HF3,(IP2^s)_{s=1}^3//C_{max}$			$IP2/r_j/C_{max}$
5	$IP2//C_{max}$	$HF3,(IP2^s)_{s=1}^3/r_j/C_{max}$		
6	$HF2,(IP2^s)_{s=1}^2//C_{max}$		$HF2,(IP2^s)_{s=1}^2/r_j/C_{max}$	
7	$HF4,(IP2^s)_{s=1}^4//C_{max}$			

Table 5.2 summarizes the problems arising in experiment 2. The sole difference to the problems in Table 5.1 is that now there are two identical parallel machines at each stage instead of only one.

5.3.2   Two-stage supply chain environment

In the second numerical study, the supply chain consists of only two stages, both possessing a single machine. The focus is still on the makespan. If they schedule separately, the stages face the problems $1//C_{max}$ and $1/r_j/C_{max}$, respectively. In the joint Supply Chain Scheduling scenario, the classic flow shop problem $F2//C_{max}$ needs to be handled. Note that these scheduling problems are all optimally solvable in polynomial-bounded computation time. The optimal solution to the joint problem, for example, can be computed using Johnson's algorithm (Johnson, 1954). By avoiding the need for heuristic solution approaches, it becomes possible to cope with even extremely large-size instances.

Remember, at the first stage, all processing sequences lead to the same makespan. However, since it is proven (Conway et al., 1967; French, 1982; Baker, 1997) that there is a permutation schedule optimizing the joint problem $F2//C_{max}$, the first stage's sequence is nevertheless of utmost importance to supply chain performance. The best reaction of the second stage is simply to adopt the first stage's sequence. The logical question is: Which dispatching rule applied at the first stage is most suitable when scheduling separately?

To answer this question, the permutation schedules resulting from the following well-known and often encountered dispatching rules are compared with Johnson's optimal overall schedules.[3] 10 000 instances are examined for 5, 50, 100, as well as 1 000 jobs. These instance are generated as explained in the previous section.

- Shortest processing time (SPT): The jobs are sequenced in non-decreasing order of their processing times. When dealing with a single machine, this rule minimizes total and mean completion time.

- Longest processing time (LPT): The jobs are sequenced in non-increasing order of their processing times. This dispatching rule is applied if jobs with long processing times tend to be more important than jobs with short ones. The more

---

[3]If the focus of this chapter were on a supply chain organized as a pull system, due date related dispatching rules such as earliest due date priority (EDD) would be more suitable.

important jobs should be processed early in order to have enough time to react in case of a machine breakdown, for example.

- First come first served (FCFS): The jobs are sequenced in the order they were received. This priority rule is applied in classic queuing systems, for example.

5.4 Computational results

Subsection 5.4.1 presents the results of the first numerical study that deals with the four-stage supply chain environment. Investigating the two-stage supply chain setting, the second study's results follow in Subsection 5.4.2.

5.4.1 Small-size instances

The commercial optimization software needs only seconds for most of the NP-hard problems. However, the hardest problems $F4//C_{max}$ and $HF4, (IP2^s)_{s=1}^4//C_{max}$ sometimes claim computation times of several hours, making it impossible to investigate instances with more jobs, stages, or machines. All computations are run on one core of a Pentium Core 2 Duo processor (1.7 GHz) using 2 048 MB RAM.

Table 5.3: Pairwise comparisons of the scenarios (p-values of the two-sample t-test)

Scenario	Machines	Scenario						
		1	2	3	4	5	6	7
0	1	0.414	0.413	0.428	0.277	0.205	0.368	0.018**
	2	0.454	0.450	0.407	0.300	0.263	0.338	0.014**
1	1		0.332	0.345	0.208	0.146	0.290	0.010**
	2		0.403	0.449	0.332	0.292	0.375	0.014**
2	1			0.485	0.357	0.275	0.453	0.030**
	2			0.360	0.261	0.225	0.294	0.011**
3	1				0.342	0.262	0.438	0.027**
	2				0.383	0.346	0.430	0.023**
4	1					0.408	0.403	0.057*
	2					0.469	0.445	0.051*
5	1						0.317	0.083*
	2						0.408	0.048**
6	1							0.038**
	2							0.029**

Table 5.3 shows the p-values of pairwise heteroscedastic two-sample t-tests comparing the mean values between all scenarios. The p-value is the probability of obtaining a test statistic that is at least as extreme as the observed one. The null hypothesis, which says that the mean values of the samples are equal, is rejected if the p-value is lower than a certain level of significance α. It turns out that only scenario 7 is significantly better than the others (**: $\alpha = 0.05$, *: $\alpha = 0.1$). In the other scenarios, information sharing and joint scheduling seem to be of marginal average usefulness at most. The number of available machines at the supply chain stages has no significant influence since experiments 1 and 2 yield almost the same results.

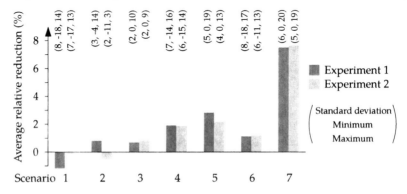

Figure 5.3: Relative makespan reductions compared to scenario 0

Some authors presume that improving information and/or sharing information with up- or downstream supply chain stages is in any case beneficial for performance (see, for example, Gavirneni and Tayur, 1999). This has already been disproved. Taylor and Xiao (2010) show that improvements in a retailer's forecasting capability can narrow the profit of a manufacturer that shares the forecasts. Figure 5.3 presents another example of a counterintuitive negative consequence of information sharing. The dark and pale gray bars illustrate the average relative reductions in the makespan. Remember, the uncoordinated status quo scenario 0 serves as a benchmark. A positive value indicates a reduction in the average makespan. Negative values mean that the scenario in question leads to a higher average makespan. Although the companies at stages 1 and 2 share their information and schedule jointly, the partially coordinated scenario 1 causes the average supply chain makespan to lengthen in both experiments.

The standard deviation, the minimum, and the maximum relative deviation are given in parenthesis above each bar in Figure 5.3. Indeed, in most cases there is an average improvement in the makespan, but the minima of the scenarios 1, 2, 4, and 6, which are all negative, show that most of the scenarios involve the risk of worsening the makespan for a given instance. It is easy to create instances in which scenarios 3 and 5 also lead to an increased makespan compared to the uncoordinated scenario 0. Only the completely coordinated scenario 7, which yields an average relative improvement of almost 8% in both experiments, is in any case safe from influencing the overall makespan negatively.

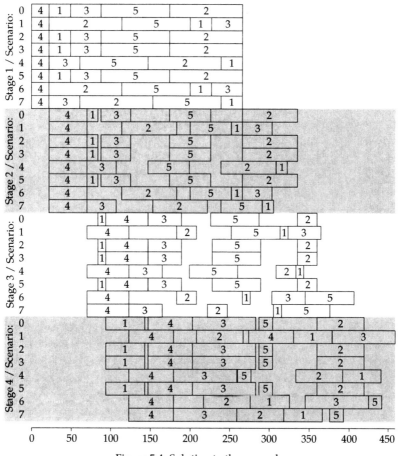

Figure 5.4: Solution to the example

Sharing information and coordinating schedules can incur considerable coordination costs such as labor input costs or license fees for new software, for example. Makespan improvements have to be carefully traded off against these costs. The fact that coordination is at the risk of worsening the supply chain makespan makes the trade-off even more critical. An example of a critical instance is depicted in Figure 5.4. There is a single machine at each stage (experiment 1). The processing times are:

$$(p) = \begin{pmatrix} p_{11} & p_{12} & \cdots & p_{1J} \\ p_{21} & & & \\ \vdots & & \ddots & \vdots \\ p_{S1} & & \cdots & p_{SJ} \end{pmatrix} \qquad (p) = \begin{pmatrix} 27 & 92 & 39 & 22 & 86 \\ 14 & 69 & 37 & 48 & 52 \\ 10 & 25 & 42 & 53 & 61 \\ 49 & 59 & 80 & 56 & 17 \end{pmatrix}$$

The partially coordinated scenarios 1, 4, and 6 result in makespans (459, 441, and 442) that are longer than the makespan of the uncoordinated benchmark scenario 0 (419). Hence, in these scenarios, information sharing and partial coordination have a negative influence on the supply chain makespan. Moreover, neither do the partially coordinated scenarios 2, 3, and 5 (419, 419, and 419) result in an improvement. Only the completely coordinated scenario 7 reduces the supply chain makespan (393). The basis for this reduction is already laid by the job sequence at the first stage. No other scenario results in this sequence. In summary, the example shows yet again that there are risks associated with Supply Chain Scheduling. Partial coordination of some but not all stages can cause the supply chain makespan to remain unchanged or even to worsen. Only total coordination of all supply chain stages guarantees that the makespan does not worsen but generally improves.

Figure 5.5 shows the average relative deviations from the optimal makespan per stage. The makespan per stage corresponds to the completion time of the last processed job at a certain stage. The optimal makespan per stage is given by the schedule of scenario 7. Only the job-processing sequences and the makespans per stage resulting from the completely coordinated scenario 7 ensure the optimal makespan at stage 4. A positive relative deviation indicates that the makespan of a stage exceeds the makespan of that stage in the schedule of scenario 7. Negative values mean that the makespan is smaller. If a scenario were to yield the same schedule as scenario 7, the result would be a straight line on the x-axis. Remember that in experiment 1, there is no difference between the makespans at the first stage in the case of only one machine and no inserted idle time. Independent of the job-processing sequence, the makespan at the first stage is given by the sum of processing times. This also becomes apparent in the solution to

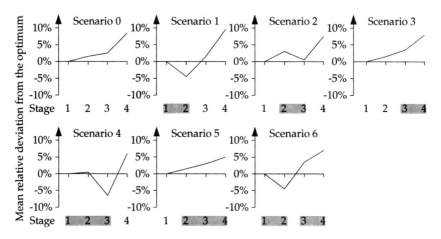

Figure 5.5: Relative makespan deviations from scenario 7 per stage (experiment 1)

the numerical example illustrated in Figure 5.4.

The graph of scenario 6 in Figure 5.5, for example, has to be interpreted as follows. The first two stages plan jointly in order to minimize the makespan at the second stage. Compared to scenario 7, this results in an average relative makespan reduction of about 5% at stage 2. Then, stages 3 and 4 schedule together with the aim to minimize the makespan at stage 4. However, due to the improved makespan at stage 2, which involves deviations from the optimal job-processing sequences and thus the schedule of scenario 7, stages 3 and 4 cannot reach the optimal makespan at the fourth stage. This problem becomes especially visible in scenario 4, where stages 1–3 schedule jointly and achieve a major relative makespan reduction of 7% at stage 3. However, this reduction is at the cost of substantial deviations from the optimal job-processing sequences at stages 1–3 causing the average relative makespan at stage 4 to be about 6% longer than the optimum.

Figure 5.6 illustrates the average relative deviations of the makespans per stage for experiment 2. Since each stage possesses two identical parallel machines, in experiment 2 the makespans at the first stage now can vary between the scenarios. However, apart from that, the observations are similar to the ones from experiment 1. Only Supply Chain Scheduling that involves all stages significantly reduces the supply chain makespan. Note that, reminiscent of the bullwhip effect, the makespan seems to build up along the supply chain in some scenarios in both figures.

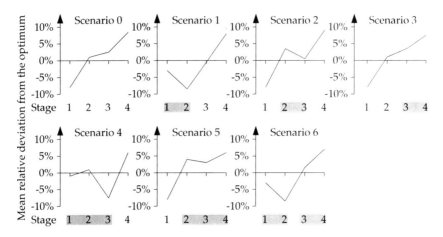

Figure 5.6: Relative makespan deviations from scenario 7 per stage (experiment 2)

5.4.2   Large-size instances

Table 5.4 summarizes the results for the two-stage supply chain environment. The average relative deviations from optimum are recorded in the third column. For example, for 100 jobs ($J = 100$) the LPT rule leads on average to supply chain makespans that are 23.24% higher than the optimal solutions computed via Johnson's algorithm.

While the average deviation from the optimum decreases with a growing number of jobs for the FCFS and the SPT rule, the mean deviation remains at about 25% for the LPT rule. Especially the SPT rule, which is in a way related to Johnson's rule, seems to be most effective in minimizing the supply chain makespan. The average relative deviation is as little as 0.5% for 100 jobs and just 0.05% for 1 000 jobs. In other words, the higher the number of jobs to be scheduled at once, the less useful joint Supply Chain Scheduling. Especially the SPT rule but also the 'random' FCFS rule lead to permutation schedules and makespans that are very close to Johnson's optima.

5.5   Summary and Outlook

Focusing on the makespan of a supply chain consisting of four stages, several joint scheduling scenarios are compared to an uncoordinated scenario in which each stage schedules separately. It turns out that partial coordination of some but not all stages of

Table 5.4: Relative makespan reductions in the two-stage supply chain scenario

J	Rule	Average relative deviation from the optimal makespan (%)	Standard deviation	Minimum reduction (%)	Maximum reduction (%)
5	LPT	25.48	13.50	0	81.73
	FCFS	15.26	11.91	0	80.66
	SPT	5.94	7.78	0	38.93
50	LPT	23.25	5.50	4.73	45.41
	FCFS	5.31	3.51	0	21.15
	SPT	0.95	1.16	0	4.67
100	LPT	23.24	4.01	8.42	35.68
	FCFS	3.62	2.44	0	15.27
	SPT	0.49	0.60	0	2.10
1 000	LPT	23.93	1.37	19.36	28.05
	FCFS	1.06	0.77	0	4.46
	SPT	0.05	0.06	0	0.20

a supply chain generally results only in minor average makespan improvements, and in some instances even worsens it. Only joint Supply Chain Scheduling of all stages brings about a significant average reduction in the supply chain makespan. The number of machines at the supply chain stages seems to have no influence on these results, which are based on small-size instances solvable by commercial optimization software. A simpler setting with only two supply chain stages allows for the investigation of real-world-size instances. Since applying the SPT rule at the first stage on average results in almost optimal permutation schedules, coordination by means of a joint Supply Chain Scheduling approach using Johnson's algorithm is unreasonable, especially when considering the costs and coordination problems involved in Supply Chain Scheduling. Hence, employing Supply Chain Scheduling to reduce the makespan in push systems seems appropriate only for small sets of jobs, if all stages are involved, and if the makespan improvements justify the costs of coordination.

Chapter 6

Supply Chain Contracting: R&D Investment sharing contracts

6.1 Motivation

As motivated in Chapter 2, the developments and discussions of the last decades suggest a tendency to focus on core competencies, which involves outsourcing parts of production or logistics to specialized suppliers (Prahalad and Hamel, 1990; Javidan, 1998; Hafeez et al., 2002, 2007; Ulrich and Ellison, 2005; Vandaele et al., 2007). However, there are some exceptions. The following examples reveal that many successful and innovating companies nevertheless have exceptionally high in-house production depth. Novel or specific components needed for product innovations are often produced in-house although their production is not one of the company's core competencies. The ability to produce a component in-house usually requires high investments in production facilities, capacity, and skills. Such investments are expected to be much lower for a specialized supplier since specific machines and know-how are already available or can easily be adjusted. Additionally, the supplier may benefit from economies of scale. So why do many innovating companies behave counterintuitively and produce a large part of the required components in-house instead of sourcing them from specialized suppliers?

For example, Miele, a manufacturer of high quality domestic appliances and commercial equipment, attaches great importance to the development of product innovations. In 2009, Miele launched the world's first domestic hybrid power cylinder vacuum cleaner. Many components, such as electronic systems and vacuum cleaner fans, are produced in-house instead of purchasing them from specialized suppliers. Hence, besides its innovativeness Miele is also characterized by a considerable in-house production depth. Miele's employees even claim that

"Miele makes the machine that makes the machine" Rohrbeck (2012), p. 47

Take Apple and its innovative tablet computer iPad, which was launched in 2010, as another example. Indeed, it is well-known that Apple sources many components needed for its iPads, iPods, Macs, iPhones, etc. from suppliers such as Foxconn and Samsung (Heuzeroth, 2012). However, this applies mainly to standard components. For example, Apple develops and produces the highly product-specific and sophisticated central processing units (CPUs) for the iPad in-house. To this end, Apple acquired CPU specialists PA Semi ($278 million) in 2008 and Intrinsity (around $121 million) in 2010 (Vance and Stone, 2010).[1] But why did Apple decide against sourcing the iPad processors from the market leaders in CPUs, Intel or MediaTek,[2] which are highly experienced and possess state-of-the-art production facilities? What is more, Apple is now said to be considering switching completely from Intel CPUs to its own processors, even for ordinary laptops and desktop computers (Satariano et al., 2012). Examples of successful and innovating companies with considerable in-house production depth are also encountered in many other industries such as agricultural engineering, consumer electronics, alternative energy, telecommunications, and apparel manufacturing, including well-known names like John Deer, Samsung, and Zara (Heuzeroth, 2012; Blume and Zimmermann, 2012; Zimmermann, 2012; Berggren and Bengtsson, 2004; Sherman, 2009; Mihm, 2010a).

In-house production not only allows companies to protect their innovations, it also gives them direct influence on the production process and in turn, on the quality of the products. Since many innovating companies such as Miele and Apple pursue high-quality strategies, product quality is an important factor in this chapter's model. Ensuring high quality standards for purchased components may require incoming goods inspection, a supplier audit, and training for the supplier's employees, for example, which can entail substantial costs. Apart from the quality of the components, sunk costs also play an important role in the make-or-buy decision. Product innovations usually require an investment in research and development (R&D) at an early stage. Strong suppliers, such as Intel with a market share of around 80% (Harvey, 2009), may use the

---

[1]Note that vertical integration decisions concerning a source of supply is considered to be equivalent to a make-or-buy decision. See for example Ulrich and Ellison (2005).
[2]Supplying Coolpad, Huawei, Lenovo, Samsung, and ZTE, MediaTek is a giant in smartphone CPUs (Yang, 2013).

innovating company's sunk R&D costs as a lever when negotiating on the component price. In order to reduce or avoid this threat, the innovating company is incentivized to choose a low R&D investment level (Klein, 2005) or even to produce the component in-house although the supplier's production costs would be lower.

The next sections cover all of these aspects and present a model which shows how to prevent inefficiencies due to the opportunistic behavior of a supplier when negotiating on the component price. Consistent with the observation that innovating companies tend to produce many components on their own instead of sourcing them from specialized suppliers, cases are identified in which the decision is in favor of in-house production. However, in-house production as well as external procurement are shown to be inefficient in many constellations. This chapter demonstrates that both the innovating company and the supplier can often benefit from jointly investing in product innovation.

The remainder is organized as follows. After a compact review of the related literature in Section 6.2, the analytical part begins with Section 6.3's basic model. In-house production, external procurement, and the first-best scenario, which assumes that both companies answer to a joint head office, are described and compared. Since commonly known contract types are unable to counter the inefficiencies revealed by the comparison, an R&D investment sharing contract is proposed and investigated in Section 6.4. Section 6.5 complements the analytical approach by a large-size numerical investigation. Section 6.6 concludes.

6.2 Literature survey

Besides cross-company new product development, make-or-buy decisions is a second topic of major importance with regard to the motivation of this chapter and the model introduced in the next sections. The classic decision between in-house production and sourcing from a supplier is studied by Dale and Cunningham (1984), Mahoney (1992), and Fine and Whitney (1996), for example. However, already in the late 1970s, an aspect was revealed that is highly relevant to this chapter's research question. Following transaction cost theory (Coase, 1937; Williamson, 1975, 1985, 1991, 2008), Klein et al. (1978) investigate the impact of opportunistic behavior of a subcontractor on a scenario where specific investments, such as R&D investments, are made. Their results suggest vertical integration as the preferable form of organization. Bad bargaining positions caused by the need to invest in R&D at a very early stage give reasons for the in-house production tendency of innovating companies.

For reviews of papers on new product development see Brown and Eisenhardt (1995), Krishnan and Ulrich (2001), Shane and Ulrich (2004), and Krishnan and Loch (2005), for example. Besides classic single-firm-centric research on new product development, recently many approaches have considered various forms of R&D collaborations between companies at adjacent supply chain stages. Kim (2000) models a manufacturer that supports its supplier's innovation activities in order to improve supply quality and delivery time. Roy et al. (2004) propose innovation generation to be a consequence of interactions between suppliers and manufacturers. Petersen et al. (2005) study the impacts of integrating a supplier into new product development on the effectiveness of the development team. The option to outsource R&D activities to research subcontractors is investigated by Lai et al. (2009). Hoetker (2005) examines how firms select a supplier for an innovative component by considering transaction costs, prior relationships with the suppliers, and the suppliers' technical capabilities. Bhaskaran and Krishnan (2009) deal with innovation and investment sharing approaches between two companies. Innovation sharing means both companies share the R&D effort and costs. By contrast, investment sharing describes a scenario in which only one company develops the innovation but both companies share the R&D costs. R&D investment sharing approaches were observed between GlaxoSmithKline and Actelion in 2008, GlaxoSmithKline and Genmab in 2006, Roche Holding and Actelion in 2006, and AstraZeneca and Athero-Genics in 2005 (Whalen, 2008). The list indicates that this type of contract originates in the pharmaceutical industry. However, as demonstrated in the next sections, R&D investment sharing can also produce win-win situations in more general supply chain environments.

6.3 Basic model

Consider a company, referred to as 'manufacturer' (he), with an idea for an innovative product. Each unit of the new product requires a specific component whose production does not count among the manufacturer's core competencies. However, if he makes some preparatory investments, he will nevertheless be able to produce the component in-house. The in-house production scenario is investigated in Subsection 6.3.1. Subsection 6.3.2 deals with the additional option to source the component from a specialized supplier (she). Finally, Subsection 6.3.3 investigates the benchmark scenario assuming that the two companies answer to a joint head office.

6.3.1 In-house production scenario

Figure 6.1 shows the timeline assumed in the in-house production scenario. Initially, the manufacturer has the idea for a new product. If he decides to carry out the innovation project, he invests in R&D (I^2). Another investment A is made after the R&D phase is successfully[3] finished, only enabling the manufacturer to produce the component in-house. The manufacturer needs to buy special machines and extend his know-how, for example. While the manufacturer must decide about the optimal level of the R&D investment I^2, the level of A is exogenously given, assuming that there is one superior investment concept that makes in-house production possible. The last step in the product innovation process is 'full production and market launch' (Cooper, 1990) which is subsumed in the timeline under 'commercialization.' The manufacturer has to determine the quantity q he wants to sell on the market, produce the required components, assemble the components to form the end products, and sell them on the market.

Figure 6.1: Timeline for in-house production

As the new product is innovative, the manufacturer is a monopolist on the market. Nevertheless, the market is assumed to be relatively transparent so he is able to properly assess the price-demand function $p(I,q)$. On the basis of this information, he chooses the level of the R&D investment I^2. The investment's effect I $(= \sqrt{I^2}, I \geq 0)$ on the market price is positive but decreasing in the investment I^2. For example, the iPad with 3G connectivity is much more expensive than the version without. Since 3G modules are relatively cheap, it is hard to justify the price difference by higher unit costs. The difference can rather be explained by the expense of additional research in order to adjust the 3G module to the iPad soft- and hardware. This additional research, however, makes the iPad more desirable and thus enables Apple to charge a higher price for the version with 3G connectivity.

Since it is likely to reflect the economic reality accurately, the price of the new prod-

---

[3]This chapter deals with a success probability of 100%. Indeed, R&D projects often harbor the risk of failure. But since incorporating a success probability parameter would strongly distract from the effects this chapter seeks to examine it is omitted here for simplicity.

uct is furthermore a decreasing and convex function in the output quantity q ($q \geq 0$), as it is commonly assumed in literature (Petruzzi and Dada, 1999):

$$\frac{\partial\, p(I,q)}{\partial\, q} < 0 \quad \text{and} \quad \frac{\partial^2\, p(I,q)}{\partial\, q^2} > 0 \tag{6.1}$$

Without loss of generality, each unit of the innovation requires one unit of the component. The manufacturer's total variable costs for producing one unit of the product innovation are denoted by κ_M which consists of $\kappa_M = k_M + k_S + f$. k_M ($k_M > 0$) symbolizes the manufacturer's variable costs for completing one unit of the end product. $k_S + f$ ($k_S, f > 0$) are his variable costs for producing the required component. The specialized supplier, who provides an external sourcing option in the next section, incurs only variable costs of k_S per component, implying that the manufacturer is not able to produce the component as cheaply as she. This is attributed to the supplier's advantages, including better know-how, more specialized machines, and economies of scale, for example.[4]

Not considering process innovation, the investment in R&D has no influence on the variable costs. This assumption can be justified by the target costing approach which is frequently applied in innovation projects (Mihm, 2010b). Following the target costing approach a company saves on other parts if one component is upgraded, so that the overall costs of the product remain unaffected. Furthermore, investments in the development of some components such as software, for example, usually do not affect the variable production costs anyway.

In Equation 6.2, all introduced elements are combined to form the manufacturer's profit function. The indices i and M denote 'in-house production' and 'manufacturer,' respectively.

$$\pi_i^M(I,q) = p(I,q)\,q - I^2 - \kappa_M\, q - A \tag{6.2}$$

The price-demand function proposed in Equation 6.3 satisfies the characteristics mentioned above and is used throughout the following investigations. The higher the parameter c ($c > 0$), the stronger the impact of the R&D investment effect I on the price.

$$p(I,q) = \frac{4\, cI}{q^{\frac{3}{4}}} \tag{6.3}$$

---

[4]Note that in-house production does not necessarily mean that production of the component takes place at the same site as the assembly of the end product. Maybe the supplier is located even closer to the final production stage. Hence, there is no reason why the manufacturer's variable component costs should be lower than the variable costs of the specialized supplier.

Lemma 1. *If there is no external source for the component, the manufacturer's optimal profit, R&D investment, and production quantity are as follows:*

$$\pi^M(I^*, q^*) = \max\left\{ \frac{4c^4}{k_M + k_S + f} - A, 0 \right\} \tag{6.4}$$

$$I^{*2} = \begin{cases} \frac{8c^4}{k_M + k_S + f} & \text{for} \quad 0 \leq \frac{4c^4}{k_M + k_S + f} - A \\ - & \text{for} \quad 0 > \frac{4c^4}{k_M + k_S + f} - A \end{cases} \tag{6.5}$$

$$q^* = \begin{cases} \frac{4c^4}{(k_M + k_S + f)^2} & \text{for} \quad 0 \leq \frac{4c^4}{k_M + k_S + f} - A \\ - & \text{for} \quad 0 > \frac{4c^4}{k_M + k_S + f} - A \end{cases} \tag{6.6}$$

Proof. Proofs appear in this chapter's Appendix 6.7.1. □

The manufacturer is assumed to be able to anticipate the subsequent events and costs associated with these events before the investment in R&D is made. He can therefore discontinue the innovation project if it were to generate a negative profit $(0 > \frac{4c^4}{k_M + k_S + f} - A)$. The decision to stop the project results in a profit of 0 since there is no investment (-) and no production quantity (-). Note that, as long as the manufacturer's profit is positive, the level of R&D investment, the product quantity, and the manufacturer's profit decrease in the variable costs κ_M and increase more than proportionally in the investment effect parameter c. Needless to say, profit is diminished by the investment in in-house production facilities and skills A.

6.3.2 External procurement scenario

This section describes the option to source the component from an external supplier via a classic wholesale price contract. Like Appel and Intel, the supplier and the manufacturer are both assumed to be more or less on a level playing field, meaning that both possess significant bargaining power. In such a scenario, applying Stackelberg competition[5] (von Stackelberg, 1934) would be inappropriate. So instead of a first moving leader and a follower, here the two parties negotiate on the component price. The sequence of events is illustrated in Figure 6.2.

---

[5]Stackelberg competition is frequently applied in supply chain contracting literature (Leng and Parlar, 2005; Cachon and Netessine, 2006; Nagarajan, 2008).

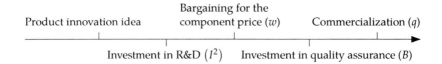

Figure 6.2: Timeline for external procurement

The first two steps are analogous to the in-house production scenario. After the investment in R&D is made, the manufacturer bargains with the supplier over the component price. Since there is usually a long period between the commencement of R&D and the start of production (Dougherty, 1992), bargaining over the component price at an earlier stage would be exceedingly difficult and expensive. The contract would have to consider each possible future environmental state, such as the economic and political situation or commodity prices, and their consequences for the component price. The necessary accuracy and extent of such a contract would lead to prohibitively high contracting costs.[6] Note that despite its deterministic character, the model reflects the uncertainties occurring in practice by separating the step of the R&D investment from the bargaining for the component price.

As mentioned in the motivation, ensuring product quality is a very important topic for many innovating companies. Since the specialization of the supplier is no sufficient guarantee of the component's quality, the manufacturer must invest in quality assurance. For example, he may arrange an audit and training for the supplier's employees. These quality assurance measures incur a one-time investment B. Finally, the manufacturer determines the quantity, orders the required components from the supplier, conducts an incoming goods inspection, processes the components to form the end product, and sells the end product on the market.

Table 6.1: Bargaining scenario for the component price w

	Successful negotiation	Failed negotiation
Supplier:	$\pi_e^S(w,q)$	0
Manufacturer:	$\pi_e^M(I,w,q)$	$-I^2$ or $\pi_i^M(I,q)$

Table 6.1 presents the bargaining scenario for the per unit wholesale price w of the

---

[6]For the theory on incomplete contracts see Hart and Moore (1988), Tirole (1999), and Schmitz (2001).

component. S and e denote 'supplier' and 'external procurement,' respectively. If the negotiation is successful, both parties achieve a certain profit. Per unit of the component, the supplier receives the negotiated price w less her variable production costs k_S. The manufacturer's profit is calculated as the revenue $p(I,q)\,q$ less the investment in R&D I^2, the variable costs $(k_M + b + w)\,q$, and the investment in quality assurance B $(B > 0)$. Since the costs of supplier audits and training are normally lower than an investment in new machines and know-how, B is assumed to be lower than A $(B < A)$. The manufacturer's variable costs comprise the agreed component price w, the production costs k_M, and the variable quality assurance costs b caused by incoming goods inspections $(b > 0)$. Equations 6.7 and 6.8 formalize the profit functions.

$$\pi_e^S(w,q) = (w - k_S)\,q \tag{6.7}$$
$$\pi_e^M(I,w,q) = p(I,q)\,q - I^2 - (k_M + b + w)\,q - B \tag{6.8}$$

The result of the negotiation on w depends fundamentally on the threat points arising from the possibility of a failed negotiation. The supplier has not spent any money before the negotiation takes place. Hence, she neither loses nor gains if the negotiation fails. Her profit would be 0. However, the manufacturer has already invested in R&D. So if the negotiation fails, he must decide between either discarding the innovation project and thus losing the investment $(-I^2)$ or producing the component in-house and generating the related profit $\pi_i^M(I,q)$. Since the manufacturer is characterized as a profit maximizer, his threat point is the maximum of both alternatives. To solve the bargaining problem, this chapter relies on the fairness principle and solution approach introduced by Nash (1950, 1953).[7] Considering differences in the bargaining powers of the two companies does not significantly contribute to explain the issues in focus of this chapter. Since different bargaining powers would only complicate the readability, here the manufacturer and the supplier are assumed to possess the same bargaining power.

Lemma 2. *Allowing for the alternative to source the component from a specialized supplier, the manufacturer's optimal profit, R&D investment, and production quantity are as follows:*

$$\pi^M(\cdot) = \begin{cases} \max\left\{\frac{4c^4}{k_M+k_S+f} - A, 0\right\} & \text{for} \quad 0 < f \leq \delta_1 \\ \max\left\{\frac{4c^4}{k_M+k_S+\frac{1}{2}(f+b)} - \frac{1}{2}(A+B), \frac{1}{2}\frac{c^4}{k_M+k_S+b} - \frac{1}{2}B, 0\right\} & \text{for} \quad \delta_1 < f \end{cases} \tag{6.9}$$

---

[7]For a discussion of common bargaining solutions see Rosenmüller (2000).

$$I^{*2} = \begin{cases} \dfrac{8c^4}{k_M+k_S+f} & \text{or} \quad - & \text{for} \quad 0 < f \le \delta_1 \\[2ex] \dfrac{8c^4}{k_M+k_S+\frac{1}{2}(f+b)} & \text{or} \quad \dfrac{c^4}{k_M+k_S+b} \quad \text{or} \quad - & \text{for} \quad \delta_1 < f \end{cases} \quad (6.10)$$

$$q^* = \begin{cases} \dfrac{4c^4}{(k_M+k_S+f)^2} & \text{or} \quad - & \text{for} \quad 0 < f \le \delta_1 \\[2ex] \dfrac{4c^4}{\left(k_M+k_S+\frac{1}{2}(f+b)\right)^2} & \text{or} \quad \dfrac{c^4}{(k_M+k_S+b)^2} \quad \text{or} \quad - & \text{for} \quad \delta_1 < f \end{cases} \quad (6.11)$$

Proposition 1. *Whenever the manufacturer decides to source the component from the supplier via a negotiated wholesale price contract, the supplier also gains a positive profit, implying that she would agree to a business relationship.*

Remember that f is the difference between the manufacturer's and the supplier's variable costs incurred by producing one unit of the component. If that difference is lower than or equal to the limit δ_1 ($0 < f \le \delta_1$), the in-house production solution described in the previous section (see Equations 6.4–6.6) holds.[8] This means that the manufacturer's profit is maximized by either in-house production or, if the in-house production profit is negative, by discarding the project. For $\delta_1 < f$, both the manufacturer and the supplier either benefit from external procurement or the manufacturer drops the project. Since there are two possible threat points in the negotiation on w, there are also two possible external procurement profits. So the manufacturer's profit for $\delta_1 < f$ is the maximum of the two alternative external procurement profits and the zero-profit discontinuation alternative. Each investment and quantity quoted in Equations 6.10 and 6.11 belongs to the profit that has the corresponding position in the profit sequence. Note that the variable quality assurance costs b negatively affect the level of R&D investment, the product quantity, and the manufacturer's external procurement profit. As expected, the one-time investment in quality assurance B has a negative impact on the manufacturer's external procurement profit. However, due to the profit distribution resulting from Nash's fairness principle, the manufacturer bears only half of these costs. The second half is borne by the supplier. Moreover, although the in-house production investment A is actually not made in the external procurement scenario, the manufacturer's profit $\dfrac{4c^4}{k_M+k_S+\frac{1}{2}(f+b)} - \frac{1}{2}(A+B)$ that results from the in-house production threat point, decreases in A. The higher A, the weaker the manufacturer's bargaining position.

---

[8]The sophisticated calculation of δ_1 from the values of the parameters $k_M, k_S, b, c, A,$ and B can be found in 'Proof of Lemma 2' in this chapter's Appendix.

6.3.3 Central control benchmark scenario

The central control scenario assumes that the supplier and the manufacturer receive their instructions from a joint head office and thus can be forced to collaborate. This scenario is the first-best case and serves as benchmark for the following investigations.

Denoting the overall profit that results from a hierarchically instructed collaboration, the central control profit is calculated as the revenue from the product $p(I,q)\,q$ less the R&D investment I^2, the variable costs $(k_M + k_S + b)\,q$, and the investment in quality assurance B. The head office's variable costs comprise the costs for producing the component k_S, for assembling the component into the end product k_M, and for quality assurance of the component b. At first sight, quality assurance measures may seem unnecessary for a fully vertically integrated company. However, subunits of big parent companies do not necessarily cooperate willingly, trustfully, and in a highly motivated way. As discussed in Section 2.2.2, variable management compensation in combination with the structural classification of subunits as investment, profit, and cost centers can cause heterogeneous goals and diverging incentives (Milgrom and Roberts, 1992). Quality levels are therefore not necessarily guaranteed just because there is a joint head office. A second and more important reason for incorporating quality assurance measures is the primary purpose of the central control scenario, which is to identify the maximum potential of the collaboration between the supplier and the manufacturer as independent companies. The index c in the following profit function denotes 'central control.'

$$\pi_c(I,q) = p(I,q)\,q - I^2 - (k_M + k_S + b)\,q - B \tag{6.12}$$

Lemma 3. *If the manufacturer and the supplier are forced by a joint head office to collaborate, the optimal overall profit, R&D investment, and product quantity are as follows:*

$$\pi_c(I^*,q^*) = \max\left\{\frac{4c^4}{k_M + k_S + b} - B, 0\right\} \tag{6.13}$$

$$I^{*2} = \begin{cases} \frac{8c^4}{k_M+k_S+b} & \text{for } \frac{4c^4}{k_M+k_S+b} - B \geq 0 \\ - & \text{for } \frac{4c^4}{k_M+k_S+h} - B < 0 \end{cases} \tag{6.14}$$

$$q^* = \begin{cases} \frac{4c^4}{(k_M+k_S+b)^2} & \text{for } \frac{4c^4}{k_M+k_S+b} - B \geq 0 \\ - & \text{for } \frac{4c^4}{k_M+k_S+b} - B < 0 \end{cases} \tag{6.15}$$

Note that if the additional variable in-house production costs are relatively low, $f < \delta_2$, the head *office would yield a higher profit by instructing the manufacturer to produce the component on his own, leaving out the supplier.*[9]

The central control profit differs from the manufacturer's in-house production profit only in that it contains b instead of f and B instead of A. Keep in mind that the solution of the central control scenario is idealized. Generally, company integration and joint head offices incur administrative overhead and other transaction costs (Coase, 1937; Williamson, 1975, 1985, 1991, 2008). However, since the maximum potential of a collaboration of independent companies is in focus, such costs are neglected here. For convenience, transaction costs remain generally unconsidered in the model. In the previous section, transaction costs such as bargaining and contracting costs are also disregarded.

Proposition 2. *If the additional variable in-house production costs f are equal to or greater than the variable quality assurance costs b, the central control profit always exceeds the manufacturer's in-house production profit. The central control profit can exceed the manufacturer's in-house production profit for $f < b$, too. If $\delta_2 < 0$, which is induced by a large difference between the one-time investments in in-house production A and external procurement B, for example, the central control profit even exceeds the in-house production profit for each $f > 0$.*

Proposition 3 can be concluded by comparing the central control profit to the sum of the supplier's and the manufacturer's external procurement profits.

Proposition 3. *No matter how high the additional variable in-house production costs f, the central control profit is equal to or greater than the sum of the supplier's and the manufacturer's external procurement profits. Equality can occur for $f = b$.*

If the variable in-house production costs are equal to the variable external procurement costs, meaning $f = b$, central control and external procurement lead to the same R&D investment, product quantity, and product price. Since the revenues from the end product market and the sum of costs are identical, the sum of both companies' external procurement profits is equal to the central control profit. Nevertheless, the external procurement profit shares between the supplier and the manufacturer can vary. They depend on the manufacturer's bargaining position, which is influenced by the profitability of his in-house production option.

For each $f \neq b$, the supplier may capitalize on the manufacturer's sunk R&D investment in the negotiation on the component price. The threat inherent in such potential opportunistic behavior causes the manufacturer to underinvest in R&D from the outset.

---

[9]The calculation of δ_2 can be found in 'Proof of Lemma 3.'

As a result, the sum of both companies' external procurement profits is lower than the central control profit. The following section examines whether it is possible to mitigate the threat of opportunistic behavior via an arrangement or a coordinating contract and, at the same time, to increase both companies' external procurement profits for $f \neq b$.

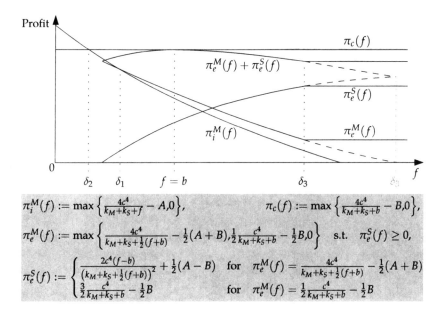

$$\pi_i^M(f) := \max\left\{\frac{4c^4}{k_M+k_S+f} - A, 0\right\}, \qquad \pi_c(f) := \max\left\{\frac{4c^4}{k_M+k_S+b} - B, 0\right\},$$

$$\pi_e^M(f) := \max\left\{\frac{4c^4}{k_M+k_S+\frac{1}{2}(f+b)} - \frac{1}{2}(A+B), \frac{1}{2}\frac{c^4}{k_M+k_S+b} - \frac{1}{2}B, 0\right\} \quad \text{s.t.} \quad \pi_e^S(f) \geq 0,$$

$$\pi_e^S(f) := \begin{cases} \frac{2c^4(f-b)}{\left(k_M+k_S+\frac{1}{2}(f+b)\right)^2} + \frac{1}{2}(A-B) & \text{for } \pi_e^M(f) = \frac{4c^4}{k_M+k_S+\frac{1}{2}(f+b)} - \frac{1}{2}(A+B) \\ \frac{3}{2}\frac{c^4}{k_M+k_S+b} - \frac{1}{2}B & \text{for } \pi_e^M(f) = \frac{1}{2}\frac{c^4}{k_M+k_S+b} - \frac{1}{2}B \end{cases}$$

Figure 6.3: Run of the profits depending on f

Figure 6.3 graphically summarizes the results of the last sections. The run of the central control profit $\pi_c(f)$, the manufacturer's in-house production profit $\pi_i^M(f)$, the manufacturer's $\pi_e^M(f)$ and the supplier's external procurement profits $\pi_e^S(f)$, and the sum of the external procurement profits $\pi_e^M(f) + \pi_e^S(f)$ are depicted in relation to the difference between the manufacturer's and the supplier's variable component production costs f. Note that the manufacturer's external procurement profit only exists if the supplier's profit is positive so she would participate in external procurement in the first place.

Four cases need to be distinguished. The first case occurs if the additional variable costs f are very low, $0 < f \leq \delta_2$, entailing that the manufacturer chooses in-house production as optimal alternative. An improvement in his profit by means of a cooperation with the supplier is impossible since his in-house production profit is greater than the central control profit, representing the maximum potential attainable by a business relationship with the supplier. Hence, there is no need to consider this case in the following investigations on bilateral contracts or arrangements. Inefficiencies arise for $f > \delta_2$. Since his in-house production profit exceeds his external procurement profit, the manufacturer chooses in-house production for $\delta_2 < f \leq \delta_1$. However, the difference between the central control profit and the manufacturer's in-house production profit $\pi_c(f) - \pi_i^M(f)$ indicates a potential that, exploited intelligently, may allow both the supplier and the manufacturer to benefit from cooperation. In the third case $\delta_1 < f \leq \delta_3$, the manufacturer and the supplier agree to external procurement. The manufacturer's external procurement profit is higher than his in-house production profit, and, at the same time, both companies' profits are positive. Since the sum of the manufacturer's and the supplier's profits $\pi_e^M(f) + \pi_e^S(f)$ is lower than the central control profit $\pi_c(f)$ (except for $f = b$), again there is a potential for a win-win situation. The same holds for the fourth case $\delta_3 < f$ in which external procurement is still beneficial, but the manufacturer switches to another threat point in the negotiation on the component price. Since it leads to a higher profit, the new threat point is dropping the project and losing the R&D investment $(-I^2)$ if the negotiations over the component price w fails. The dashed lines in the interval for $\delta_3 < f$ indicate the runs of the optimal external procurement profit if the new threat point were to lead to a negative profit. In that case, δ_3 would be the x-coordinate of the intersection of the manufacturer's external procurement profit $\pi_e^M(f)$ and the x-axis. If so, in-house production and external procurement would both mean a negative profit for the manufacturer, given $\delta_3 < f$. Hence, he would discontinue the innovation project before investing in R&D although a potential win-win situation is revealed by the positive central control profit.

Finally, some special cases should be mentioned:

- The product innovation is unprofitable if $\delta_2 < 0$ and $\pi_c(f) = 0$. In-house production as well as a collaboration enforced by a joint head office result in negative profits. So there is no way for a coordinating contract to improve the situation.

- If δ_1, δ_2, and δ_3 are all negative and the manufacturer's second threat point $(-I^2)$ leads to a negative external procurement profit for him, neither in-house production nor external procurement are profitable. Note that the central control profit can nevertheless be positive and shared such that both the supplier and the manufacturer benefit from collaboration.

- 'Proof of Proposition 2' shows that $\delta_2 < \delta_1$. Hence, apart from the situation $\delta_2 < \delta_1 < \delta_3$, which is depicted in Figure 6.3, the two situations $\delta_3 < \delta_2 < \delta_1$ and $\delta_2 < \delta_3 < \delta_1$ can also occur. In both situations, only the three cases $0 < f \leq \delta_2$, $\delta_2 < f \leq \delta_1$, and $\delta_1 < f$ need to be taken into consideration when describing the manufacturer's optimal decision depending on f. In order to account for all possible cases, the investigations in the following sections rely on the more sophisticated situation $\delta_2 < \delta_1 < \delta_3$, which entails the four cases described on the basis of Figure 6.3.

6.4 R&D investment sharing contracts

The classic contract types discussed in the supply chain management literature (Tsay et al., 2003; Cachon, 2003) do not bring about win-win situations in the described scenarios. See this chapter's Appendix 6.7.2 for the impacts of a revenue sharing contract, a quantity discount contract, and a contract with a two-part tariff on the companies' profits. This section investigates whether a contract based on shared R&D investment (Bhaskaran and Krishnan, 2009) is able to coordinate the supply chain, meaning to fully exploit the potential indicated by the central control solution. Sharing the R&D investment implies that the manufacturer and the supplier agree to cooperate at an early stage, in an attempt to safeguard their business relationship (Christy and Grout, 1994; Williamson, 2008). The sequence of events in the R&D investment sharing scenario is illustrated in Figure 6.4.

In order to realize his product innovation idea, the manufacturer asks the supplier to enter into a business relationship based on a shared R&D investment. Note that he only asks for the financial support. Know-how participation is not considered here. Since the R&D process can be lengthy, it is difficult to bargain over the component price at the same time as for the investment share g. See page 122 for the argumentation on incomplete contracts and prohibitively high contracting costs. Hence, the component price w is negotiated after the R&D phase has ended and just before the manufacturer invests in quality assurance.

The manufacturer's threat point in the negotiation on the supplier's share g depends on his optimal decision in the previous section's basic model. For example, the manufacturer produces the component in-house for $\delta_2 < f \leq \delta_1$. So this option is his threat point when bargaining for g. Subsections 6.4.1, 6.4.2, and 6.4.3 deal with the cases $\delta_2 < f \leq \delta_1$, $\delta_1 < f \leq \delta_3$, and $\delta_3 < f$, respectively.

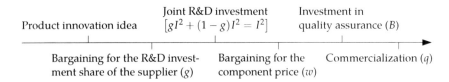

Figure 6.4: Timeline for R&D investment sharing

Note that the extremal values for the supplier's R&D investment share $g \in]0,1[$ are excluded. The case $g = 0$ corresponds to the external procurement scenario discussed in Section 6.3.2. By contrast, $g = 1$ expresses that the supplier pays for the whole R&D investment herself. In that case, it holds that the higher the investment level, the higher the manufacturer's and the lower the supplier's profit. Consequently, the manufacturer would choose the investment level such that the supplier has only a marginal profit, ensuring that she barely participates.

6.4.1 In-house production threat point

If the negotiation on the R&D investment share g fails, the manufacturer's best alternative is to produce the component in-house. The supplier neither loses nor gains anything, so Table 6.2's bargaining scenario results. The index *is* denotes 'investment sharing' referring to the R&D investment.

Table 6.2: Bargaining scenario for the supplier's investment share g (scenario 6.4.1)

	Successful negotiation	Failed negotiation
Supplier:	$\pi_{is}^{S}[w_{is}(g), q_{is}(g)]$	0
Manufacturer:	$\pi_{is}^{M}[I_{is}(g), w_{is}(g), q_{is}(g)]$	$\pi_{i}^{M}(I_i, q_i)$

While bargaining for the supplier's share g, both the manufacturer and the supplier anticipate the next steps on the timeline, specifically the negotiation on the component price w. The resulting component price $w^*(g)$, production quantity $q^*(g)$, and investment level $I^{*2}(g)$, all as a function of g, are therefore known by both in the negotiation on g.

Table 6.3 illustrates the anticipated future bargaining scenario for the component price w. The rights to the R&D output are assumed to be owned by both parties jointly if the R&D investment is shared. Hence, no party can launch the product without the

Table 6.3: Bargaining scenario for the component price w (R&D investment sharing)

	Successful negotiation	Failed negotiation
Supplier:	$\pi_{is}^S(w,q,g)$	$-gI^2$
Manufacturer:	$\pi_{is}^M(I,w,q,g)$	$-(1-g)I^2$

agreement of the other, implying that, if the negotiation on w fails, both parties may lose all of their R&D investment.

The sole difference between the investment sharing profit functions and the external procurement profit functions is that the investment I^2 is divided into the manufacturer's part $(1-g)I^2$ and the supplier's part gI^2.

$$\pi_{is}^M(I,w,q,g) = p(I,q)q - (1-g)I^2 - (k_M + b + w)q - B \tag{6.16}$$
$$\pi_{is}^S(w,q,g) = (w - k_S)q - gI^2 \tag{6.17}$$

Calculating the Nash bargaining solution for the component price w, inserting the solution for w into the manufacturer's profit function and then maximizing the profit function with respect to I^2 and q yields the following investment, production quantity, component price, market price, and profits, all as a function of g:

$$\pi_{is}^M[I_{is}(g),w_{is}(g),q_{is}(g)] = \frac{1}{2}\frac{c^4}{(1-g)^2(k_M+k_S+b)} - \frac{1}{2}B \tag{6.18}$$

$$\pi_{is}^S[w_{is}(g),q_{is}(g)] = \frac{1}{2}\frac{(3-5g)c^4}{(1-g)^3(k_M+k_S+b)} - \frac{1}{2}B \tag{6.19}$$

$$I_{is}^2(g) = \frac{c^4}{(1-g)^3(k_M+k_S+b)^2} \tag{6.20}$$

$$q_{is}(g) = \frac{c^4}{(1-g)^2(k_M+k_S+b)^2} \tag{6.21}$$

$$w_{is}(g) = \frac{1}{2}\left[3k_M + 5k_S + 3b - \frac{B(1-g)^2(k_M+k_S+b)^2}{c^4}\right] \tag{6.22}$$

$$p_{is}[I_{is}(g),q_{is}(g)] = 4(k_M+k_S+b) \tag{6.23}$$

The product price is constant in the investment share g and equal to the central control product price (see Proof of Lemma 3 in the Appendix). The higher the supplier's investment share g, the better the manufacturer's bargaining position, so the R&D investment, the product quantity, and the manufacturer's profit all rise in g. The same holds for a higher component price $w_{is}(g)$, which is also beneficial for the supplier. However, the higher her share g, the weaker her bargaining position.

Proposition 4. *The supplier's profit is maximized by an R&D investment share of 40%. Furthermore, her profit is in any case negative for investment shares equal to or greater than 60%.*

The supplier's profit increases for g going up to 0.4. For higher values, the component price cannot compensate for the weakening bargaining position so that her profit decreases in g. Note that some parameter constellations induce that the supplier's profit is negative for each $g \in]0,1[$. If so, there is no chance the supplier agrees to R&D investment sharing.

Table 6.4: Bargaining scenario with anticipated profits (scenario 6.4.1)

	Successful negotiation	Failed negotiation
Supplier:	$\frac{1}{2}\frac{(3-5g)\,c^4}{(1-g)^3(k_M+k_S+b)} - \frac{1}{2}B$	0
Manufacturer:	$\frac{1}{2}\frac{c^4}{(1-g)^2(k_M+k_S+b)} - \frac{1}{2}B$	$\frac{4c^4}{k_M+k_S+f} - A$

Table 6.4's bargaining scenario for g follows from inserting the in-house production profit and the anticipated profit functions resulting from the future negotiation on w (Equations 6.18 and 6.19) into the initial bargaining scenario presented in Table 6.2. Maximizing the Nash product with respect to g yields the first-order condition shown in Equation 6.24.[10] The explicit solution for g cannot be quoted here because of its extent.

$$0 = \frac{1}{2}\frac{c^4\left[(3-5g_{is})\,c^4 - B(1-g_{is})^3(k_M+k_S+b)\right]}{(1-g_{is})^6(k_M+k_S+b)^2} + \frac{c^4(2-5g_{is})\left[\frac{\frac{1}{2}c^4}{(1-g_{is})^2(k_M+k_S+b)} - \frac{4c^4}{k_M+k_S+f} + A - \frac{1}{2}B\right]}{(1-g_{is})^4(k_M+k_S+b)}$$

(6.24)

The following numerical constellation is used to demonstrate the impacts of the supplier's negotiated R&D investment share g on the profits: $k_M = k_S = 5$, $b = 2.5$, $A = 1\,000$, $B = 900$, and $c = 7.4$. Figure 6.5 illustrates the results for g as a function of f. The Nash bargaining solution $g_{is}(f)$ is depicted by the dashed line. Furthermore, the solid lines plot upper and lower bounds. For g being equal to the lower bound curve $\underline{g}(f)$, the manufacturer would obtain the same profit as in the in-house production scenario. The greater the supplier's R&D investment share g, the greater the manufacturer's profit. On the other hand, for g being equal to the upper bound curve $\bar{g}(f)$, the

---

[10]Note that the corresponding graph may intersect the x-axis several times in the interval $]0,1[$. If so, the optimum is that g which induces a win-win situation and at the same time maximizes the sum of both companies' profits. If there is no $g \in]0,1[$ involving a win-win situation, the negotiation on g fails.

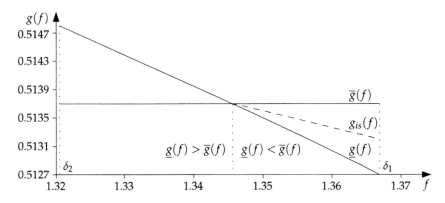

Figure 6.5: The R&D investment share g as a function of f (scenario 6.4.1)

supplier obtains a profit of 0. The lower her share g, the higher her profit. Consequently, the Nash bargaining solution $g_{is}(f)$, for which both benefit from R&D investment sharing, must be within these bounds. A win-win situation cannot be attained if the lower bound is higher than the upper bound $[\underline{g}(f) > \overline{g}(f)]$. This case occurs to the left of the intersection of $\underline{g}(f)$ and $\overline{g}(f)$ in Figure 6.5.

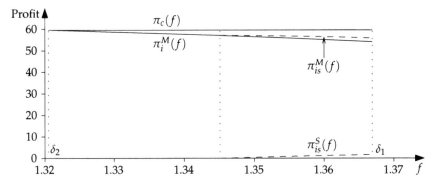

Figure 6.6: Profitability of R&D investment sharing (scenario 6.4.1)

Figure 6.6 compares the manufacturer's and supplier's investment sharing profits with the in-house production profit. The central control profit is also illustrated as a benchmark. For f lower than 1.345, the manufacturer prefers to produce the component in-house since his investment sharing profit would be lower than his in-house production profit. Obviously, the supplier's profit is 0. For greater values of f the manufacturer and the supplier agree to the R&D investment sharing contract. Both obtain a higher profit, illustrated by the dashed lines, than in the in-house production scenario. Indeed, the profit enhancements achieved by investment sharing are relatively low in the example. There are numerous examples with much higher profit improvements. The proposed parameter setting is chosen since, without the need for adjustments, it can be used throughout the next sections, too.

6.4.2 External procurement threat point

In the basic model, the manufacturer and the supplier agree to external procurement with a classic wholesale price contract for $\delta_1 < f \leq \delta_3$. So, if bargaining for the supplier's investment share g fails, the manufacturer would propose the wholesale price contract instead. Table 6.5 summarizes the resulting bargaining scenario for g.

Table 6.5: Bargaining scenario for the supplier's investment share g (scenario 6.4.2)

	Successful negotiation	Failed negotiation
Supplier:	$\pi_{is}^S\left[w_{is}(g), q_{is}(g)\right]$	$\pi_e^S(w_e, q_e)$
Manufacturer:	$\pi_{is}^M\left[I_{is}(g), w_{is}(g), q_{is}(g)\right]$	$\pi_e^M(I_e, w_e, q_e)$

Remember that the supplier and the manufacturer anticipate all following steps while bargaining for g, and both would lose their part of the investment in R&D if the future negotiation on the component price w fails. Bargaining for w and the subsequent optimization of the manufacturer's profit function yield the same investment, production quantity, component price, market price, and profits, all as a function of g, as quoted in Equations 6.18–6.23. Inserting the anticipated profits in the bargaining scenario for g leads to Table 6.6.

Table 6.6: Bargaining scenario with anticipated profits (scenario 6.4.2)

	Successful negotiation	Failed negotiation
Supplier:	$\frac{1}{2}\frac{(3-5g)\,c^4}{(1-g)^3(k_M+k_S+b)} - \frac{1}{2}B$	$\frac{2c^4(f-b)}{\left(k_M+k_S+\frac{1}{2}(f+b)\right)^2} + \frac{1}{2}(A-B)$
Manufacturer:	$\frac{1}{2}\frac{c^4}{(1-g)^2(k_M+k_S+b)} - \frac{1}{2}B$	$\frac{4c^4}{k_M+k_S+\frac{1}{2}(f+b)} - \frac{1}{2}(A+B)$

Maximizing the Nash product with respect to g results in the following first-order condition:

$$0 \overset{!}{=} \frac{\frac{c^4}{2}\left[\frac{(3-5g_{is})c^4}{(1-g_{is})^3(k_M+k_S+b)} - \frac{4c^4(f-b)}{(k_M+k_S+\frac{1}{2}(f+b))^2} - A\right]}{(1-g_{is})^3(k_M+k_S+b)} + \frac{\frac{c^4}{2}(2-5g_{is})\left[\frac{c^4}{(1-g_{is})^2(k_M+k_S+b)} - \frac{8c^4}{k_M+k_S+\frac{1}{2}(f+b)} + A\right]}{(1-g_{is})^4(k_M+k_S+b)}$$

(6.25)

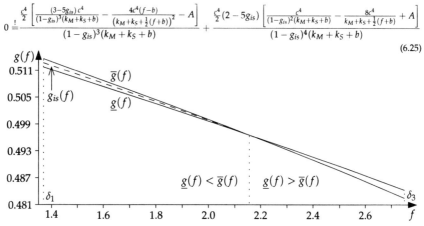

Figure 6.7: The R&D investment share g as a function of f (scenario 6.4.2)

Here too, the impact of the investment share g on profits is demonstrated with the help of the numerical example proposed in Section 6.4.1. The results are illustrated in Figure 6.7. Again, the dashed line depicts the Nash bargaining solution g_{is} as a function of f. The upper bound curve $\overline{g}(f)$ and the lower bound curve $\underline{g}(f)$ are given by solid lines. The lower bound exceeds the upper bound in the right-hand part of Figure 6.7 ($f > 2.17$) which means there is no R&D investment sharing contract that improves both parties' profits at the same time. Consequently, the negotiation on g fails.

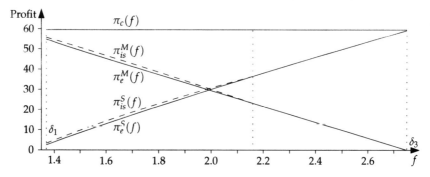

Figure 6.8: Profitability of R&D investment sharing (scenario 6.4.2)

Figure 6.8 compares the manufacturer's and supplier's investment sharing profits with their external procurement profits. For lower values of f ($f \leq 2.17$), the supplier and the manufacturer agree to R&D investment sharing. Both obtain a higher profit, illustrated by the dashed lines, than in the external procurement scenario. However, as already revealed by the results in Figure 6.7, R&D investment sharing fails for $f > 2.17$.

6.4.3   External procurement or discontinuing threat point

Remember, in the basic model two cases can occur if the manufacturer's additional variable costs f for in-house production are greater than δ_3. The threat point in the negotiation on supplier's R&D investment share g depends on whether the manufacturer's external procurement profit calculated under the failure-condition of discontinuing the whole innovation project is positive or not (see Section 6.3.2).

For the numerical example introduced in Section 6.4.1 holds $\frac{1}{2}\frac{c^4}{k_M+k_S+b} - \frac{1}{2}B < 0$, which means that the manufacturer would not realize the innovation project if the negotiation on g fails. Hence, the threat point in the bargaining scenario for g is 0 and not external procurement. Before the numerical example is further investigated in Subsection 6.4.3.2, the alternative scenario with a positive external procurement profit as threat point is analyzed in 6.4.3.1.

6.4.3.1   External procurement threat point

Table 6.7 provides the bargaining scenario for g if the manufacturer's external procurement profit calculated under the failure condition of discontinuing the innovation project were positive $0 \leq \frac{1}{2}\frac{c^4}{k_M+k_S+b} - \frac{1}{2}B$. Obtained analogously to the results of the previous sections, Proposition 5 summarizes the results for this scenario.

Table 6.7: Bargaining scenario with anticipated profits (scenario 6.4.3.1)

	Successful negotiation	Failed negotiation
Supplier:	$\frac{1}{2}\frac{(3-5g)\,c^4}{(1-g)^3(k_M+k_S+b)} - \frac{1}{2}B$	$\frac{3}{2}\frac{c^4}{k_M+k_S+b} - \frac{1}{2}B$
Manufacturer:	$\frac{1}{2}\frac{c^4}{(1-g)^2(k_M+k_S+b)} - \frac{1}{2}B$	$\frac{1}{2}\frac{c^4}{k_M+k_S+b} - \frac{1}{2}B$

Proposition 5. *Independently of the parameter constellation, bargaining for the supplier's R&D investment share g leads to $g_{is} = \frac{21-\sqrt{185}}{16} \approx 0.46$. Both the supplier and the manufacturer obtain a higher profit than in the external procurement scenario. Since the sum of their*

profits is furthermore close to the maximum potential $\pi_C(f)$ and constant in f, the R&D invest-
ment sharing contract almost coordinates the supply chain for $\delta_3 < f$ and $0 \le \frac{1}{2}\frac{c^4}{k_M+k_S+b} - \frac{1}{2}B$.

$$\pi_{is}^M(f) = \frac{128c^4}{(\sqrt{185}-5)^2(k_M+k_S+b)} - \frac{1}{2}B \tag{6.26}$$

$$\pi_{is}^S(f) = \frac{128(5\sqrt{185}-57)\,c^4}{(\sqrt{185}-5)^3(k_M+k_S+b)} - \frac{1}{2}B \tag{6.27}$$

$$\pi_{is}^M(f) + \pi_{is}^S(f) \approx \frac{3.94\,c^4}{k_M+k_S+b} - B < \frac{4c^4}{k_M+k_S+b} - B = \pi_C(f) \tag{6.28}$$

6.4.3.2 Discontinuing the innovation project threat point

Since the manufacturer's external procurement profit is negative $\frac{1}{2}\frac{c^4}{k_M+k_S+b} - \frac{1}{2}B < 0$, external procurement is no option in case of a failed negotiation on g. Failed bargaining over g entails that the innovation project is dropped and profits are 0. Table 6.8 shows the bargaining scenario for g. Proposition 6 summarizes the results.

Table 6.8: Bargaining scenario with anticipated profits (scenario 6.4.3.2)

	Successful negotiation	Failed negotiation
Supplier:	$\frac{1}{2}\frac{(3-5g)\,c^4}{(1-g)^3(k_M+k_S+b)} - \frac{1}{2}B$	0
Manufacturer:	$\frac{1}{2}\frac{c^4}{(1-g)^2(k_M+k_S+b)} - \frac{1}{2}B$	0

Proposition 6. *Independently of the parameter constellation, bargaining for the supplier's R&D investment share g yields $g_{is} = \frac{1}{2}$. The R&D investment sharing contract capitalizes on 100% of the potential promised by a positive central control profit, and thus coordinates the supply chain for $\delta_3 < f$ and $\frac{1}{2}\frac{c^4}{k_M+k_S+b} - \frac{1}{2}B < 0$. Both parties equally share the total profit which is constant in f.*

$$\pi_{is}^M(f) = \pi_{is}^S(f) = \frac{2c^4}{k_M+k_S+b} - \frac{1}{2}B \tag{6.29}$$

$$\pi_{is}^M(f) + \pi_{is}^S(f) = \frac{4c^4}{k_M+k_S+b} - B = \pi_L(f) \tag{6.30}$$

Table 6.9 summarizes the example. The preferred business relationship and the prof-
its are quoted in relation to f. For $f > 2.751 = \delta_3$ holds $\pi_{is}^M(f) = \pi_{is}^S(f) = 29.785$. Note
that, because of the changing bargaining scenarios, the manufacturer's profit is greater

Table 6.9: Summary of the example

	$0 < f \leq 1.3452$	$1.3452 < f \leq 2.17$	$2.17 < f \leq 2.751$	$2.751 < f$
Decision in favor of	in-house production	investment sharing	external procurement	investment sharing
Manufacturer's profit	$[199.46, 57.24]$	$]57.24, 22.41]$	$]22.41, 0.01]$	29.785
Supplier's profit	0	$]0, 37]$	$]37, 59.44]$	29.785

for high additional in-house production costs $f > 2.751$ than for some lower values of f, so his profit is more or less U-shaped in his cost disadvantage f. This finding leads to the counterintuitive conclusion that it sometimes may even be disadvantageous for a manufacturer to be able to produce a required component in-house in the first place.

6.5   Numerical robustness evaluation

This section is inspired by Cachon and Swinney (2011) and Boyabatli et al. (2011) who also carry out numerical studies to complement their analytical findings. However, instead of combining the required instances from predefined sets of values for each model parameter (Cachon and Swinney, 2011), here the parameter values attributed to a certain instance are randomly generated from reasonable intervals. The heterogeneity of the resulting parameter constellations in conjunction with the large number of 1 000 000 instances reveals additional insights into the robustness and behavior of the model. For each instance, the manufacturer's optimal decision is computed. The aim is to identify parameter constellations which are characteristic of in-house production, external procurement, R&D investment sharing, and discontinuation of the innovation project. Since the results of the previous sections feature sophisticated interdependencies, it is impossible to derive most of the following insights analytically.

Each of the 1 000 000 instances investigated during the numerical study is generated in the same way. The variable costs incurred per unit of the product innovation k_M, k_S, f, and b are created as real numbers, each independently and randomly drawn from the interval $]0, 10]$. Since it holds for most real world cases, investments A and B should be likely to exceed the variable cost parameters. Hence, the manufacturer's investments in in-house production A and external procurement B are drawn from $]0, 1\,000]$ and $]0, A[$, respectively. Each parameter introduced so far is generated as a realization of a uniform distribution over the respective interval. By contrast, the R&D investment effect parameter c is obtained from a truncated normal distribution with an expected value of 5, a standard deviation of 1, and the limits 0.1 and 10. The normal distribution implies that values close to 0.1 and 10 are rather unlikely. Since a relatively low c requires a very high R&D investment to stimulate the market, low c's are likely to result in the decision to discontinue the project. Remember that the main goal of the numerical examination is not to estimate how often R&D investment sharing contracts are advantageous in practice, but to identify parameter constellations that are typical of the dominance of a certain option. Hence, in order to generate c such that each of the manufacturer's options occurs sufficiently frequently, ensuring reliable results, the truncated normal distribution is chosen.[11]

Table 6.10: Frequency of occurrence and average parameter values

	%	A	B	k_M	k_S	f	b	c	A	B	k_M	k_S	f	b	c
Discontinuation	49.4	629	368	5.36	5.37	5.04	5.31	4.55	→	↑	→	→	→	→	↓
In-house production	7.5	208	131	3.93	3.94	2.33	6.82	5.66	↓	→	→	→	↓	↑	↑
External procurement	17.4	252	89	4.80	4.81	5.23	4.36	5.66	↓	↓	→	→	→	→	↑
Investment sharing (6.4.1)	0.2	469	168	3.22	3.19	1.53	7.55	5.44	→	→	↓	↓	↓	↑	↑
Investment sharing (6.4.2)	5.8	317	141	3.91	3.91	6.02	3.15	5.63	↓	→	→	→	→	↓	↑
Investment sharing (6.4.3.1)	4.0	588	26	5.06	5.08	5.44	4.67	4.96	→	↓	→	→	→	→	→
Investment sharing (6.4.3.2)	15.7	554	156	4.99	5.00	5.44	4.58	5.08	→	→	→	→	→	→	→

In the second column, Table 6.10 contains each possible scenario's frequency of occurrence (in %). Furthermore, the rounded mean parameter values are calculated from all instances leading to the respective scenario. For example, the manufacturer decides in favor of in-house production in around $7.5\% \cdot 1\,000\,000 = 75\,000$ cases. The average investment A in these $75\,000$ instances is 208. To the right, with a down arrow in the in-house production row, is a second column titled A. This down arrow indicates that the mean investment of 208 is in the lowest of the three ranges defined by the theoretical tertiles. Since A is generated as a realization of a random variable uniformly distributed over the interval $]0, 1\,000]$, the theoretical tertiles delimit the ranges $]0, 333]$, $]333, 667]$, and $]667, 1\,000]$. Right and up arrows indicate that the mean parameter value is in the medium and upper range, respectively.[12] The illustration by arrows provides a simple overview that facilitates the interpretation of the mean values. Based on the arrows, Table 6.10 suggest the following conclusions.

---

[11]Barring only very few exceptions, the proposed way of generating instances leads to profits which, from a real-world view, are in a reasonable proportion to the values of the cost parameters.

[12]The assumption $B < A$, causing the tertiles of B to depend on the distribution of A, leads to the ranges $]0, 101]$, $]101, 305]$, and $]305, 1\,000[$ for B. Given the truncated normal distribution, the ranges for c are $[0.1, 4.57]$, $]4.57, 5.43]$, and $]5.43, 10]$. The ranges of the uniformly distributed parameters k_M, k_S, f, and b are $]0, 3.33]$, $]3.33, 6.67]$, and $]6.67, 10]$, respectively.

- As expected, if the R&D investment effect parameter c is relatively low, the man-ufacturer should seriously consider discontinuing the innovation project. Due to the strong influence on the price-demand function, the product innovation is likely to be unprofitable.

  Although the mean investment in in-house production A is only in the medium range in the discontinuation scenario, no other scenario exhibits a higher mean A. High A's primarily have a strong negative impact on the profitability of in-house production, but also on the manufacturer's bargaining position in other scenar-ios. The mean investment in external procurement B, however, is in the upper range, making all external procurement and R&D investment sharing scenarios unprofitable. Yet keep in mind that A and B must be interpreted very carefully and jointly. The model assumption $A > B$ causes only high values for A to allow for B to be high as well.

  The mean values of all other parameters are in the medium range. Statements on their influence on the discontinuation decision cannot be made, or only made to a limited extent, since a low and a high value as well as two medium range values both result in a medium range mean.

- The average values in the in-house production row are self-explanatory. If the investment in in-house production A and the additional variable in-house pro-duction costs f are low and, furthermore, the variable external procurement costs b and the investment effect parameter c are high, in-house production is obviously advantageous.

- In the external procurement scenario (Section 6.3.2), there are two possible threat points that may take effect when negotiating on the component price: First, pro-ducing the component in-house and second, dropping the whole innovation pro-ject. Since the external procurement scenario resulting from the second threat point is strictly dominated by the R&D investment sharing scenario introduced in Section 6.4.3.1, only the external procurement scenario with the threat point of producing the component in-house occurs in the numerical study. This scenario is advantageous for the manufacturer if the investment effect parameter c is high and the investment in external procurement B is low. Moreover, the investment in in-house production A, which negatively influences the manufacturer's bargain-ing power, should be relatively low. Unlike the in-house production scenario, the external procurement scenario seems to have no need for clear requirements on the means of f and b, which may explain why external procurement occurs more frequently than in-house production. It is especially notable that the variable external procurement costs b do not have to be low for external procurement.

- The requirements for the optimality of R&D investment sharing according to Section 6.4.1 turn out to be very specific, which is likely the reason why only about 2 000 instances result in that scenario. On average, the variable cost parameters $(k_M, k_S,$ and $f)$ are low, while the manufacturer's additional variable costs for external procurement b and the investment effect parameter c are characterized by high means. It seems counterintuitive that the variable additional in-house production costs f are low and the variable external procurement costs b are high and nonetheless, the decision is in favor of a collaboration. However, remember that, in Section 6.4.1, the manufacturer's threat point in the negotiation on the supplier's investment share g is his in-house production profit. In order for this to be an effective threat, the manufacturer's in-house production profit should be relatively high, which is induced by a low average f and a medium range A.

- The R&D investment sharing scenario introduced in Section 6.4.2 relies on the external procurement scenario examined in the third row. This relation justifies the similarity of the results for the average values of A, B, k_M, k_S, f, and c. However, there is a significant difference in the variable external procurement costs b. R&D investment sharing seems preferable to external procurement if b is relatively low, ceteris paribus.

- Regarding the arrows that belong to R&D investment sharing according to Sections 6.4.3.1 and 6.4.3.2, it becomes apparent that these scenarios differ only in the mean value of the investment in external procurement B. While the average B of R&D investment sharing 6.4.3.1 is very close to 0, the mean B of scenario 6.4.3.2 is in the medium range. Hence, the requirements for the optimality of scenario 6.4.3.1 are more stringent, explaining why it occurs less frequently (4%) than scenario 6.4.3.2 (15.7%). However, except for B being especially low in scenario 6.4.3.1, no parameter tendency becomes apparent to characterize the R&D investment sharing scenarios 6.4.3.1 and 6.4.3.2. Nevertheless, it should be highlighted that there are around 157 000 instances for which neither in-house production nor external procurement are profitable. Only R&D investment sharing 6.4.3.2 entails positive profits for both the manufacturer and the supplier.

Table 6.11 focuses on the effectiveness of the four R&D investment sharing scenarios. The three columns headlined 'Potential (%)' contain the minimum, mean, and max-

Table 6.11: Effects of R&D investment sharing

	Potential (%)			Used potential (%)			Supplier's share g		
	Min	Mean	Max	Min	Mean	Max	Min	Mean	Max
Investment sharing (6.4.1)	3.1	37.3	99.8	0.4	66.3	99.9	0.50	0.54	0.59
Investment sharing (6.4.2)	2_{10}^{-6}	8.5	74.2	4_{10}^{-5}	71.7	100	0.40	0.50	0.57
Investment sharing (6.4.3.1)	50.0	57.5	66.7	97.2	97.2	97.2	0.46	0.46	0.46
Investment sharing (6.4.3.2)	100	100	100	100	100	100	0.50	0.50	0.50

imum potential for improvement. The improvement potential is defined as the additional profit achievable, which is the central control profit, minus the status quo sum of profits given by either the manufacturer's in-house production profit (6.4.1), the sum of the supplier's and the manufacturer's external procurement profits (6.4.2 and 6.4.3.1), or 0 (6.4.3.2). This difference is the maximum gain attainable by R&D investment sharing.

Dividing the difference by the central control profit produces a percentage, allowing for comparability. For example, in scenarios 6.4.2 and 6.4.3.1, the potential is calculated as $\frac{\pi_c(f) - \pi_e^M(f) - \pi_e^S(f)}{\pi_c(f)}$ (see Figure 6.3 on page 127). The records within the row 'Investment sharing (6.4.1)' have to be interpreted as follows: The mean potential of the 2 000 instances, which result in scenario 6.4.1, is 37.3%. The minimum and maximum potentials are 3.1 and 99.8%, respectively.

These percentages describe the maximum possible improvement achievable by R&D investment sharing. But remember that except for scenario 6.4.3.2, R&D investment sharing does not guarantee it will be possible to capitalize on the whole potential. For example, in scenario 6.4.1, only 66.3% of the improvement potential is used on average. Straight following from the 66.3%, R&D investment sharing here causes a mean increase in total profit of almost 40%.[13] In scenarios 6.4.2 and 6.4.3.1, the average increase in the total profit is 7 and 132%, respectively. The average increase cannot be calculated for scenario 6.4.3.2 since there would be no profit without R&D investment sharing.

There is (almost) no unused potential in scenarios 6.4.3.1 and 6.4.3.2, so R&D investment sharing (almost) coordinates the supply chain. However, the low minimum values in the rows for scenarios 6.4.1 and 6.4.2 suggest that there are also instances for which R&D investment sharing is only marginally useful.

---

[13]66.3% of the mean potential (37.3%) is used on average which implies that it is possible to capitalize on 87.43% $[= (100\% - 37.3\%) + 37.3\% \cdot 66.3\%]$ of the central control profit. Hence, R&D investment sharing on average achieves an increase in the total profit of almost 40% $\left[= \frac{87.43\% - (100\% - 37.3\%)}{100\% - 37.3\%}\right]$.

Last but not least, the three columns headed 'Supplier's share g' record the minimum, mean, and maximum R&D investment share g for the four scenarios. Note that the simulation's results in the rows for scenarios 6.4.3.1 and 6.4.3.2 correspond to the previous section's analytical findings.

6.6 Summary and outlook

This chapter provides an explanation for the observation that many innovating companies produce many required components in-house instead of sourcing them from specialized suppliers. However, in many scenarios in-house production as well as external procurement via a classic wholesale price contract turn out to be inefficient. Hence, the concept of R&D investment sharing contracts, which is encountered in the pharmaceutical industry, for example, is examined with regard to its ability to coordinate the supply chain. Using this type of contract, almost perfect coordination is attainable if the manufacturer's variable production costs clearly exceed the supplier's. But in many other cases, too, both the manufacturer and the supplier can benefit from R&D investment sharing contracts. Even if neither in-house production nor common external procurement is profitable, meaning that the innovation project would normally be discontinued, positive profits for both parties can be achieved. The results of this chapter suggest that innovating companies should seriously contemplate R&D investment sharing contracts with strong suppliers before embarking on an R&D process. Financial cooperation at an early stage can be beneficial for both parties.

Future research should extend the model to include transaction cost considerations. The benefits of R&D investment sharing contracts need to be traded off against additional contracting and implementation costs. Stochastic influences on the price-demand function, cost parameters, and, above all, the results of the R&D process may also reveal further insights. For example, if there is a possibility that the R&D phase fails, the supplier may want a risk premium, which impairs his cost advantage. Furthermore, the collaboration should not be limited only to financial support by the supplier. Collaboration in the R&D effort may produce other benefits such as technological product enhancements due to improved component fit, for example. Affecting R&D effort levels, team production considerations (Alchain and Demsetz, 1972) could be incorporated into the model as well.

Also, future research should address a general issue in Supply Chain Contracting. Like this chapter, too, the Supply Chain Contracting literature mainly deals with relationships between two companies. In practice, supply chains often consist of many more companies in arborescent network structures. So restricting the focus to bilateral contracts may have negative impacts on other supply chain partners. The challenge is to design a system of contracts that coordinates all companies within one corporate network. Chapter 5 reveals that Supply Chain Scheduling can cause similar problems. Compared to the fully uncoordinated benchmark scenario, only joint Supply Chain Scheduling of all stages brings about a significant average reduction in the supply chain makespan. Partial coordination of some but not all stages can even worsen it.

6.7 Appendix

6.7.1 Proofs

Proof of Lemma 1

Inserting the price-demand function (Equation 6.3) into the manufacturer's profit function (Equation 6.2) and then maximizing the profit function with respect to I and q results in the following R&D investment, product quantity, price, and profit:

$$I_i^2 = \frac{8c^4}{k_M + k_S + f} \tag{6.31}$$

$$q_i = \frac{4c^4}{(k_M + k_S + f)^2} \tag{6.32}$$

$$p_i(I_i, q_i) = 4(k_M + k_S + f) \tag{6.33}$$

$$\pi_i^M(I_i, q_i) = \frac{4c^4}{k_M + k_S + f} - A \tag{6.34}$$

A straight transformation of $\pi_i^M(I_i, q_i) \geq 0$ reveals that the manufacturer's in-house production profit is positive for $0 < f \leq \delta_4$.

$$\pi_i^M(I_i, q_i) \begin{cases} \geq 0 & \text{for } 0 < f \leq \delta_4 \\ < 0 & \text{for } \delta_4 < f \end{cases} \tag{6.35}$$

$$\delta_4 = \frac{4c^4}{A} - k_M - k_S \quad \square \tag{6.36}$$

Proof of Lemma 2

Inserting the Nash bargaining solution for w into the manufacturer's profit function (Equation 6.8) and then maximizing the profit function with respect to I and q leads to the following R&D investment, production quantity, component price, market price, and profits:

$$\pi_e^M(I_e, w_e, q_e) = \begin{cases} \frac{4c^4}{k_M + k_S + \frac{1}{2}(f+b)} - \frac{1}{2}(A + B) & \text{for } 0 < f \leq \delta_{3a} \ \left[\text{threat: } \pi_i^M(I, q)\right] \\ \frac{1}{2}\frac{c^4}{k_M + k_S + b} - \frac{1}{2}B & \text{for } \delta_{3a} < f \quad\quad \left[\text{threat: } -I^2\right] \end{cases} \tag{6.37}$$

$$\pi_e^S(w_e, q_e) = \begin{cases} \dfrac{2c^4(f-b)}{\left(k_M + k_S + \frac{1}{2}(f+b)\right)^2} + \frac{1}{2}(A-B) & \text{for} \quad 0 < f \leq \delta_{3a} \\[2ex] \dfrac{3}{2}\dfrac{c^4}{k_M + k_S + b} - \frac{1}{2}B & \text{for} \quad \delta_{3a} < f \end{cases} \tag{6.38}$$

$$I_e^2 = \begin{cases} \dfrac{8c^4}{k_M + k_S + \frac{1}{2}(f+b)} & \text{for} \quad 0 < f \leq \delta_{3a} \\[2ex] \dfrac{c^4}{k_M + k_S + b} & \text{for} \quad \delta_{3a} < f \end{cases} \tag{6.39}$$

$$q_e = \begin{cases} \dfrac{4c^4}{\left(k_M + k_S + \frac{1}{2}(f+b)\right)^2} & \text{for} \quad 0 < f \leq \delta_{3a} \\[2ex] \dfrac{c^4}{(k_M + k_S + b)^2} & \text{for} \quad \delta_{3a} < f \end{cases} \tag{6.40}$$

$$w(I_e, q_e) = \begin{cases} k_S + \frac{1}{2}(f-b) + \dfrac{\left(k_M + k_S + \frac{1}{2}(f+b)\right)^2}{8c^4}(A-B) & \text{for} \quad 0 < f \leq \delta_{3a} \\[2ex] \frac{1}{2}(3k_M + 5k_S + 3b) - \dfrac{(k_M + k_S + b)^2}{2c^4}B & \text{for} \quad \delta_{3a} < f \end{cases} \tag{6.41}$$

$$p(I_e, q_e) = \begin{cases} 4\left(k_M + k_S + \frac{1}{2}(f+b)\right) & \text{for} \quad 0 < f \leq \delta_{3a} \\[2ex] 4(k_M + k_S + b) & \text{for} \quad \delta_{3a} < f \end{cases} \tag{6.42}$$

$$\delta_{3a} = \dfrac{16c^4(k_M + k_S + b)}{(k_M + k_S + b)A + c^4} - 2(k_M + k_S) - b \tag{6.43}$$

δ_{3a} denotes a critical value up to which the manufacturer will produce the component in-house if negotiations on the component price fails. For f greater than δ_{3a}, the manufacturer discontinues the innovation project and loses his R&D investment I^2 in case the negotiation fails. In-house production would lead to a profit lower than $-I^2$.

Obviously, the manufacturer as well as the supplier only consider external procurement if their external procurement profits are positive. Different cases need to be distinguished. The manufacturer's external procurement profit is in any case positive if $0 \leq \frac{1}{2}\frac{c^4}{k_M + k_S + b} - \frac{1}{2}B$. If so, the manufacturer's external procurement profit calculated under the threat of losing the R&D investment $[\text{threat}: -I^2]$ is necessarily positive, too. While the manufacturer's external procurement profit calculated with the in-house production threat $[\text{threat}: \pi_i^M(I, q)]$ strictly decreases in f (see Equation 6.37), his external procurement profit under the threat $-I^2$ is constant in f. δ_{3a} is the x-coordinate of the point where his profit functions intersect. Given these properties, the manufacturer's external procurement profit under the threat $\pi_i^M(I, q)$ must be also positive for $0 < f \leq \delta_{3a}$.

$$\pi_e^M(I_e, w_e, q_e) \geq 0 \qquad \text{for} \quad 0 \leq \frac{1}{2}\frac{c^4}{k_M + k_S + b} - \frac{1}{2}B \tag{6.44}$$

If $0 > \frac{1}{2}\frac{c^4}{k_M+k_S+b} - \frac{1}{2}B$, his profit is only positive for $f \leq \delta_{3b}$ which can be obtained from a straightforward transformation of $\frac{4c^4}{k_M+k_S+\frac{1}{2}(f+b)} - \frac{1}{2}(A+B) \geq 0$.

$$\pi_e^M(I_e, w_e, q_e) \begin{cases} \geq 0 & \text{for} \quad 0 < f \leq \delta_{3b} \\ < 0 & \text{for} \quad \delta_{3b} < f \end{cases} \tag{6.45}$$

$$\delta_{3b} = \frac{16c^4}{A+B} - 2(k_M + k_S) - b \tag{6.46}$$

Let $\delta_3 := \min\{\delta_{3a}, \delta_{3b}\}$, then, for $f \leq \delta_3$, the manufacturer's threat point in the bargaining for the component price is the in-house production option. Now consider the case $f > \delta_3$. If $\delta_3 = \min\{\delta_{3a}, \delta_{3b}\} = \delta_{3a}$, his threat point is losing the R&D investment. If $\delta_3 = \delta_{3b}$, the manufacturer anticipates his external procurement profit to be negative and thus decides to abandon the innovation project before investing in R&D, resulting in a profit of 0.

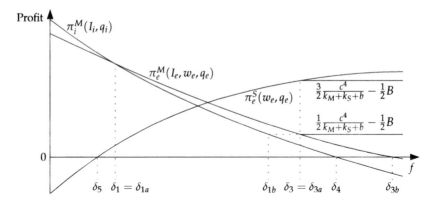

Figure 6.9: Run of the profits depending on f (Proof of Lemma 2)

Comparing the manufacturer's in-house production and external procurement profits leads to the following results:

$$\pi_i^M(I_i, q_i) \begin{cases} \geq \pi_e^M(I_e, w_e, q_e) & \text{for} \quad 0 < f \leq \delta_1 \\ < \pi_e^M(I_e, w_e, q_e) & \text{for} \quad \delta_1 < f \end{cases} \tag{6.47}$$

$$\delta_1 = \min\{\delta_{1a}, \delta_{1b}\} \tag{6.48}$$

$$\delta_{1a} = \frac{\sqrt{\lambda} - (A - B)(3k_M + 3k_S + b) - 8c^4}{2(A - B)} \tag{6.49}$$

$$\text{with} \quad \lambda = (A - B)^2(k_M + k_S + b)^2 + 48c^4(A - B)(k_M + k_S + b) + 64c^8$$

$$\delta_{1b} = \frac{8c^4(k_M + k_S + b)}{c^4 + (2A - B)(k_M + k_S + b)} - (k_M + k_S) \tag{6.50}$$

The manufacturer decides in favor of external procurement for $f > \delta_1 = \min\{\delta_{1a}, \delta_{1b}\}$. The x-coordinates δ_{1a} and δ_{1b} of the two possible intersections of the manufacturer's in-house production and external procurement profit functions result from the two possible external procurement threat points.[14] Figure 6.9 summarizes the insights graphically. Here, the term $\frac{1}{2}\frac{c^4}{k_M+k_S+b} - \frac{1}{2}B$ is assumed to be positive but relatively small so that the x-coordinate of the intersection of the manufacturer's in-house production profit $\pi_i^M(I_i, q_i)$ and his external procurement profit $\pi_e^M(I_e, w_e, q_e)$ is $\delta_1 = \min\{\delta_{1a}, \delta_{1b}\} = \delta_{1a}$.
□

Proof of Proposition 1

For $f > \delta_1$, the manufacturer prefers external procurement to in-house production (see Proof of Lemma 2). However, the supplier will only agree to external procurement if her profit is also positive. Two cases must be distinguished (see Equation 6.37 and Figure 6.9). First, the manufacturer decides in favor of external procurement and $f \leq \delta_{3a}$. Second, the manufacturer decides in favor of external procurement and $f > \delta_{3a}$.

1. **External procurement and $f \leq \delta_{3a}$:**[15]
   A straightforward transformation of $0 \leq \frac{2c^4(f-b)}{\left(k_M+k_S+\frac{1}{2}(f+b)\right)^2} + \frac{1}{2}(A - B)$ reveals that the supplier's profit is positive for $f \geq \delta_5$ (see Equation 6.38).

$$\pi_e^S(w_e, q_e) \begin{cases} < 0 & \text{for} \quad 0 < f < \delta_5 \\ \geq 0 & \text{for} \quad \delta_5 \leq f \end{cases} \tag{6.51}$$

$$\delta_5 = \frac{4\sqrt{(A - B)(k_M + k_S + b)2c^4 + 4c^8} - (A - B)(2k_M + 2k_S + b) - 8c^4}{A - B} \tag{6.52}$$

---

[14]There is also a negative interval for f leading to $\pi_i^M(I_i, q_i) < \pi_e^M(I_e, w_e, q_e)$, which can be neglected since f is greater than 0 by assumption.

[15]In this scenario, it holds that the greater the differences between the variable costs $f - b$ and the investments $A - B$, the higher the profit of the supplier (see Equation 6.38). An increase in these differences strengthens the arguments for external procurement and thus the supplier's position.

Furthermore, the scenario 'external procurement and $f \leq \delta_{3a}$' implies that $\delta_1 = \min\{\delta_{1a}, \delta_{1b}\} = \delta_{1a}$ (see Figure 6.9). From $\delta_5 < \delta_{1a}$ follows $-k_M - k_S < b$ which holds true since k_M, k_S, and b are strictly positive. Hence, the supplier's profit is positive and she will therefore agree if the manufacturer proposes external procurement.

2. **External procurement and $f > \delta_{3a}$:**
   The manufacturer's external procurement profit must be positive $0 \leq \frac{1}{2}\frac{c^4}{k_M+k_S+b} - \frac{1}{2}B$ since he would abandon the innovation project otherwise (see Equation 6.37). The supplier's profit $\frac{3}{2}\frac{c^4}{k_M+k_S+b} - \frac{1}{2}B$ is obviously higher than the manufacturer's and thus also positive.

Consequently, both the manufacturer and the supplier generate positive external procurement profits for

$$\delta_5 \leq f \leq \begin{cases} \infty & \text{if } 0 \leq \frac{1}{2}\frac{c^4}{k_M+k_S+b} - \frac{1}{2}B \\ \delta_3 & \text{if } 0 > \frac{1}{2}\frac{c^4}{k_M+k_S+b} - \frac{1}{2}B \end{cases} \quad \square \tag{6.53}$$

Proof of Lemma 3

Maximizing the central control profit function (Equation 6.12) with respect to I and q leads to the following R&D investment, production quantity, market price, and profit:

$$I_c^2 = \frac{8c^4}{k_M + k_S + b} \tag{6.54}$$

$$q_c = \frac{4c^4}{(k_M + k_S + b)^2} \tag{6.55}$$

$$p_c(I_c, q_c) = 4(k_M + k_S + b) \tag{6.56}$$

$$\pi_c(I_c, q_c) = \frac{4c^4}{k_M + k_S + b} - B \tag{6.57}$$

From a straightforward transformation of $\pi_i^M(I_i, q_i) \geq \pi_c(I_c, q_c)$ follows

$$\pi_i^M(I_i, q_i) \begin{cases} \geq \pi_c(I_c, q_c) & \text{for } 0 < f \leq \delta_2 \\ < \pi_c(I_c, q_c) & \text{for } \delta_2 < f \end{cases} \tag{6.58}$$

$$\delta_2 = \frac{(B-A)(k_M+k_S)(k_M+k_S+b) + 4c^4 b}{(A-B)(k_M+k_S+b) + 4c^4} \quad \square \tag{6.59}$$

Proof of Proposition 2

A straightforward transformation of $\delta_2 < b$ results in $-k_M - k_S < b$ which holds true since k_M, k_S, and b are assumed to be strictly positive. □

Besides, note that $\delta_2 < \delta_5$, $\delta_5 < \delta_{1a}$, $\delta_5 < \delta_{1b}$ and $\delta_{1a} < b$ can all be transformed to $-k_M - k_S < b$, implying that the following orders hold:

$$\delta_2 < \delta_5 < \delta_{1a} < b \tag{6.60}$$

$$\delta_2 < \delta_5 < \delta_{1b} \tag{6.61}$$

$$\delta_2 < \delta_5 < \delta_1 = \min\{\delta_{1a}, \delta_{1b}\} \tag{6.62}$$

Note that there are parameter constellations which lead to $b < \delta_{1b}$.

Proof of Proposition 3

Two cases must be distinguished (see Equations 6.37 and 6.38 and Figure 6.9). First, $f \leq \delta_{3a}$ and, second, $f > \delta_{3a}$.

1. $f \leq \delta_{3a}$:
   In this case, the manufacturer's and the supplier's external procurement profits are $\pi_e^M(I_e, w_e, q_e) = \frac{4c^4}{k_M + k_S + \frac{1}{2}(f+b)} - \frac{1}{2}(A+B)$ and $\pi_e^S(w_e, q_e) = \frac{2c^4(f-b)}{(k_M + k_S + \frac{1}{2}(f+b))^2} + \frac{1}{2}(A-B)$, respectively. A straight transformation of $\pi_c(I_c, q_c) \geq \pi_e^M(I_e, w_e, q_e) + \pi_e^S(w_e, q_e)$ yields $\frac{1}{4}(f-b)^2 \geq 0$ which is fulfilled regardless of the parameter constellation. Note that the equality holds for $f = b$.

2. $f > \delta_{3a}$:
   Here, the external procurement profits of the manufacturer and the supplier are $\pi_e^M(I_e, w_e, q_e) = \frac{1}{2}\frac{c^4}{k_M + k_S + b} - \frac{1}{2}B$ and $\pi_e^S(w_e, q_e) = \frac{3}{2}\frac{c^4}{k_M + k_S + b} - \frac{1}{2}B$, respectively. The sum of these profits is $\pi_e^M(I_e, w_e, q_e) + \pi_e^S(w_e, q_e) = \frac{2c^4}{k_M + k_S + b} - B$ which is obviously smaller than $\pi_c(I_c, q_c) = \frac{4c^4}{k_M + k_S + b} - B$ ($B, c, k_M, k_S, b > 0$). □

Proof of Proposition 4

Proposition 4 can be easily deduced by analyzing Equation 6.19 with respect to g. □

Proof of Proposition 5

Maximizing the Nash product with respect to g leads to the optimal g_{is}. Inserting g_{is} into the manufacturer's and the supplier's investment sharing profit functions yields the profits quoted in Equations 6.26–6.27. Inequalities 6.63 and 6.64 compare these profits to the external procurement profits. It becomes apparent that, independently of f, the investment sharing profits of both the supplier and the manufacturer are higher than the external procurement profits. Hence, investment sharing dominates the second external procurement scenario (see Equations 6.37 and 6.38) which is calculated under the threat of discontinuing the whole innovation project.

$$\pi_{is}^M(f) = \frac{128c^4}{(\sqrt{185}-5)^2(k_M+k_S+b)} - \frac{1}{2}B > \frac{1}{2}\frac{c^4}{k_M+k_S+b} - \frac{1}{2}B \qquad (6.63)$$

$$\Leftrightarrow \qquad \frac{128}{(\sqrt{185}-5)^2} \approx 1.73 > \frac{1}{2}$$

$$\pi_{is}^S(f) = \frac{128(5\sqrt{185}-57)c^4}{(\sqrt{185}-5)^3(k_M+k_S+b)} - \frac{1}{2}B > \frac{3}{2}\frac{c^4}{k_M+k_S+b} - \frac{1}{2}B \qquad (6.64)$$

$$\Leftrightarrow \qquad \frac{128(5\sqrt{185}-57)}{(\sqrt{185}-5)^3} \approx 2.21 > \frac{3}{2}$$

$$\pi_{is}^M(f) + \pi_{is}^S(f) = \frac{256(3\sqrt{185}-31)c^4}{(\sqrt{185}-5)^3(k_M+k_S+b)} - B \approx \frac{3.94\,c^4}{k_M+k_S+b} - B \quad \square \qquad (6.65)$$

Proof of Proposition 6

Maximizing the Nash product with respect to g results in $g_{is} = \frac{1}{2}$. Inserting g_{is} into the investment sharing profit functions yields the profits recorded in Equation 6.29.

6.7.2 Common contract types

Tsay et al. (2003) and Cachon (2003) discuss various well-known types of contracts. While some are not applicable in this chapter's supply chain environment, revenue sharing, quantity discount, and two-part tariffs appear promising at first glance. In the next subsections, basic variants of these contract types are considered instead of the wholesale price contract (see the external procurement timeline in Figure 6.2). Note that many other and more sophisticated variants were also investigated, but since these approaches were all unsuccessfully either, only the following three simple examples are presented here.

Revenue sharing contract

Under a revenue sharing contract (Cachon and Lariviere, 2001, 2005), the manufacturer pays to the supplier a percentage $s \in [0,1]$ of his total revenue plus a wholesale price for each unit ordered. First, the manufacturer determines the percentage and offers the revenue sharing (rs) contract to the supplier. Given the profit functions in Equations 6.66 and 6.67, the parties then bargain for the component price w.

$$\pi_{rs}^M(I,w,q) = (1-s)\, p(I,q)\, q - I^2 - (k_M + b + w)\, q - B \qquad (6.66)$$
$$\pi_{rs}^S(w,q) = s\, p(I,q)\, q + (w - k_S)\, q \qquad (6.67)$$

Nash bargaining and profit maximization result in a production quantity, an investment level, and profits equal to those obtained under the classic wholesale price contract (see Section 6.3.2). A high revenue share s leads to a low unit price and vice versa. Hence, independently of the value of s, neither the manufacturer nor the supplier benefit or suffer from this revenue sharing contract.

Quantity discount contract

Quantity discount (qd) means that the supplier charges the manufacturer a component price $w(q)$ per unit ordered, with $w(q)$ being a decreasing function in the product quantity q. The greater the quantity, the lower the component price. This section assumes the component price function $w(q) = \frac{4d}{q^{\frac{3}{4}}}$. Taking account of the following profit functions, the price parameter d is a matter of negotiation:

$$\pi_{qd}^M(I,q,d) = p(I,q)\, q - I^2 - (k_M + b)\, q - \frac{4d}{q^{\frac{3}{4}}} q - B \qquad (6.68)$$
$$\pi_{qd}^S(q,d) = \frac{4d}{q^{\frac{3}{4}}} q - k_S q \qquad (6.69)$$

Nash bargaining leads to a d that causes the component price to be equal to the price in the external procurement scenario. Since the investment level, the production quantity, and the profits again remain unaffected, coordination cannot be achieved through a quantity discount contract either.

Two-part tariff

Under a two-part tariff (tp), the supplier receives a fixed fee L plus a payment per unit ordered by the manufacturer. Here, the payment is assumed to be equal to the supplier's marginal production costs k_S. The fixed fee L is negotiated. The profit functions are:

$$\pi_{tp}^M(I, q, L) = p(I, q) q - I^2 - (k_M + b + k_S) q - B - L \tag{6.70}$$
$$\pi_{tp}^S(q, L) = (k_S - k_S) q + L \tag{6.71}$$

Nash bargaining entails an L that is equal to the supplier's profit in the external procurement scenario. Again, the investment level, the production quantity, and the profits neither improve nor worsen.

Chapter 7

Concluding remarks

The previous chapters show that Supply Chain Scheduling and Contracting are promising supply chain management approaches. In the following, the most important findings of this dissertation are briefly summarized.

- **Chapter 3. Supply Chain Scheduling: Integrated machine scheduling and vehicle routing**
  Despite the inherent complexity, it is possible to reduce total tardiness by integrating and simultaneously solving machine scheduling and vehicle routing problems. A tailor-made holistic genetic algorithm approach outperforms classic decomposition heuristics that break down the integrated problem, solve the subproblems successively, and then merge the subsolutions to form a solution to the overall problem. Within an acceptable computation time, the genetic algorithm provides good solutions for instances with up to 50 jobs, 5 machines, and 10 vehicles. In the special case of only one job destination, the genetic algorithm's performance for instances with even up to 70 jobs, 5 machines, and 10 vehicles is acceptable.

- **Chapter 4. Supply Chain Scheduling: Cost-cutting potential**
  The sum of a supplier's and a manufacturer's costs produced by a successive and separate scheduling approach is compared with the total costs resulting from joint Supply Chain Scheduling. While joint Supply Chain Scheduling is found to greatly reduce tardiness and inventory holding costs, the reduction in transportation costs is moderate at best. The cost-cutting potential increases with the relationship intensity between the supplier and the manufacturer. Given a very close business relationship, there is a mean savings potential of up to 24% (35%

for small-size instances). Note that this chapter also contributes to scheduling research in general. The innovative Excel-based evolutionary algorithm approach, developed to cope with the NP-hard scheduling problems, can be easily adjusted to many types of problems including batching, sequencing, scheduling, and routing decisions. Accordingly, it may serve as a benchmark heuristic to compare with new algorithms designed to solve almost every kind of vehicle routing and machine scheduling problem, for example.

- **Chapter 5. Supply Chain Scheduling: Makespan reduction potential**
  Focusing on the supply chain makespan, several joint scheduling scenarios are compared to an uncoordinated scenario in which each stage schedules separately. It turns out that partial coordination of some but not all stages of a supply chain generally results only in minor average reductions in the overall makespan, and in some instances even worsens it. Only joint Supply Chain Scheduling of all stages leads to a significant average reduction in the supply chain makespan. Aiming to reduce the makespan, Supply Chain Scheduling emerges as reasonable only for small sets of jobs, if all stages are involved, and if the makespan improvements justify the incurred coordination costs such as labor input costs or license fees for new software, for example.

- **Chapter 6. Supply Chain Contracting: R&D investment sharing contracts**
  This chapter provides an explanation for the observation that many innovating companies produce a huge part of the required components in-house instead of sourcing them from specialized suppliers. However, in many cases, in-house production as well as external procurement via a classic wholesale price contract turn out to be inefficient. Hence, the concept of R&D investment sharing contracts, which are commonplace in the pharmaceutical industry, is examined with regard to its ability to coordinate the supply chain. Almost perfect coordination can be achieved if the manufacturer's variable production costs clearly exceed the supplier's. But in many other cases, too, both the manufacturer and the supplier can benefit from R&D investment sharing contracts. Even if neither in-house production nor common external procurement is profitable, which means that the innovation project would normally be discontinued, positive profits for both parties can be achieved.

The motivating research questions of chapters 3–6 are answered to the greatest possible extent. However, as is the dilemma with research in general, when closely investigating a specific topic, very often new problems arise that need to be addressed. This is also the case here. The chapters' motivations and outlooks discuss many relevant issues resulting from the research goals, approaches, and findings. Any attempt to write an exhaustive scientific work that leaves no question unanswered is likely to become a Sisyphean task. At some point, a dissertation project has to be brought to a conclusion. Future research may take up the issues left open here.

Bibliography

Agnetis, A., Hall, N. G., Pacciarelli, D., 2006. Supply Chain Scheduling: Sequence coordination. Discrete Applied Mathematics 154 (15), 2044–2063.

Akkerman, R., Farahani, P., Grunow, M., 2010. Quality, safety and sustainability in food distribution: A review of quantitative operations management approaches and challenges. OR Spectrum 32 (4), 863–904.

Albright, S. C., Winston, W. L., 2012. Management Science Modeling, 4th Edition. Cengage Learning, South-Western.

Alchain, A. A., Demsetz, H., 1972. Production, information costs, and economic organization. American Economic Review 62 (5), 777–795.

Alshawi, S., 2001. Logistics in the internet age: Towards a holistic information and process picture. Logistics Information Management 14 (4), 235–241.

Alvarenga, G. B., Mateus, G. R., de Tomi, G., 2007. A genetic and set partitioning two-phase approach for the vehicle routing problem with time windows. Computers & Operations Research 34 (6), 1561–1584.

Anderson, E. T., Fitzsimons, G. J., Simester, D., 2006. Measuring and mitigating the costs of stockouts. Management Science 52 (11), 1751–1763.

Arrow, K., Harris, T., Marschak, J., 1951. Optimal inventory policy. Econometrica 19 (3), 250–272.

Averbakh, I., 2010. On-line integrated production-distribution scheduling problems with capacitated deliveries. European Journal of Operational Research 200 (2), 377–384.

Averbakh, I., Baysan, M., 2012. Semi-online two-level Supply Chain Scheduling problems. Journal of Scheduling 15 (3), 381–390.

Averbakh, I., Xue, Z., 2007. On-line Supply Chain Scheduling problems with preemption. European Journal of Operational Research 181 (1), 500–504.

Aydinliyim, T., Vairaktarakis, G. L., 2013. A cooperative savings game approach to a time sensitive capacity allocation and scheduling problem. Decision Sciences 44 (2), 357–376.

Aytug, H., Khouja, M., Vergara, F. E., 2003. Use of genetic algorithms to solve production and operations management problems: A review. International Journal of Production Research 41 (17), 3955–4009.

Baker, K. R., 1997. Elements of Sequencing and Scheduling. Dartmouth College, Hanover.

Barboza, D., Bradsher, K., 2012. Foxconn factory in china is closed after worker riot. The New York Times (September 23).

Barnes, D., 2006. Competing supply chains are the future. Financial Times (November 8).

Bean, J. C., 1994. Genetic algorithms and random keys for sequencing and optimization. Informs Journal on Computing 6 (2), 154–160.

Berger, J., Barkaoui, M., 2003. A new hybrid genetic algorithm for the capacitated vehicle routing problem. Journal of the Operational Research Society 54 (12), 1254–1262.

Berger, P. D., Zeng, A. Z., 2006. Single versus multiple sourcing in the presence of risks. Journal of the Operational Research Society 57 (3), 250–261.

Berggren, C., Bengtsson, L., 2004. Rethinking outsourcing in manufacturing: A tale of two telecom firms. European Management Journal 22 (2), 211–223.

Bhaskaran, S. R., Krishnan, V., 2009. Effort, revenue, and cost sharing mechanisms for collaborative new product development. Management Science 55 (7), 1152–1169.

Bhattarai, A., 2012. Wal-Mart tests same-day delivery in Northern Virginia. The Washington Post (October 10).

Biskup, D., Feldmann, M., 2001. Benchmarks for scheduling on a single machine against restrictive und unrestrictive common due dates. Computers & Operations Research 28 (8), 787–801.

Biskup, D., Herrmann, J., Gupta, J. N. D., 2008. Scheduling identical parallel machines to minimize total tardiness. International Journal of Production Economics 115 (1), 134–142.

Blume, S., Zimmermann, T., 2012. WEC today and tomorrow - An LCA approach. Proceedings of International Conference on Efficiency, Cost, Optimization, Simulation and Environmental Impact of Energy Systems (ECOS) 2012.

Bowman, E. H., 1959. The schedule-sequencing problem. Operations Research 7 (5), 621–624.

Boyabatli, O., Kleindorfer, P. R., Koontz, S. R., 2011. Integrating long-term and short-term contracting in beef supply chains. Management Science 57 (10), 1771–1787.

Brah, S. A., 1996. A comparative analysis of due date based sequencing rules in a flow shop with multiple processors. Production Planning & Control 7 (4), 362–373.

Bray, R. L., Mendelson, H., 2012. Information transmission and the bullwhip effect: An empirical investigation. Management Science 58 (5), 860–875.

Brinkhoff, A., Thonemann, U., 2007. Perfekte Projekte in der Lieferkette. Harvard Business Manager 29 (7), 6–9.

Brown, S. L., Eisenhardt, K. M., 1995. Product development: Past research, present findings, and future directions. Academy of Management Review 20 (2), 243–378.

Bruce, M., Daly, L., 2011. Adding value: Challenges for UK apparel supply chain management - A review. Production Planning & Control 22 (3), 210–220.

Bruce, M., Daly, L., Towers, N., 2004. Lean or agile - A solution for supply chain management in the textiles and clothing industry? International Journal of Operations & Production Management 24 (2), 151–170.

Bräysy, O., Gendreau, M., 2005. Vehicle routing problem with time windows, Part II: Metaheuristics. Transportation Science 39 (1), 119–139.

Burgess, K., Singh, P. J., Koroglu, R., 2006. Supply chain management: A structured literature review and implications for future research. International Journal of Operations & Production Management 26 (7), 703–729.

Cachon, G., Fisher, M., 1998. Campbell Soup's continuous replenishment program: Evaluation and enhanced inventory decision rules. In: Lee, H. L., Ng, S. M. (Eds.), Global supply chain and technology management. Vol. 1. POMS series in technology and operations management, Miami, Florida, pp. 130–140.

Cachon, G. P., 2003. Supply chain coordination with contracts. In: Graves, S., de Kok, T. (Eds.), Handbooks in operations research and management science 11. North-Holland, Amsterdam, pp. 229–340.

Cachon, G. P., Kök, A. G., 2007. Implementation of the newsvendor model with clearance pricing: How to (and how not to) estimate a salvage value. Manufacturing & Service Operations Management 9 (3), 276–290.

Cachon, G. P., Lariviere, M. A., 2001. Turning the supply chain into a revenue chain. Harvard Business Review 79 (3), 20–21.

Cachon, G. P., Lariviere, M. A., 2005. Supply chain coordination with revenue-sharing contracts: Strenghts and limitations. Management Science 51 (1), 30–44.

Cachon, G. P., Netessine, S., 2006. Game theory in supply chain analysis. In: Johnson, M. P., Norman, B., Secomandi, N., Gray, P. (Eds.), Tutorials in Operations Research - Models, Methods, and Applications for Innovative Decision Making. INFORMS, Hanover, pp. 95–233.

Cachon, G. P., Swinney, R., 2011. The value of fast fashion: Quick response, enhanced design, and strategic consumer behavior. Management Science 57 (4), 778–795.

Cakici, E., Mason, S. J., Kurz, M. E., 2012. Multi-objective analysis of an integrated Supply Chain Scheduling problem. International Journal of Production Research 50 (10), 2624–2638.

Caro, F., Gallien, J., 2010. Inventory management of a fast-fashion retail network. Operations Research 58 (2), 257–273.

Caro, F., Gallien, J., Díaz, M., García, J., Corredoira, J. M., Montes, M., Ramos, J. A., Correa, J., 2010. Zara uses operations research to reengineer its global distribution process. Interfaces 40 (1), 78–84.

Çetinkaya, S., Lee, C.-Y., 2000. Stock replenishment and shipment scheduling for vendor-managed inventory systems. Management Science 46 (2), 217–232.

Chang, Y.-C., Lee, C.-Y., 2004. Machine scheduling with job delivery coordination. European Journal of Operational Research 158 (2), 470–487.

Chen, B., Lee, C.-L., 2008. Logistics scheduling with batching and transportation. European Journal of Operational Research 189 (3), 871–876.

Chen, J.-S., Liu, H.-S., Nien, H.-Y., 2007. Minimizing makespan in single machine scheduling with job deliveries to one customer area. International Journal of Industrial Engineering 14 (2), 203–211.

Chen, Z.-L., 1996. Scheduling and common due date assignment with earliness-tardiness penalties and batch delivery costs. European Journal of Operational Research 93 (1), 49–60.

Chen, Z.-L., 2004. Integrated production and distribution operations - Taxonomy, models, and review. In: Simchi-Levi, D., Wu, S. D., Shen, Z.-J. (Eds.), Handbook of Quantitative Supply Chain Analysis. Kluwer Academic Publishers, Boston, pp. 711–740.

Chen, Z.-L., 2010. Integrated production and outbound distribution scheduling: Review and extension. Operations Research 58 (1), 130–148.

Chen, Z.-L., Hall, N. G., 2007. Supply Chain Scheduling: Conflict and cooperation in assembly systems. Operations Research 55 (6), 1072–1089.

Chen, Z.-L., Pundoor, G., 2006. Order assignment and scheduling in a supply chain. Operations Research 54 (3), 555–572.

Chen, Z.-L., Pundoor, G., 2009. Integrated order scheduling and packing. Production and Operations Management 18 (6), 672–692.

Chen, Z.-L., Vairaktarakis, G. L., 2005. Integrated scheduling of production and distribution operations. Management Science 51 (4), 614–628.

Cheng, T. C. E., Gordon, V. S., 1994. Batch delivery scheduling on a single machine. Journal of the Operational Research Society 45 (10), 1211–1215.

Cheng, T. C. E., Gordon, V. S., Kovalyov, M. Y., 1996. Single machine scheduling with batch deliveries. European Journal of Operational Research 94 (2), 277–283.

Cheng, T. C. E., Kahlbacher, H. G., 1993. Scheduling with delivery and earliness penalties. Asia-Pacific Journal of Operational Research 10 (2), 145–152.

Cheng, T. C. E., Kovalyov, M. Y., Lin, B. M.-T., 1997. Single machine scheduling to minimize batch delivery and job earliness penalties. Siam Journal on Optimization 7 (2), 547–559.

Chiu, C.-H., Choi, T.-M., Tang, C. S., 2010. Price, rebate, and returns supply contracts for coordinating supply chains with price dependent demand. Production and Operations Management 20 (1), 30–44.

Chopra, S., Meindl, P., 2012. Supply Chain Management - Strategy, Planning, and Operation, 5th Edition. Pearson, London.

Christopher, M., 1992. Logistics and Supply Chain Management, 1st Edition. Financial Times / Pitman, London.

Christy, D. P., Grout, J. R., 1994. Safeguarding supply chain relationships. International Journal of Production Economics 36 (3), 233–242.

Chung, T.-P., Liao, C.-J., Su, L.-H., 2010. Scheduling on identical machines with batch arrivals. International Journal of Production Economics 123 (1), 179–186.

Clifford, S., 2012. Same-day delivery test at Wal-Mart. The New York Times (October 9).

Coase, R. H., 1937. The nature of the firm. Economica 4 (16), 386–405.

Conway, R., Johnson, B., Maxwell, W., 1960. An experimental investigation of priority dispatching. Journal of Industrial Engineering 11 (3), 221 – 229.

Conway, R. W., Maxwell, W. L., Miller, L. W., 1967. Theory of Scheduling. Addison-Wesley, Reading.

Cooper, M. C., Lampert, D. M., Pagh, J. D., 1997. Supply chain management: More than a new name for logistics. International Journal of Logistics Management 8 (1), 1–14.

Cooper, R. G., 1990. Stage-Gate systems: A new tool for managing new products. Business Horizons 33 (3), 44–54.

Corbett, C. J., de Groote, X., 2000. A supplier's optimal quantity discount policy under asymmetric information. Management Science 46 (3), 444–450.

Cournot, A. A., 1838. Recherches sur les Principes Mathématiques de la Théorie des Richesses. Chez L. Hachette, Paris.

Cournot, A. A., 1897. Research into the Mathematical Principles of the Theory of Wealth. MacMillian, New York.

Croom, S. R., 2005. The impact of e-business on supply chain management: An empirical study of key developments. International Journal of Operations & Production Management 25 (1), 55–73.

Czaja, L., 2009. Qualitätsfrühwarnsysteme für die Automobilindustrie. Gabler, Wiesbaden.

Dale, B., Cunningham, M., 1984. The importance of factors other than cost considerations in make or buy decisions. International Journal of Operations & Production Management 4 (3), 43–54.

Davis, L., 1991. Handbook of Genetic Algorithms. Van Nostrand Reinhold, New York.

Dawande, M., Geismar, H. N., Hall, N. G., 2006. Supply Chain Scheduling: Distribution systems. Production and Operations Management 15 (2), 243–261.

Desrochers, M., Lenstra, J. K., Savelsbergh, M. W. P., 1990. A classification scheme for vehicle routing and scheduling problems. European Journal of Operational Research 46 (3), 322–332.

Dinkelbach, W., 1964. Zum Problem der Produktionsplanung in Ein- und Mehrprodukttunternehmen. Physica-Verlag, Würzburg.

Disney, S. M., Towill, D. R., 2003. The effect of vendor managed inventory (VMI) dynamics on the bullwhip effect in supply chains. International Journal of Production Economics 85 (2), 199–215.

Dolan, K. A., Meredith, R., 2001. Ghost cars, ghost brands. Forbes Magazine 167 (10, April 30), 106–110.

Dougherty, D., 1992. Interpretive barriers to successful product innovation in large firms. Organization Science 3 (2), 179–202.

Du, J., Leung, J. Y.-T., 1990. Minimizing total tardiness on one machine is NP-hard. Mathematics of Operations Research 15 (3), 483–495.

Dudek, G., Stadtler, H., 2005. Negotiation-based collaborative planning between supply chain partners. European Journal of Operational Research 163 (3), 668–687.

Edgeworth, F. Y., 1888. The mathematical theory of banking. Journal of the Royal Statistical Society 51 (1), 113–127.

Erengüç, S. S., Simpson, N. C., Vakharia, A. J., 1999. Integrated production/distribution planning in supply chains: An invited review. European Journal of Operational Research 115 (2), 219–236.

Ewert, R., Wagenhofer, A., 2008. Interne Unternehmensrechnung, 7th Edition. Springer, Berlin.

Fahimnia, B., Farahani, R. Z., Marian, R., Luong, L., 2013. A review and critique on integrated production–distribution planning models and techniques. Journal of Manufacturing Systems 32 (1), 1–19.

Fandel, G., Giese, A., Raubenheimer, H., 2009. Supply Chain Management. Springer, Berlin.

Farahani, P., Grunow, M., Guenther, H.-O., 2012. Integrated production and distribution planning for perishable food products. Flexible Services and Manufacturing Journal 24 (1), 28–51.

Fine, C. H., Whitney, D. E., 1996. Is the make-buy decision process a core competence? Working Paper 140-96, Sloan School of Management, Massachusetts Institute of Technology, Cambridge, MA.

Fleischmann, B., 1990. The discrete lot-sizing and scheduling problem. European Journal of Operational Research 44 (3), 337–348.

Fleischmann, B., Meyr, H., Wagner, M., 2008. Advanced planning. In: Stadtler, H., Kilger, C. (Eds.), Supply Chain Management and Advanced Planning – Concepts, Models, Software and Case Studies. Vol. 4. Springer, New York, pp. 81–106.

Forrester, J. W., 1958. Industrial dynamics: A major breakthrough for decision makers. Harvard Business Review 36 (4), 37–66.

Framinan, J. M., Gupta, J. N. D., Leisten, R., 2004. A review and classification of heuristics for permutation flow-shop scheduling with makespan objective. Journal of the Operational Research Society 55 (12), 1243–1255.

Freitag, M., Noé, M., 2005. Wir werden genauer prüfen. manager magazin 3.

French, S., 1982. Sequencing and scheduling: An introduction to the mathematics of job-shop. Wiley, New York.

Fu, B., Huo, Y., Zhao, H., 2012. Coordinated scheduling of production and delivery with production window and delivery capacity constraints. Theoretical Computer Science 422 (9), 39–51.

Garcia, J. M., Lozano, S., Canca, D., 2004. Coordinated scheduling of production and delivery from multiple plants. Robotics and Computer-Integrated Manufacturing 20 (3), 191–198.

Garcia, J. M., Lozano, S., Smith, K., Kwok, T., Villa, G., 2002. Coordinated scheduling of production and delivery from multiple plants and with time windows using genetic algorithms. Proceedings of the 9th International Conference on Neuronal Information Processing (ICONP'02) 3, 1153–1158.

Garey, M. R., Johnson, D. S., 1979. Computers and intractability. W. H. Freemann and Company, New York.

Garey, M. R., Johnson, D. S., Sethi, R., 1976. The complexity of flowshop and jobshop scheduling. Mathematics of Operations Research 1 (2), 117–129.

Gavirneni, S., K. R., Tayur, S., 1999. Value of information in capacitated supply chains. Management Science 45 (1), 16–24.

Geismar, H. N., Dawande, M., Sriskandarajah, C., 2011. Pool-point distribution of zero-inventory products. Production and Operations Management 20 (5), 737–753.

Geismar, H. N., Laporte, G., Lei, L., Sriskandarajah, C., 2008. The integrated production and transportation scheduling problem for a product with a short lifespan. Journal on Computing 20 (1), 21–33.

Gendreau, M., Potvin, J.-Y., 2010. Handbook of Metaheuristics, 2nd Edition. Operations Research & Management Science. Springer, New York, Dordrecht, Heidelberg, London.

Gharbi, A., Haouari, M., 2002. Minimizing makespan on parallel machines subject to release dates and delivery times. Journal of Scheduling 5 (4), 329–355.

Goldberg, D. E., 1989. Genetic Algorithms in Search, Optimization, and Machine Learning. Addison-Wesley, Reading.

Göpfert, I., 2004. Einführung, Abgrenzung und Weiterentwicklung des Supply Chain Managments. In: Busch, A., Dangelmaier, W. (Eds.), Integriertes Supply Chain Management: Theorie und Praxis unternehmensübergreifender Geschäftsprozesse. Vol. 2. Gabler, Wiesbaden.

Graham, R. L., Lawler, E. L., Lenstra, J. K., Rinnooy Kan, A. H. G., 1979. Optimization and approximation in deterministic sequencing and scheduling: A survey. Annals of Discrete Mathematics 5, 278–326.

Greenhalgh, D., Marshall, S., 2000. Convergence criteria for genetic algorithms. SIAM Journal on Computing 30 (1), 269–282.

Grunow, M., Stefánsdóttir, B., 2012. Transportation planning/vehicle scheduling (TP/VS). In: Stadtler, H., Fleischmann, B., Grunow, M., Meyr, H., Sürie, C. (Eds.), Advanced Planning in Supply Chains: Illustrating the Concepts Using an SAP® APO Case Study. Springer, Berlin, Heidelberg, Ch. 9, pp. 249–285.

Grupp, K., 1998. Mit Supply Chain Management globale Transparenz in der Distribution. PPS Management 3 (2), 50–52.

Hafeez, K., Malak, N., Zhang, Y. B., 2007. Outsourcing non-core assets and competences of a firm using analytic hierarchy process. Computers & Operations Research 34 (12), 3592–3608.

Hafeez, K., Zhang, Y. B., Malak, N., 2002. Core competence for sustainable competitive advantage: A structured methodology for identifying core competence. IEEE Transactions on Engineering Management 49 (1), 28–35.

Hall, N. G., 2011. Supply Chain Scheduling: Origins and application to sequencing, batching and lot sizing. Wiley Encyclopedia of Operations Research and Management Science.

Hall, N. G., Lesaoana, M., Potts, C. N., 2001. Scheduling with fixed delivery dates. Operations Research 49 (1), 134–144.

Hall, N. G., Potts, C. N., 2003. Supply Chain Scheduling: Batching and delivery. Operations Research 51 (4), 566–584.

Hall, N. G., Potts, C. N., 2005. The coordination of scheduling and batch deliveries. Annals of Operations Research 135 (1), 41–64.

Hamidinia, A., Khakabimamaghani, S., Mazdeh, M. M., Jafari, M., 2012. A genetic algorithm for minimizing total tardiness/earliness of weighted jobs in a batched delivery system. Computers and Industrial Engineering 62 (1), 29–38.

Handfield, R. B., Nichols, E. L., 1999. Introduction to Supply Chain Management. Prentice Hall, New Jersey.

Hariri, A. M. A., Potts, C. N., 1989. A branch and bound algorithm to minimize the number of late jobs in a permutation flow shop. European Journal of Operational Research 38 (2), 228–238.

Harris, F. W., 1913. How many parts to make at once. Factory, The Magazine of Management 10 (2), 135–136.

Hart, O., Moore, J., 1988. Incomplete contracts and renegotiation. Econometrica 56 (4), 755–785.

Harvey, M., 2009. Intel sales rise as optimism to computing. The Times (October 13).

Heizer, J., Render, B., 2011. Operations Management, 10th Edition. Pearson, Upper Saddle River.

Hejazi, S. R., Saghafian, S., 2005. Flowshop-scheduling problems with makespan criterion: A review. International Journal of Production Research 43 (14), 2895–2929.

Herrmann, J., 2010. Supply Chain Scheduling. Gabler, Wiesbaden.

Herrmann, J. W., Lee, C.-Y., 1993. On scheduling to minimize earliness-tardiness and batch delivery costs with a common due date. European Journal of Operational Research 70 (3), 272–288.

Heuzeroth, T., 2012. Die Hass-Liebe zwischen Apple und Samsung. Die Welt (December 31).

Höhn, W., König, F. G., Möhring, R. H., Lübbecke, M. E., 2011. Integrated sequencing and scheduling in coil coating. Management Science 57 (4), 647–666.

Ho, D. C. K., Au, K. F., Newton, E., 2002. Empirical research on supply chain management: A critical review and recommendations. International Journal of Production Research 40 (17), 4415–4430.

Hoetker, G., 2005. How much you know versus how well I know you: Selecting a supplier for a technically innovative component. Strategic Management Journal 26 (1), 75–96.

Hofmann, C., 2000. Supplier's pricing policy in a just-in-time environment. Computers & Operations Research 27 (14), 1357–1373.

Holland, J. H., 1975. Adaptation in natural and artificial systems. University of Michigan Press, Ann Arbor.

Houlihan, J. B., 1985. International supply chain management. International Journal of Physical Distribution & Materials Management 15 (1), 22–38.

Humphrey, J., 2003. Globalization and supply chain networks: The auto industry in Brazil and India. Global Networks 3 (2), 1470–2266.

Huo, Y., Leung, Y.-T., Wang, X., 2010. Integrated production and delivery scheduling with disjoint windows. Discrete Applied Mathematics 158 (8), 921–931.

Hurter, A. P., Van Buer, M. G., 1996. The newspaper production/distribution problem. Journal of Business Logistics 17 (1), 85–107.

Iba, H., Paul, T. K., Hasegawa, Y., 2009. Applied Genetic Programming and Machine Learning. CRC Press, Boca Raton.

Jain, J., Dangayach, G. S., Agarwal, G., Banerjee, S., 2010. Supply chain management: Literature review and some issues. Journal of Studies on Manufacturing 1 (1), 11–25.

Javidan, M., 1998. Core competence: What does it mean in practice? Long Range Planning 31 (1), 60–71.

Ji, M., He, Y., Cheng, T. C. E., 2007. Batch delivery scheduling with batch delivery cost on a single machine. European Journal of Operational Research 176 (2), 745–755.

Johnson, S. M., 1954. Optimal two- and three-stage production schedules with setup times included. Naval Research Logistics 1 (1), 61–68.

Jones, T. C., Riley, D. W., 1985. Using inventory for competitive advantage through supply chain management. International Journal of Physical Distribution & Materials Management 15 (5), 16–26.

Katok, E., Yan Wu, D., 2009. Contracting in supply chains: A laboratory investigation. Management Science 55 (12), 1953–1968.

Kim, B., 2000. Coordinating an innovation in supply chain management. European Journal of Operational Research 123 (3), 568–584.

Klein, B., Crawford, R. G., Alchian, A. A., 1978. Vertical integration, appropriable rents, and the competitive contracting process. Journal of Law and Economics 21 (2), 297–326.

Klein, P., 2005. The make-or-buy decision: Lessons from empirical studies. In: Menard, C., Shirley, M. (Eds.), Handbook of New Institutional Economics. Springer US, pp. 435–464.

Koulamas, C., 1994. The total tardiness problem: Review and extensions. Operations Research 42 (6), 1025–1041.

Kreipl, S., Pinedo, M., 2004. Planning and scheduling in supply chains: An overview of issues in practice. Production and Operations Management 13 (1), 77–92.

Krishnan, V., Loch, C. H., 2005. A retrospective look at production and operations management articles on new product development. Production and Operations Management 14 (4), 433–441.

Krishnan, V., Ulrich, K. T., 2001. Product development decisions: A review of the literature. Management Science 47 (1), 1–21.

Kurt Salmon Associates, author unknown, 1988. Quick response implementation. Technical Report Kurt Salmon Associates.

Lai, E. L.-C., Riezman, R., Wang, P., 2009. Outsourcing of innovation. Eononomic Theory 38, 485–515.

Lancioni, R. A., Schau, H. J., Smith, M. F., 2003. Internet impacts on supply chain management. Industrial Marketing Management 32 (3), 173–175.

Lariviere, M. A., Porteus, E. L., 2001. Selling to the newsvendor: An analysis of price-only contracts. Manufacturing & Service Operations Management 3 (4), 293–305.

Lee, C. C., Chu, W. H. J., 2005. Who should control inventory in a supply chain? European Journal of Operational Research 164 (1), 158–172.

Lee, C.-Y., Chen, Z.-L., 2001. Machine scheduling with transportation considerations. Journal of Scheduling 4 (1), 3–24.

Lee, H. L., Padmanabhan, V., Whang, S., 1997a. The bullwhip effect in supply chains. Sloan Management Review 38 (3), 93–102.

Lee, H. L., Padmanabhan, V., Whang, S., 1997b. Information distortion in a supply chain: The bullwhip effect. Management Science 43 (4), 546–558.

Lee, I. S., Yoon, S. H., 2010. Coordinated scheduling of production and delivery stages with stage-dependent inventory costs. Omega 38 (6), 509–521.

Lehmer, D. H., 1951. Mathematical methods in large-scale computing units. In: Proceedings of the second symposium on large-scale digital calculating machinery. Harvard University Press, pp. 141–146.

Leng, M., Parlar, M., 2005. Game theoretic applications in supply chain management: A review. Information Systems and Operational Research 43 (3), 187–220.

Lenstra, J., Rinooy Kan, A., Bruckner, P., 1977. Complexity of machine scheduling problems. Annals of Discrete Mathematics 1, 343–362.

Li, C.-L., Ou, J., 2005. Machine scheduling with pickup and delivery. Naval Research Logistics 52 (7), 617–630.

Li, C.-L., Vairaktarakis, G. L., 2007. Coordinating production and distribution of jobs with bundling operations. IIE Transactions 39 (2), 203–215.

Li, S., Yuan, J., 2009. Scheduling with families of jobs and delivery coordination under job availability. Theoretical Computer Science 410 (47-49), 4856–4863.

Li, S., Yuan, J., Fan, B., 2011. Unbounded parallel-batch scheduling with family jobs and delivery coordination. Information Processing Letters 111 (12), 575–582.

Lin, G., Ettl, M., Buckley, S., Yao, D. D., Naccarato, B. L., Allan, R., Kim, K., Koenig, L., 2000. Extended-enterprise supply-chain management at IBM personal systems group and other divisions. Interfaces 30 (1), 7–25.

Linn, R., Zhang, W., 1999. Hybrid flow shop scheduling: A survey. Computers & Industrial Engineering 37 (1), 57–61.

Liu, Z., Cheng, T. C. E., 2002. Scheduling with job release dates, delivery times and preemption penalties. Information Processing Letters 82 (2), 107–111.

Lozano, J. A., Larrañaga, P., Graña, Albizuri, F. X., 1999. Genetic algorithms: Bridging the convergence gap. Theoretical Computer Science 229 (1-2), 11–22.

Machlup, F., Taber, M., 1960. Bilateral monopoly, successive monopoly, and vertical integration. Economica 27 (106), 101–119.

Mahoney, J. T., 1992. The choice of organizational form: Vertical financial ownership versus other methods of vertical integration. Strategic Management Journal 13 (8), 559–584.

manager magazin, author unknown, 2005a. GM ruft 155.000 Fahrzeuge zurück. manager magazin online (February 11).

manager magazin, author unknown, 2005b. Zwangsurlaub bei DaimlerChrysler. manager magazin online (January 31).

Manne, A. S., 1960. On the job-shop scheduling problem. Operations Research 8 (2), 219–223.

Manoj, U. V., Gupta, J. N. D., Gupta, S. K., Sriskandarajah, C., 2008. Supply Chain Scheduling: Just-in-time environment. Annals of Operational Research 161 (1), 53–86.

Manoj, U. V., Sriskandarajah, C., Wagneur, E., 2012. Coordination in a two-stage production system: Complexity, conflict and cooperation. Computers & Operations Research 39 (6), 1245–1256.

Martini, J. T., 2007. Verrechnungspreise zur Koordination und Erfolgsermittlung. Deutscher Universitäts-Verlag, Wiesbaden.

Matsuo, H., 1988. The weighted total tardiness problem with fixed shipping times and overtime utilization. Operations Research 36 (2), 293–307.

Mazdeh, M. M., Sarhadi, M., Hindi, K. S., 2007. A branch-and-bound algorithm for single-machine scheduling with batch delivery minimizing flow times and delivery costs. European Journal of Operational Research 183 (1), 74–86.

Mazdeh, M. M., Sarhadi, M., Hindi, K. S., 2008. A branch-and-bound algorithm for single-machine scheduling with batch delivery and job release times. Computers & Operations Research 35 (4), 1099–1111.

Mazdeh, M. M., Shashaani, S., Ashouri, A., Hindi, K. S., 2011. Single-machine batch scheduling minimizing weighted flow times and delivery costs. Applied Mathematical Modelling 35 (2), 563–570.

Mentzer, J. T., DeWitt, W., Keebler, J. S., Min, S., Nix, N. W., Smith, C. D., Zacharia, Z. G., 2001. Defining supply chain management. Journal of Business Logistics 22 (2), 1–25.

Mentzer, J. T., Stank, T. P., Myers, M. B., 2007. Why global supply chain management? In: Mentzer, J. T., Myers, M. B., Stank, T. P. (Eds.), Handbook of global supply chain management. Sage, Thousand Oaks, pp. 1–18.

Mihm, B., 2010a. Fast fashion in a flat world: Global sourcing strategies. International Business & Economics Research Journal 9 (6), 55–64.

Mihm, J., 2010b. Incentives in new product development projects and the role of target costing. Management Science 56 (8), 1324–1344.

Milgrom, P. R., Roberts, J., 1992. Economics, Organization & Management. Prentice Hall, Englewood Cliffs, New Jersey.

Min, L., Cheng, W., 1999. A genetic algorithm for minimizing the makespan in the case of scheduling identical parallel machines. Artificial Intelligence in Engineering 13 (4), 399–403.

Monczka, R. M., Handfield, R. B., Giunipero, L. C., Patterson, J. L., 2009. Purchasing and Supply Chain Management, 4th Edition. Cengage Learning, South-Western.

Moyaux, T., Chaib-draa, B., D'Amours, S., 2007. Information sharing as a coordination mechanism for reducing the bullwhip effect in a supply chain. IEEE Transactions on Systems, Man, and Cybernetics, Part C: Applications and Reviews 37 (3), 396–409.

Nagarajan, M. S., 2008. Game-theoretic analysis of cooperation among supply chain agents: Review and extensions. European Journal of Operational Research 187 (3), 719–745.

Nash, J. F., 1950. The bargaining problem. Econometrica 18 (2), 155–162.

Nash, J. F., 1953. Two-person cooperative games. Econometrica 21 (1), 128–140.

Ng, C. T., Lingfa, L., 2012. On-line integrated production and outbound distribution scheduling to minimize the maximum delivery completion time. Journal of Scheduling 15 (3), 391–398.

Ohno, T., 1988. Toyota Production System: Beyond large-scale production. Productivity Press, Portland.

Oliver, R. K., Webber, M. D., 1982. Supply chain management: Logistics catches up with strategy. Outlook, Booz, Allen and Hamilton Inc.

Oliver, R. K., Webber, M. D., 1992. Supply-chain management: Logistics catches up with strategy (reprint from Outlook 1982). In: Christopher, M. (Ed.), Logistics – The strategic issues. Chapman & Hall, London, pp. 63–75.

Pan, J. C.-H., Wu, C.-L., Huang, H.-C., Su, C.-S., 2009. Coordinating scheduling with batch deliveries in a two-machine flow shop. International Journal of Advanced Manufacturing Technologie 40 (5-6), 607–616.

Petersen, K. J., Handfield, R. B., Ragatz, G. L., 2005. Supplier integration into new product development: Coordinating product, process and supply chain design. Journal of Operations Management 23 (3-4), 371–388.

Petruzzi, N. P., Dada, M., 1999. Pricing and the newsvendor: A review and extensions. Operations Research 47 (2), 183–194.

Pongcharoen, P., Hicks, C., Braiden, P. M., Stewardson, D. J., 2002. Determining optimum genetic algorithm parameters for scheduling the manufacturing and assembly of complex products. International Journal of Production Economics 78 (3), 311–322.

Potts, C., Strusevich, V., 2009. Fifty years of scheduling: A survey of milestones. Journal of the Operational Research Society 60 (1), 41–68.

Potts, C. N., 1980. Analysis of a heuristic for one machine sequencing with release dates and delivery times. Operations Research 28 (6), 1436–1441.

Prahalad, C. K., Hamel, G., 1990. The core competence of the corporation. Harvard Business Review 68 (3), 79–92.

Prins, C., 2004. A simple and effective evolutionary algorithm for the vehicle routing problem. Computers & Operations Research 31 (12), 1985–2002.

Pundoor, G., Chen, Z.-L., 2005. Scheduling a production-distribution system to optimize the tradeoff between delivery tardiness and distribution cost. Naval Research Logistics 52 (6), 571–589.

Qi, X., 2005. A logistics scheduling model: Inventory cost reduction by batching. Naval Research Logistics 52 (4), 312–320.

Qi, X., 2006. A logistics scheduling model: Scheduling and transshipment for two processing centers. IIE Transactions 38 (7), 537–546.

Qi, X., 2008. Coordinated logistics scheduling for in-house production and outsourcing. IEEE Transactions on Automation Science and Engineering 5 (1), 188–192.

Reeves, C. R., 2010. Genetic algorithms. In: Gendreau, M., Potvin, J.-Y. (Eds.), Handbook of Metaheuristics, 2nd Edition. Springer, New York, Dordrecht, Heidelberg, London, pp. 109–139.

Ribas, I., Leisten, R., Framiñan, J. M., 2010. Review and classification of hybrid flow shop scheduling problems from a production system and a solution procedure perspective. Computers & Operations Research 37 (8), 1439–1454.

Rohde, J., Meyr, H., Wagner, M., 2000. Die Supply Chain Planning Matrix. PPS-Management (5), 10–15.

Rohrbeck, F., 2012. Die Qualitätsfanatiker. Impulse 5, 46–47.

Rosenmüller, J., 2000. Game Theory - Stochastics, Information, Strategies and Cooperation. Kluwer Academic Publishers, Boston.

Ross, D. F., 1998. Competing through supply chain management. Kluwer Academic Publishers, Dordrecht.

Roy, S., Sivakumar, K., Wilkinson, I. F., 2004. Innovation generation in supply chain relationships: A conceptual model and research propositions. Journal of the Academy of Marketing Science 32 (1), 61–79.

Ruiz, R., Vázquez-Rodriguez, J. A., 2010. The hybrid flow shop scheduling problem. European Journal of Operational Research 205 (1), 1–18.

Sachan, A., Datta, S., 2005. Review of supply chain management and logistics research. International Journal of Physical Distribution & Materials Management 35 (9), 664–705.

Sarac, A., Absi, N., Dauzère-Pérès, 2010. A literature review on the impact of RFID technologies on supply chain management. International Journal of Production Economics 128 (1), 77–95.

Sarmiento, A. M., Nagi, R., 1999. A review of integrated analysis of production-distribution systems. IIE Transactions 31 (11), 1061–1074.

Satariano, A., Burrows, P., King, I., 2012. Apple said to be exploring switch from Intel chips for Mac. The Washington Post with Bloomberg online (November 6).

Sauvant, K. P., 2008. The rise of transnational corporations from emerging markets – Threat or opportunity? Edward Elgar Publishing Limited, Cheltenham.

Savelsbergh, M. W. P., 1985. Local search in routing problems with time windows. Annals of Operations Research 4 (1), 285–305.

Schenkenbach, J. B., 2009. Collaborative planning in detailed scheduling. Ph.D. thesis, Universität Hamburg.

Schifrin, M., 2001. Partner or perish. Forbes Magazine 167 (12, May 21), 26–28.

Schmitz, P. W., 2001. The hold-up problem and incomplete contracts: A survey of recent topics in contract theory. Bulletin of Economic Research 53 (1), 1–17.

Selvarajah, E., Steiner, G., 2006. Batch scheduling in customer-centric supply chains. Journal of the Operations Research Society of Japan 49 (3), 174–187.

Selvarajah, E., Steiner, G., 2009. Approximation algorithms for the supplier's Supply Chain Scheduling problem to minimize delivery and inventory holding costs. Operations Research 57 (2), 426–438.

Shane, S. A., Ulrich, K. T., 2004. Technological innvotion, product development, and entrepreneurship in management science. Management Science 50 (2), 133–144.

Sherman, L., 2009. Rethinking outsourcing in the recession. Forbes.com, (February 2).

Simchi-Levi, D., Kaminsky, P., Simchi-Levi, E., 2008. Designing and managing the supply chain: Concepts, Strategies, and Cases, 3rd Edition. McGraw-Hill, New York.

Simon, H. A., 1952. On the application of servomechanism theory to the study of production control. Econometrica 20 (2), 247–268.

Sivrikaya-Şerifoğlu, F., Ulusoy, G., 1999. Parallel machine scheduling with earliness and tardiness penalties. Computers & Operations Research 26 (8), 773–787.

Soukhal, A., Oulamara, A., Martineau, P., 2005. Complexity of flow shop scheduling problems with transportation constraints. European Journal of Operational Research 161 (1), 32–41.

Spekman, R. E., Kamauff Jr, J. W., Myhr, N., 1998. An empirical investigation into supply chain management. International Journal of Physical Distribution & Logistics Management 28 (8), 630–650.

Spengler, J. J., 1950. Vertical restraints and antitrust policy. Journal of Political Economy 58 (4), 347–352.

Stadtler, H., 2005. Supply chain management and advanced planning - Basics, overview and challenges. European Journal of Operational Research 163 (3), 575–588.

Stadtler, H., 2008. Supply chain management – An overview. In: Stadtler, H., Kilger, C. (Eds.), Supply chain management and advanced planning, 4th Edition. Springer, Berlin, pp. 7–37.

Stadtler, H., Fleischmann, B., Grunow, M., Meyr, H., Sürie, C., 2012. Advanced Planning in Supply Chains - Illustrating the Concepts Using an SAP® APO Case Study. Springer, Heidelberg.

Stadtler, H., Kilger, C., 2005. Supply Chain Management and Advanced Planning: Concepts, Models, Software, 3rd Edition. Springer, Berlin.

Stecke, K., Zhao, X., 2007. Production and transportation integration for a make-to-delivery business mode. Manufacturing & Service Operations Management 9 (2), 206–224.

Steiner, G., Zhang, R., 2009. Approximation algorithms for minimizing the total weighted number of late jobs with late deliveries in two-level supply chains. Journal of Scheduling 12 (6), 565–574.

Suzuki, J., 1995. A Markov chain analysis on simple genetic algorithms. IEEE Transactions on Systems, Man, and Cybernetics 25 (4), 655–659.

Swenseth, S. R., Godfrey, M. R., 2002. Incorporating transportation costs into inventory replenishment decisions. International Journal of Production Economics 77 (2), 113–130.

Tadei, R., Gupta, J. N. D., Croce, F. D., Cortesi, M., 1998. Minimising makespan in two-machine flow-shop with release times. Journal of Operational Research Society 49 (1), 77–85.

Taylor, T., 2002. Supply chain coordination under channel rebates with sales effort effects. Management Science 48 (8), 992–1007.

Taylor, T. A., Xiao, W., 2010. Does a manufacturer benefit from selling to a better-forecasting retailer? Management Science 56 (9), 1584–1598.

Thomas, D. J., Griffin, P. M., 1996. Coordinated supply chain management. European Journal of Operational Research 94 (1), 1–15.

Ting, C.-J., Huang, C.-H., 2005. An improved genetic algorithm for vehicle routing problem with time windows. International Journal of Industrial Engineering 12 (3), 218–228.

Tiplady, R., 2006. Zara: Taking the lead in fast-fashion. Bloomberg Businessweek (April 4).

Tirole, J., 1988. The theory of industrial organization, 2nd Edition. MIT Press, Cambridge.

Tirole, J., 1999. Incomplete contracts: Where do we stand? Econometrica 67 (4), 741–781.

Tokatli, N., 2008. Global sourcing: Insights from the global clothing industry – The case of Zara, a fast fashion retailer. Journal of Economic Geography 8 (1), 21–38.

Tokatli, N., Wrigley, N., Kizilgün, O., 2008. Shifting global supply networks and fast fashion: Made in Turkey for Marks & Spencer. Global Networks 8 (3), 261–280.

Tsay, A. A., Nahamias, S., Agrawal, N., 2003. Modeling supply chain contracts: A review. In: Sridhar, T., Ganeshan, R., Magazine, M. (Eds.), Quantitative models for supply chain management, 6th Edition. Kluwer Academic Publishers, Norwell, Massachusatts, pp. 299–336.

Ullrich, C. A., 2012. Supply Chain Scheduling: Makespan reduction potential. International Journal of Logistics Research and Applications 15 (5), 323–336.

Ullrich, C. A., 2013. Integrated machine scheduling and vehicle routing with time windows. European Journal of Operational Research 227 (1), 152–165.

Ulrich, K. T., Ellison, D. J., 2005. Beyond make-buy: Internalization and integration of design and production. Production and Operations Management 14 (3), 315–330.

Valente, J. M. S., Gonçalves, J. F., 2009. A genetic algorithm approach for the single machine scheduling problem with linear earliness and quadratic tardiness penalties. Computers & Operations Research 36 (10), 2707–2715.

Van Buer, M. G., Woodruff, D. L., Olson, R. T., 1999. Solving the medium newspaper production/distribution problem. European Journal of Operational Research 115 (2), 237–253.

Vance, A., Stone, B., 2010. Apple buys intrinsity, a maker of fast chips. The New York Times (April 27).

Vandaele, D., Rangarajan, D., Gemmel, P., Lievens, A., 2007. How to govern business services exchanges: Contractual and relational issues. International Journal of Management Reviews 9 (3), 237–258.

Vidal, T., Crainic, T. G., Gendreau, M., Prins, C., 2013. A hybrid genetic algorithm with adaptive diversity management for a large class of vehicle routing problems with time windows. Computers & Operations Research 40 (1), 475–489.

von Stackelberg, H., 1934. Marktform und Gleichgewicht. Springer, Wien.

Wagner, H. M., 1959. An integer linear-programming model for machine scheduling. Naval Research Logistics 6 (2), 131–140.

Wan, G., Yen, B. P.-C., 2002. Tabu search for single machine scheduling with distinct due windows and weighted earliness/tardiness penalties. European Journal of Operational Research 142 (2), 271–281.

Wang, G., Cheng, T. C. E., 2000. Parallel machine scheduling with batch delivery costs. International Journal of Production Economics 68 (2), 177–183.

Wang, H., Lee, C.-Y., 2005. Production and transport logistics scheduling with two transport mode choices. Naval Research Logistics 52 (8), 796–809.

Wang, X., Cheng, T. C. E., 2007. Machine scheduling with an availability constraint and job delivery coordination. Naval Research Logistics 54 (1), 11–20.

Wang, X., Cheng, T. C. E., 2009a. Logistics scheduling to minimize inventory and transport costs. International Journal of Production Economics 121 (1), 266–273.

Wang, X., Cheng, T. C. E., 2009b. Production scheduling with supply and delivery considerations to minimize the makespan. European Journal of Operational Research 194 (3), 743–752.

Warren, A., Peers, M., 2002. Video retailers have day in court – Plaintiffs say supply deals between blockbuster inc. and studios violate laws. Wall Street Journal (June 13).

Whalen, J., 2008. Glaxo gives actelion sweet deal for drug. Wall Street Journal (July 15).

White, C. H., Wilson, R. C., 1977. Sequence dependent set-up times and job sequencing. International Journal of Production Research 15 (2), 191–202.

Williamson, O. E., 1975. Markets and Hierarchies: Analysis and Antitrust Implications, A Study in the Economics of Internal Organizations. Free Press, New York.

Williamson, O. E., 1985. The Economic Institutions of Capitalism. Free Press, New York.

Williamson, O. E., 1991. Comparative economic organization: The analysis of discrete structural alternatives. Administrative Science Quarterly 36 (2), 269–296.

Williamson, O. E., 2008. Outsourcing: Transaction cost economics and supply chain management. Journal of Supply Chain Management 44 (2), 5–16.

Woeginger, G. J., 1994. Heuristics for parallel machine scheduling with delivery times. Acta Informatica 31 (6), 503–512.

Woeginger, G. J., 1998. A polynomial-time approximation scheme for single-machine sequencing with delivery times and sequence-indepent batch set-up times. Journal of Scheduling 1 (1), 79–87.

Yang, L., 2013. Providing a template to challenge Apple. The New York Times (Januar 6).

Yang, X., 2000. Scheduling with generalized batch delivery dates and earliness penalties. IIE Transactions 32 (8), 735–741.

Yuan, J., 1996. A note on the complexity of single-machine scheduling with a common due date, earliness-tardiness, and batch delivery costs. European Journal of Operational Research 94 (1), 203–205.

Yuan, J., Soukhal, A., Chen, Y., Lu, L., 2007. A note on the complexity of flow shop scheduling with transportation constraints. European Journal of Operational Research 178 (3), 918–925.

Zdrzalka, S., 1995. Analysis of approximation algorithms for single-machine scheduling with delivery times and sequence independent batch setup times. European Journal of Operational Research 80 (2), 371–380.

Zhao, X., Flynn, B. B., Roth, A. V., 2007. Decision sciences research in China: Current status, opportunities, and propositions for research in supply chain manangement, logistics, and quality management. Decision Sciences 38 (1), 39–80.

Zhong, W., Dósa, G., Tan, Z., 2007. On the machine scheduling problem with job delivery coordination. European Journal of Operational Research 182 (3), 1057–1072.

Zhu, H., 2012. A two stage scheduling with transportation and batching. Information Processing Letters 112 (19), 728–731.

Zimmermann, T., 2012. Parameterized tool for site specific LCAs of wind energy converters. International Journal of Life Cycle Assessment, (forthcoming).